Policies and Practices in Global Human Resource Systems

Michael J. Duane

QUORUM BOOKS
Westport, Connecticut • London

Library of Congress Cataloging-in-Publication Data

Duane, Michael John.
    Policies and practices in global human resource systems / Michael J. Duane.
       p. cm.
    Includes bibliographical references and index.
    ISBN 1–56720–428–7 (alk. paper)
    1. International business enterprises—Personnel management.   2. International business
enterprises—Management.   3. International business enterprises—Employees. I. Title.
    HF5549.5.E45D8   2001
    658.3—dc21   2001016132

British Library Cataloguing in Publication Data is available.

Library of Congress Catalog Card Number: 2001016132
ISBN: 1–56720–428–7

First published in 2001

Quorum Books, 88 Post Road West, Westport, CT 06881
An imprint of Greenwood Publishing Group, Inc.
www.quorumbooks.com

Printed in the United States of America

The paper used in this book complies with the
Permanent Paper Standard issued by the National
Information Standards Organization (Z39.48–1984).

10 9 8 7 6 5 4 3 2 1

Copyright Acknowledgments

The author and publisher gratefully acknowledge permission for use of the following material:

Table 3.1 reprinted with permission, Page 2-104, from "Human Resource Planning Employment
and Placement, ASPA/BNA Series No. 3, edited by Wayne Casio." Copyright © 1989 by The Bureau of National Affairs, Inc., Washington, DC. For copies of BNA Books publications call toll-free
1–800–960–1220.

Tables 4.5–4.9 are reprinted with the kind permission of C. J. Brewster.

Contents

Tables   vii

1   INTRODUCTION   1

Failure of the Expatriate Approach   2
Plan of the Book   6
Organization of the Book   6

2   LABOR MARKET CONTEXT   9

The United States and Canada   9
Western Europe   12
Eastern Europe and the New Independent States   18
The Middle East   22
Chapter Summary   28

3   ACQUIRING HUMAN RESOURCES   31

The United States and Canada   31
Western Europe   37
Eastern Europe and the New Independent States   46
The Middle East   49
Chapter Summary   50

4   DEVELOPING HUMAN RESOURCES   53

The United States and Canada   53
Western Europe   58

Eastern Europe and the New Independent States   68
The Middle East   71
Chapter Summary   74

5   REWARDING HUMAN RESOURCES   77

Performance Appraisal   77
The United States and Canada   81
Western Europe   88
Eastern Europe and the New Independent States   98
The Middle East   104
Chapter Summary   110

6   PROTECTING HUMAN RESOURCES   111

The United States and Canada   111
Western Europe   114
Eastern Europe and the New Independent States   120
The Middle East   124
Chapter Summary   130

7   MANAGING LABOR RELATIONS   131

The United States and Canada   131
Western Europe   135
Eastern Europe and the New Independent States   143
The Middle East   148
Chapter Summary   152

8   CONCLUSIONS   155

Acquiring Human Resources   155
Developing Human Resources   156
Rewarding Human Resources   156
Protecting Human Resources   157
Managing Labor Relations   158
A Final Note   159

Appendix   161
References   167
Name and Source Index   177
Subject Index   181

Tables

1.1	Reasons for Expatriate Failure	5
2.1	The Erosion of Real Wages in the United States	10
2.2	Labor Market Statistics for the United States and Canada, 1997	11
2.3	Labor Market Indicators, 1998	14
2.4	Annual Fixed Income for Representative Managerial Positions (Netherlands = 100), 1992	16
2.5	Indexes of Hourly Compensation Costs for Production Workers in Manufacturing (United States = 100)	17
2.6	Labor Market Data	20
2.7	Breakdown of Gender Distribution of Employment	24
2.8	Labor Market Statistics	25
3.1	Sources of Recruitment	33
3.2	Selection Methods	35
3.3	Evaluation of Selection Methods	36
3.4	Human Resource Planning Techniques by Country (Percentage)	38
3.5	Time Horizons for Human Resource Planning (Percentage)	39
3.6	Recruiting Problems by Job Categories (Percentage)	41
3.7	Practices to Assist in Recruitment (Percentage)	42
3.8	Employee Selection Methods (Percentage)	44
4.1	Percentage of Adults Scoring on Four Levels of the Prose Literacy Scale	54

4.2   Percent of Total Training Hours Spent in Various Types of Formal
       Training by Industry, May-October 1995   57

4.3   Selected Expenditures per Employee, by Size of Establishment,
       1994   58

4.4   School Expectancy in Years, 1998   59

4.5   Methods of Needs Assessment for Training Programs   62

4.6   Average Number of Days of Training per Year   63

4.7   Methods of Management Development   64

4.8   Areas in Which at Least a Third of Managers Have Been Trained   66

4.9   Methods Used to Monitor the Effectiveness of Training Programs   67

4.10   Average Days of Training per Year, by Profession
       (Percentage of Organizations)   70

4.11   Literacy and Education Data for Countries in the
       Middle East, 1995   72

5.1   Participation in Selected Benefits for Full-time Employees in
       Goods-producing Industries, 1997 (Percentage)   86

5.2   Comparative Hourly Compensation Costs   91

5.3   1992 Average Wages in Representative Professions
       (Netherlands = 100), Adjusted for Purchasing Power   92

5.4   Variable Pay Programs in West European Countries
       (Percentage)   93

5.5   Monthly Average Wages for Workers in Eastern Europe,
       in U.S. Dollars   100

5.6   Base Salaries Paid to Russian Employees, 1992   101

5.7   Incentive Programs in the Czech Republic (Percentage)   102

5.8   Employee Benefits in Russian Organizations, by Profession   103

5.9   Average Annual Wage in Manufacturing, in U.S. Dollars   107

5.10   Premium Pay Options in Middle East Countries   109

6.1   Organizations Monitoring Equal Opportunity in Employment
       Activities, by Group (Percentages)   116

6.2   Employment Laws in Eastern Europe and the
        New Independent States   122

6.3   Employment Laws in the Middle East   126

7.1   1998 Union Membership in the United States and
        Canada (Percentages)   133

7.2   Union Density in West European Countries, 1998   137

7.3   Impasses Resolution Framework in Western Europe   139

7.4   Strike Activity in West European Countries   141

7.5   Management-Labor Legislation   149

CHAPTER 1

Introduction

Globalization has become a buzz term used by both academics and managers to describe today's business environment. Although many large firms such as Exxon and General Motors have long been active in international ventures, many medium-sized and small businesses are now becoming more involved globally. Organizations in even the world's strongest economies have had to respond to international competition and changing market forces. In the 1960s, for example, only 6 percent of the United States economy was exposed to international competition. By the 1980s, this ballooned to more than 70 percent—and continues to grow. In his timely book, *The Competitive Advantage of Nations* (1998), Michael Porter comments on this trend by observing that in addition to price, product quality, rapid product development, and unique product features, a keen grasp of international dynamics is essential to succeed in today's world marketplace. He suggests further that a domestic competitive advantage does not guarantee a comparative advantage internationally. Thus, the task for multinationals has become one of developing strategic approaches to international business that, in many respects, differ from domestic ventures.

Traditionally, U.S. businesses have attempted to improve productivity in domestic operations by cutting investments in human resources. Some organizations in other regions of the world, however, have followed precisely the opposite strategy by increasing human resource investments. These conflicting expectations about how to improve productivity have been problematic for many multinationals, as the case of General Electric illustrates.

> GE purchased a majority interest in Tungsram, a manufacturer of lighting products in Hungary. Tungsram was attractive to GE because of its low wage rates and the possibility of using the company to export lighting products to Western Europe. GE transferred some of its best managerial talent to Tungsram. However, GE ran into many problems. The Hungarians expected higher Western-style wages, not low wages.

Americans wanted strong sales and marketing functions that would service customers, while the Hungarians believed these would take care of
themselves. The American managers found the workers to lack motivation. The Hungarian employees believed the American managers were
pushy. To turn the Tungsram plant around, GE had to invest an additional $400 million in new plant and equipment and in retraining em-
ployees. GE also had to lay off half of the work force! (Noe, Hollenbeck, Gehart, & Wright, 2000)

The GE experience underscores the importance of effective human resource management (HRM) to the success of global undertakings.

The GE case also illustrates that multinationals have at least in the past
used and viewed expatriate managers as strategic and control mechanisms in their
ever-expanding global operations (Adler 1991; Bartlett & Ghoshal 1987; Boyacigiller 1990; Edstrom & Galbraith 1977; Hedlund 1986; Kobrin 1988; Morrison &
Roth 1992; Yip 1989). Under this approach, the problem becomes one of selecting
individuals who, on the one hand, have the skills required to perform a particular
job and, on the other, have the ability and willingness to move and fit into the host
country. Organizations that at first strongly advocated this practice were Procter &
Gamble, Philips NV, and Matsushita. The Dutch firm Philips, for example, filled
all their important positions with Dutch nationals, who were mockingly referred to
by their non-Dutch colleagues as the "Dutch Mafia." To be sure, many other organizations (e.g., Toyota and Matsushita) continue to staff their key jobs in international operations with expatriates, or parent-country nationals (Hill, 1997).

The expatriate approach is pursued for two reasons. First, the executives
at the home office believe that they will be unable to find qualified senior management and professional employees in the host country. Second, it is believed that
staffing key jobs with parent nationals will advance the corporate culture. According to Hill (1997), many Japanese organizations "prefer their foreign operations to
be headed by expatriate Japanese managers because the managers will have been
socialized into the firm's culture while employed in Japan" (p. 519). He notes further that until recently, Procter & Gamble followed the same approach, for the
same reason. The protocol was to require several years of experience in a U.S.
Procter & Gamble operation, where managers would learn the corporate culture,
prior to an expatriate assignment.

FAILURE OF THE EXPATRIATE APPROACH

The expatriate approach presents unique HRM challenges. Most obvious
is that, by and large, expatriate assignments are reserved for key positions only,
leaving the rest of the operation to be staffed by domestics. But even in the case of
key positions, the expatriate approach has tended to be unsatisfactory. In their
analysis of expatriate assignments, Black, Mendenhall, and Oddou (1991) hint at
some of the insurmountable problems associated with them.

1. Individuals who have been selected based on a wide array of relevant criteria will experience easier and quicker cross-cultural adjustment compared to individuals who have been selected based on only job-related criteria.
2. Self-efficacy, including self-esteem, self-confidence, and mental well being, will have a positive relationship with degree of host-country adjustment.
3. Relational skills will be positively related to degree of host-country adjustment.
4. Perceptual skills will be positively related to host-country adjustment.
5. Role clarity and role discretion will be positively associated with international adjustment, especially work adjustment.
6. International transfers that involve high role discretion will be associated with individuals utilizing modes of adjustment characterized by efforts to change the situation (e.g., the work role), whereas such transfers that involve low role discretion will be associated with individuals utilizing modes of adjustment characterized by efforts to change themselves.
7. International transfers that involve low role novelty will be associated with individuals utilizing modes of adjustment characterized by efforts to change the situation (e.g., work role), whereas such transfers that involve high role novelty will be associated with individuals utilizing modes of adjustment characterized by efforts to change themselves.
8. High organizational culture differences between the parent and host operations will be negatively associated with degree of international adjustment, especially work adjustment.
9. Social support from organizational members will be positively associated with degree of international adjustment, especially work adjustment.
10. Logistical support, including housing, schools, and grocery stores, from the organization will be positively associated with degree of international adjustment, especially interaction and general adjustment.
11. Institutional socialization tactics will be associated with low role innovation, and individual socialization tactics will be associated with high role innovation as modes of adjustment during international transfers.
12. High culture novelty will be negatively associated with degree of international adjustment, especially interaction and general adjustment.
13. Family adjustment, especially spouse adjustment, will be positively related to employee international degree of adjustment.

At first glance, the expatriate approach seemed to be a logical staffing extension for international operations—after all, only our "own kind" can do the job. But as companies continue to expand globally, several impracticalities of expatriate assignments have emerged. First, the expense of staffing international positions with expatriates is by itself astronomical. According to a survey by Foster (2000), the average cost of an expatriate hire is 2.5 times that of a domestic employee. To be sure there is a wide variation in this cost. For example, U.S. based multinationals spend 23 percent more on assignments to the Netherlands than on their domestic ones, compared with 253 more on assignments to Korean-based operations. Regarding expatriate assignments to China, Cui (1998) notes that the average compensation for expatriate managers is $350,000, along with additional costs associated with maintaining them and their families. He concludes that continued growth of multinational corporations (MNCs) in China would require localization of management. Swaak (1995) argues further that the cost of a poor staffing decision overseas is likely to range from $200,000 to $1.2 million, estimates which include only compensation, training, development, and, when applicable, termination. Other cost considerations might well consist of lost business; the potential damage to customers, suppliers, and even government officials; as well as the negative effects of poor domestic HRM decisions made by the expatriate.

Second, it is extremely difficult to provide expatriates with adequate training in language and culture as well as a thorough understanding of local business practices and conditions. To this point, Digh (1997) provides the example of a U.S. expatriate manager working in a China-based firm who caught an employee stealing. Following company policy, she fired the employee and notified local authorities. Later she found out that the employee had been summarily executed. Although this may be an extreme case, it does illustrate the importance of cultural differences in successfully managing international operations. In any event, host country managers are less likely to make mistakes arising from cultural misunderstandings.

Third, Minehan (1996) notes that most countries want foreign subsidiaries to employ their citizens. One measure that is commonly used to advance this preference is to apply immigration laws that require the employment of host-country nationals when they are qualified. Even the United States requires firms to provide extensive documentation if they wish to hire a non-U.S. citizen. As Bachler (1996) notes:

> Sometimes the best—or only—candidates are found outside the United States. It is true that few companies go out of their way to hire foreign workers. It is generally easier to hire domestically. There are numerous costly and time-consuming immigration restrictions to clear when hiring outside our borders. For one thing, the Department of Labor (DOL) encourages U.S. companies to hire U.S. citizens whenever possible. To be approved by the Attorney General for importing a foreigner as an *H-2 worker* (the label for a temporary employee), a petitioner must apply to the Secretary of Labor for a certification that:
>
> 1. There are not sufficient workers who are able, willing and qualified, and who will be available at the time and place needed, to perform the labor or services involved in the petition, and
> 2. The employment of the alien in such labor or services will not adversely affect the wages and working conditions of workers in the United States similarly employed. (p. 55)

Fourth, in many cases the expatriate approach fails due to personal reasons. Tung (1987) insists that many expatriates return early or are terminated from their foreign assignments. She identifies several factors that account for this trend (see Table 1.1).

TABLE 1.1

Reasons for Expatriate Failure

1. Inability of spouse to adjust
2. Inability of expatriate to adjust
3. Other family-related problems
4. Expatriate's personality or lack of emotional maturity
5. Expatriate's inability to cope with overseas work
6. Expatriate's lack of technical competence
7. Expatriate's lack of motivation to work overseas

Source: Adopted from Tung (1987).

Fifth, in most cases, an expatriate assignment is temporary, thus an often-overlooked problem is repatriation—preparing the person to return home. Recent research suggests that almost 70 percent of those returning from a foreign assignment had no idea what their positions would be when they returned. Indeed 77 percent took jobs that were actually at lower levels in their parent organizations than in their foreign positions (Hill, 1997). The message to others in an organization is all too clear: " Steer clear of foreign assignments."

Finally, Groh and Allen (1998) insist that multinational corporations with greater numbers of expatriates generally have lower total returns to shareholders. In contrast, multinationals that deemphasized the use of expatriates and tended to use regional transfers along with domestic workers performed much better.

In sum, the expatriate approach is coming to be a thing of the past. As Roberts (1998) indicates, "this arrangement was adequate in yesterday's international organization because leadership, decision-making authority, and organizational power flowed from the parent site to the foreign subsidiaries. Today, however, new technologies, new markets, innovation, and new talent no longer solely emanate from headquarters but are found cross-nationally, making the *expatriate model obsolete*" [italics added] (p. 96). In underscoring this point, Forster (2000) refers to the expatriate assignment as the *myth of the international manager*.

PLAN OF THE BOOK

Given the problems with the expatriate approach, it is not unexpected that firms are changing HRM practices in their international operations. Indeed there is a trend toward hiring, whenever possible, host-country nationals, even at the upper management and professional levels. This is not to say that expatriate assignments will always be inadvisable or inappropriate. To be sure, if host-country nationals are unavailable in adequate numbers or do not have the necessary skills, the expatriate approach, if allowed by host-country policies, may be the only alternative. But multinationals will gain a competitive advantage only when they adopt the expatriate approach as an exception rather than the rule. Accordingly, the purpose of the book is to discuss HRM policies and practices in several regions of the world, with a focus on those governmental, societal, and business policies that affect them.

Granted this information will assist multinationals in their selection and training of expatriates. The intent, however, is to provide researchers and practitioners with a comparative analysis regarding the management of human resources in host countries.

ORGANIZATION OF THE BOOK

Separate chapters are devoted to each of the various HRM functions: the labor market context, acquiring human resources, developing human resources, rewarding human resources, protecting human resources, and managing labor relations. The final chapter presents conclusions and limitations of the book. An appendix is also included that provides a brief discussion of resources for global HRM systems.

Labor Market Context

Chapter 2 provides an overview of the economic conditions in various regions of the world. In addition to wages, many other factors define the dynamics of labor markets: the quantity and quality of employment, the levels of employment and unemployment, the occupational and industrial structures of employment. The educational and training requirements behind the structure of employment will be discussed in Chapter 4.

Acquiring Human Resources

Chapter 3 discusses the variations in practices and policies among countries concerning each level of the human-resource-acquisition process. The stages in this process typically involve a procedure by which organizations anticipate future staffing needs (human resource planning), a program that identifies and attracts a qualified applicant pool (recruiting), and a hiring procedure to fill vacant positions (selecting).

Developing Human Resources

In Chapter 4, it is argued that investments in human resource development are not simply the responsibility of individual organizations, but of society as a whole. Accordingly, the role of government in providing opportunities for citizens to receive education and training is addressed. Policies and practices of employee training for individual organizations within countries will also be examined.

Rewarding Human Resources

It is a common practice to draw a distinction between direct compensation, which allows employees to purchase goods and services in the marketplace, and indirect compensation, which provides them with benefits in the form of health-care coverage and pensions as well as time off, including vacation and sick days. Taken together, both types of compensation are designed to attract the talent an organization needs, to reward employees, and to motivate them in terms of developing and utilizing their skills and abilities. In the international arena, cultural, economic, and social differences play a central role in shaping compensation systems. These differences are particularly reflected in compensation legislation and in pay and benefits systems. In Chapter 5, these differences will serve as a general framework for a comparative analysis of compensation systems. Inasmuch as performance appraisal is so closely tied to compensation, the chapter begins with a brief discussion of how workers are evaluated, with some attention given to regional trends.

Protecting Human Resources

The labor force throughout the world is composed of individuals of different races, genders, ages, cultural backgrounds, and national origins. This diversity has both positive and negative aspects. On the positive side, it provides organizations with a pool of applicants that have a wide range of abilities, experiences, and ideas. On the down side, diversity may lead to increased tensions and conflicts in the workplace, including objections to hiring people with different backgrounds or characteristics. As a result, governments have had to impose laws and regulations to protect certain groups of individuals in the employment relationship. Chapter 6 covers a number of issues aimed at preventing discrimination against *protected classes*, which vary across countries, but typically include such characteristics as race, gender, national origin, age, and religion. Other issues that are addressed include child-labor laws as well as working-conditions regulations.

Managing Labor Relations

In 1958, John Dunlop introduced a conceptual framework that can be used to analyze the similarities and differences that exist in industrial relations practices among firms, industries, and countries. This framework spells out how individuals and institutions relate to each other, how the terms of employment are determined, and how labor problems are handled. Elaborating on the Dunlop framework, Mills (1989) notes that the industrial relations systems of a society may be seen as overlapping with other social systems, including "important aspects of the social, economic, and legal systems of a country as they relate to the industrial workforce and the relationship among employees and managers" (pp. 8-9). In Chapter 7, the industrial relations systems of the various regions are examined regarding their legal frameworks as well as the structure of their collective-bargaining processes and labor-management cooperation. Accordingly, there is a focus on the role of unions in the industrial relations systems.

Within the book's framework, four regions of the world are investigated in terms of their human resource practices. A brief summary of each of these regions will help to clarify the structure of the book.

The United States and Canada. Both the United States and Canada have robust economies and are very competitive internationally. HRM practices in these countries are more extensive, and in many respects, more sophisticated than those practices found elsewhere.

Western Europe. This region includes those countries in the British Isles (Ireland and the United Kingdom) and the continental European countries of Austria, Belgium, Denmark, Finland, France, Germany, Greece, Italy, Liechtenstein, the Netherlands, Norway, Portugal, Spain, Sweden, and Switzerland, along with smaller entities (e.g., Andorra, San Marino). Many of the countries in this region are members of the European Union, which is establishing standards for business practices—including HRM.

Eastern Europe and the New Independent States. Many of the countries in this region became independent states after the fall of the Soviet regime. Today this region consists of Albania, Armenia, Azerbaijan, Belarus, Bosnia and Herzegovina, Bulgaria, Croatia, the Czech Republic, Estonia, Georgia, Hungary, Kazakhstan, the Kyrgyz Republic, Latvia, Lithuania, the former Yugoslav Republic of Macedonia, Moldova, Poland, Romania, Russia, Serbia, Slovakia, Slovenia, Tajikistan, the Ukraine, and Uzbekistan. Although some countries (e.g., the Czech Republic) in this region are attempting to modernize their business practices, including HRM, most have made little progress.

The Middle East. The Middle East consists of those countries around the southern and eastern shores of the Mediterranean Sea, extending from Morocco to the Arabian Peninsula and Iran. So defined, the Middle East includes Cyprus, Egypt, Iran, Iraq, Israel, Jordan, Lebanon, Syria, The Sudan, Turkey, and the various states of Arabia proper (Bahrain, Kuwait, Oman, Qatar, Saudi Arabia, the United Arab Emirates, and Yemen). Due to their closely connected cultures and foreign policies with the Arab countries, the four North African countries of Algeria, Libya, Morocco, and Tunisia are often included in the Middle East. The most notable HRM issue in this region is that, with the exception of Israel, most countries still openly discriminate against women in employment decisions.

CHAPTER 2

Labor Market Context

Any discussion of HRM must include the context in which labor markets function. Many factors define the dynamics of labor markets: the quantity and quality of employment, the levels of employment and unemployment, and the occupational and industrial structures of employment. Although there will be some discussion of wage and salary patterns, they will be addressed in greater detail in Chapter 5. In what follows, the labor market conditions are examined in the four world regions.

THE UNITED STATES AND CANADA

The U.S. economy is immense. In 1998, it included more than 270 million consumers and 20 million businesses. U.S. consumers purchased more than $5.5 trillion of goods and services, and businesses invested over a trillion dollars more for factories and equipment. Moreover, the Gross Domestic Product (GDP), the value of goods and services produced, was $8.40 trillion. It is not surprising, therefore, that the experience in the United States has stood out among the industrialized nations as a unique one: enough so that the U. S. economy during the last years of the 20th century came to be dubbed "The Great American Jobs Machine." Between 1980 and 1997, total employment in the United States grew by some 30.5 percent, creating over 30 million new jobs. To Europeans, who looked about their generally bleaker economic landscape and saw employment grow in West Germany—the strongest Continental economy—over the same period by some 4 percent (and about half that in France), this was indeed a miraculous performance. There were other features of strength in the American model as well. Besides the tremendous growth in employment of women, blacks and Hispanics increased their shares of professional and managerial employment from 5.6 and 3.0 percent in 1983 to 7.4 and 5.0 percent in 1997.

There were, however, a number of negative features to the cornucopia of jobs pouring out of the Great American Jobs Machine. On the one hand, so-called voluntary part-time jobs (i.e., those held by workers who were not on part time due to economic difficulties faced by their employers) grew more rapidly than total employment, and especially so for men. From 1980 to 1997, total male employment rose by 21.9 percent, with voluntary part-time employment by 35.8 percent. For women, the rate of increase was even greater (40.2%), although lower than total employment growth (42.2%), so that the share of female employment in such positions declined from 27 to 26 percent.

Second, the new jobs did not seem to be doing much for the quality of employment, at least as measured by real wages. As measured by the U.S. Bureau of Labor Statistics, real wages for most broad industrial groups appear to have peaked sometime in the 1970s, and then declined to the present. Table 2.1 shows the estimated loss of real wages for the major groups. The biggest success of the U.S. economy, as measured by employment figures, is its unique achievement among all industrialized nations in reducing the level of unemployment. Even the Canadian economy so closely intertwined with that of its southern neighbor, was unable to buck the worldwide trend toward higher unemployment, which is still high in comparison with the United States rate (see Table 2.2).

TABLE 2.1

The Erosion of Real Wages in the United States

Group	Year of Peak (Real Wage)	1997 Real Wage, as a Percent of Peak
Total	1972	83
Mining	1978	92
Construction	1973	75
Manufacturing	1978	92
Transportation	1978	81
Wholesale Trade	1972	91
Retail Trade	1973	70
Services	1973	97

Source: Bureau of Labor Statistics (1999).

The fact that the overall population of the United States is nearly nine times that of Canada is reflected in the comparative data on the civilian labor force (i.e., noninstitutionalized people who are older than 16 years of age and who are either working or looking for work). Although the unemployment rate for Canada is almost twice that of the United States, participation rates are quite compatible, suggesting that the proportion of Canadians looking for work is higher than it is for their American counterparts.

The U.S. labor market stands in sharp contrast with those of other industrialized nations. For the most part, these other nations have more regulated labor markets—higher levels of unionization, stricter governmental rules about termination of employment, legislated shorter workweeks, among other factors. Indeed many European policymakers would like to see more U.S.-style flexibility in their labor markets. But the question remains: Would they accept the decline in quality of jobs that might accompany increased flexibility?

TABLE 2.2

Labor Market Statistics for the United States and Canada, 1997

Characteristic	United States	Canada
Civilian Labor Force (in thousands)	136,297	15,354
Labor Force Participation Rate (Total)	67.1	64.8
Labor Force Participation Rate (Men)	75.0	72.5
Labor Force Participation Rate (Women)	59.8	57.4
Unemployment Rate	4.9	9.2

Source: Bureau of Labor Statistics (1999).

Conventional wisdom has it that U.S. workers are richer than their Canadian counterparts. Data for production workers indicate that the average hourly compensation costs in U.S. dollars in the United States increased by 3.1 percent from 1996 ($17.70) to 1997 ($18.24). (As will be noted again in Chapter 5, any comparisons of wages converted to U.S. dollars at prevailing commercial market exchange rates must be interpreted with caution, since they do not compensate for relative living standards or purchasing power.) The wages of comparable Canadian workers increased by only .8 percent over the same period when measured in Canadian currency—1996 ($22.73), 1997 ($22.92). When measured in U.S. dollars, Canadian wages actually declined from 1996 ($16.66) to 1997 ($16.55), reflecting in large measure the U.S. dollar's appreciation against the Canadian dollar. These findings are consistent with the study conducted by Wolfson and Murphy (1998), which found that on average U.S. workers make more money than their Canadian counterparts. They also point out:

> Employees in the United States are not necessarily better off in terms of disposable income, than their Canadian counterparts. Indeed roughly half of the Canadian families had disposable incomes in 1995 that gave them higher purchasing power than otherwise comparable U.S. families. The reason is that the very rich in the United States pull up the average income much more than in Canada, while those at the bottom of the U.S. income spectrum have less purchasing power than those at the bottom in Canada. (p. 3)

WESTERN EUROPE

Various turn-of-the-century European observers thought that a general European war was no longer possible. The nationalism that soon developed proved them wrong. After World War I, economic problems culminating in the Great Depression reinforced the independent nature of the nation states. The problems experienced by Western Europe during the period of the Great Depression from the late 1920s through World War II made it difficult for this region to make any serious attempts at economic integration. When the war ended, however, a spirit of cooperation gradually emerged. A major indication of this was the establishment of the Organization for European Economic Cooperation (OEEC) in 1948. Although the primary purpose of the OEEC was to administer the Marshall Plan, thereby limited to economic reconstruction, its success set the stage for more profound integrative efforts. In 1952, for example, West Germany, France, Italy, Belgium, the Netherlands, and Luxembourg formed the European Coal and Steel Community (ECSC). The objective of the ECSC was to provide a practical basis for gradual concrete economic and political achievements by creating a common market in coal, steel, and iron ore for member countries (Czinkota, Rivoli, & Ronkainen, 1990).

In 1957, the European Economic Community was established by the Treaty of Rome. Since then, its name changed to the European Community (EC) and finally the Maastricht Treaty transformed the EC into the European Union (EU). The original members—including the now unified Germany—consisted of those countries in the ECSC. By 1995, nine other countries had joined: Great Britain (1973), Ireland (1973), Denmark (1973), Greece (1981), Spain (1986), Portugal (1986), Austria (1995), Finland (1995), and Sweden (1995). EU overtures toward Norway were rejected by its citizens in a late November 1994 referendum primarily on the basis of fishing rights in the North Sea (McIvor, 1994). Recent membership considerations consist of Central and East European countries, particularly Hungary, Poland, the Czech Republic, Slovakia, Bulgaria, and Romania. Many of these countries are eager to join despite the EU's failure to deal with the war in Bosnia.

Of paramount importance to the EU is advancement of the mobility of goods, service, labor, and capital among countries in the region. Another major goal has been to implement the Economic and Monetary Union (EMU), which established a single currency for EU members. To accomplish these goals, the EU has passed several pieces of legislation, many of which directly affect HRM. For example, Article 118 of the Single European Act (1987), which amended the Treaty of Rome, focuses on making improvements in workplace conditions and on promoting contacts between labor and management. Moreover, the Union Charter of the Fundamental Social Rights of Workers (the Social Charter, 1989), endorsed by all EU members other than the United Kingdom, covers several HRM issues: employment and remuneration; improvement of living and working conditions; freedom of association; vocational training; equal treatment for men and women; information, consultation, and participation of workers; health protection; and protection of children and adolescents within the workplace. Finally, the Social Protocol of the Maastricht Treaty (1991), again not supported by the United Kingdom, states:

> The Union and the Member States shall have as their objectives the promotion of employment, improved living and working conditions, proper social protection, dialogue between management and labour, the development of human resources with a view to lasting high employment and the combating of exclusion. To this end the Community and Member States shall implement measures which take account of the diverse forms of national practices, in particular in the field of contractual relations, and the need to maintain the competitiveness of the Community economy.

The EU's ability to achieve its goals has been limited by disagreements among member states. For example, the EU officially agreed in May 1998 to adopt a single European currency: the euro. Although Britain, Sweden, and Denmark met the economic criteria to join in the adoption of the euro, they opted not to participate. Greece had hoped to take part but did not meet the criteria. As a result only 11 nations began to use the euro for electronic money transfers and for accounting purposes in 1999. By 2002, the euro will become the legal tender in these countries. Furthermore, the legislation enacted, and still being developed, by the EU tends to encourage the standardization of HRM practices in Western Europe. Yet significant differences remain. As Brewster, Hegewisch, and Mayne (1994) observe, "over the next decade or so we anticipate increasing steps toward a common European understanding of the key issues in human resource management—but a continuing divergence in how organizations handle these key issues" (p. 130).

With regard to labor-market indicators, Blanchard and Jimeno (1995) note that "the increase in European unemployment over the past two decades has made clear that the natural rate of unemployment is all but natural, and all but constant" (p. 221). In March 1995, seasonally adjusted unemployment across the 15 EU countries was 10.8 percent, exactly double the jobless rate in the United States for the same period. As Table 2.3 indicates, the West European country experiencing the highest unemployment rate is Spain. The Spanish unemployment rate was below the EU average until 1977. After that, however, it began to rise dramatically with a moderate correction during the economic boom of 1986-90. But how can Spain and Portugal, having remarkably similar histories over the past 20 years, differ so much in their unemployment rates? Blanchard and Jimeno (1995) argue that at least in part the variation in their rates can be attributed to regulations governing unemployment benefits, in particular those dealing with eligibility. In Spain, workers are eligible for such benefits if they have worked six months out of the last four years (one year out of the last four, since a 1992 reform). Workers in Portugal, however, are eligible only if they have worked a year and one-half within the last two years. As a result, 59 percent of the unemployed receive benefits in Spain, compared to 41 percent in Portugal. Blanchard and Jimeno (1995) conclude that unemployment benefits have a direct influence on persistence.

TABLE 2.3

Labor Market Indicators, 1998

Countries	Unemployment	Employment (thousands)
Austria	4.2	3,723.3
Belgium	9.1	3,839.1[1]
Denmark	5.5	2,692.4
Finland	11.3	2,247.0
France	11.8	22,705.0
Germany	9.7	35,860.0
Greece	10.3[1]	3,854.1[1]
Ireland	7.8	1,494.5
Italy	12.3[1]	20,087.0[1]
Luxembourg	3.1	219.4
Netherlands	4.4	7,398.0
Norway	4.1[1]	2,242.0
Portugal	5.0	4,751.9
Spain	18.8	13,204.9
Sweden	6.5	3,979.0
Switzerland	3.6	3,850.0
United Kingdom	6.1	26,947.4

Source: LABORSTA, International Labor Organization: laborsta.ilo.org/cgi-bin/broker.exe
[1]1997 data

The Finnish experience is quite unique. From 1960 to 1991, the unemployment rate in Finland remained relatively low, generally 1 to 3 percent below the EU average. In the early 1990s, however, Finland experienced a dramatic surge in unemployment, from about 3 to 22 percent. The sharp deterioration of the employment situation can be attributed in large measure to the collapse of the Soviet Union, one of Finland's major customers; to the banking crisis; and to the process of financial consolidation in the private sector. But as the labor statistics indicated, economic conditions are improving somewhat in Finland.

One of the most defining developments in West European labor markets occurred in 1989, when the collapse of communism in Eastern Europe paved the way for a reunification of East Germany with the highly successful West German economy. This process, however, has produced some mixed economic conditions. For example, although it pushed western Germany into its deepest recession since World War II, shrinking its economy by 1.9 percent, the economy of eastern Germany grew by 7.1 percent. But overall the effects of unification on the Federal Republic's labor markets have been mostly negative. Unemployment in western Germany rose to 8.2 percent by 1995, up more than 3 percent from 1991. It also increased in eastern Germany during this period, from 10.8 percent in 1991 to 15.1 percent in 1995. Women have been hard hit. In 1993, unemployment for women in n the eastern region stood at 21.7 percent, whereas the figure for men was 11 percent. One explanation is that prior to German unification, women in East Germany worked primarily in the health, social work, education, and retail organizations, which were among the first to go bankrupt or be dismantled in the transition from a command to a market economy.

A problem that almost all West European countries have been experiencing is long-term unemployment. In an attempt to improve employment opportunities, the EU established the European Social Fund. According to Article 123 of the Maastricht Treaty, the aim of the European Social Fund is to enhance the employment of workers, to increase their geographical and occupational mobility within the Community, and to facilitate their adaptation to industrial changes by providing them with vocational training. Another effort to address long-term unemployment has included the establishment of such special projects as Lunar European Demonstration Approach (LEDA). Under this program, officials of the European Space Agency are seeking some $350 million from member states to pay for the first in a series of lunar programs that could culminate in a manned-station on the moon within the next 25 years. Needless to say, LEDA will result in considerable human-resource demands.

In recent years, salary and wage trends in Western Europe have been interesting. Table 2.4 provides comparative indexes of gross annual salaries for three different management positions in various countries. As the data indicate, Austria, Switzerland, and Germany tend to have the highest indexes in all three management categories. Kmitch, Laboy, and Van Damme (1995) provide indexes of hourly compensation costs for production workers in a variety of West European countries and selected regions (see Table 2.5). In complying with the Bureau of Labor Statistics' approach to collecting wage data, they first analyzed total labor costs, which include both direct and indirect compensation. They note that total hourly compensation for production workers increased on average about 5.5 percent each year between 1975 and 1994, although this rate decreased to 3.5 percent from 1990 to 1994. In terms of trade-weighted averages for the West European economies, hourly compensation costs rose at an annual average rate of 14.5 percent in the 1975-80 period, fell 4 percent each year between 1980 and 1985, rose about 16.5 percent per year between 1985 and 1990, and slowed its annual average increase to 2.5 percent each of the following years. Kmitch et al. (1995) explain that several factors account for this roller-coaster experience:

> The decline over the 1980-85 period reflected the dollar's appreciation, which resulted in a decline in the trade-weighted value of the European currencies of 11 1/2 percent per year. The sharp increase for Europe in the 1985-90 percent reflected the subsequent depreciation of the U.S. dollar, which resulted in an increase in the trade-weighted value of the European currencies of 10 1/2 percent per year. The U.S. dollar rose about 2 percent per year over the full 1990-94 period against the European currencies, largely because the average European currency valued had fallen about 10 1/2 percent in 1993. (p. 4)

Finally, the trade-weighted average labor costs across Western Europe in 1975 was 81 percent of the U.S. rate and reached a low of 62 percent in 1985, but peaked at 123 percent in 1992, before declining to 115 percent in 1994. The Kmitch et al. (1995) study also revealed that in 1994 Germany had the highest total hourly compensation costs of approximately $28.00 an hour, compared with the U.S. cost of $17.10. Compensation costs for Switzerland and Belgium were comparatively high at 145 percent and 134 percent of the U.S. level, respectively. Many of the southern countries were at the low end, particularly Portugal, where the compensation cost level was 27 percent of the U.S. level.

TABLE 2.4

Annual Fixed Income for Representative Managerial Positions (Netherlands = 100), 1992

Country	Lower Management	Middle Management	Senior Management
Austria	137.2	147.9	138.0
Switzerland	147.2	147.5	136.8
Germany	139.9	144.9	148.9
Italy	95.5	121.8	118.8
Spain	113.2	120.4	120.7
Denmark	112.0	110.9	99.7
Belgium	107.2	109.1	106.0
France	98.7	100.1	93.5
Netherlands	100.0	100.0	100.0
Sweden	100.2	99.3	85.1
Ireland	93.3	90.1	92.0
Finland	90.7	86.4	76.8
United States	85.0	83.1	81.0
Portugal	73.9	82.8	81.8
United Kingdom	79.0	81.4	79.5
Norway	93.2	80.0	67.1
Greece	57.3	63.1	67.0

Source: Logger et al. (1995).

When direct compensation costs, or pay for time worked, are isolated, it is noteworthy that they account for about 70 percent of U.S. total compensation costs. Direct-pay data also indicate that they account for 80 to 85 percent of total compensation costs in Denmark, and for about 50 to 60 percent in France, Germany, and Italy. Kmitch et al. (1995) suggest that the high direct-pay rate in Denmark largely reflects very low social insurance expenditures for employers, only about 5 percent of total compensation, whereas the rates in France, Germany, and Italy are due to comparatively high social insurance rates, ranging from 24 percent to over 30 percent of total compensation.

TABLE 2.5

Indexes of Hourly Compensation Costs for Production Workers in Manufacturing (United States = 100)

Country	1975	1990	1994
Germany	–	147	160
Switzerland	96	140	145
Belgium	101	119	134
Austria	71	119	127
Norway	106	144	122
Netherlands	103	123	122
Denmark	99	120	120
Finland	72	141	110
Sweden	113	140	110
France	71	102	100
United States	100	100	100
Italy	73	119	95
United Kingdom	53	85	80
Spain	40	76	67
Portugal	25	25	27
Ireland	48	79	–
Greece	27	45	–
Europe	82	118	115
European Union	80	116	114

Source: Kmitch et al. (1995).

This combination of wage and unemployment developments has led to two parallel policy concerns in Western Europe. The first of these appears to represent an attempt to draw lessons from the perceived virtues of the American labor market, and takes the form of a quest for "labor market flexibility." In general, it was thought that much of North American job creation was due to the greater ability of employers to shed excess workers and to greater levels of competition in the labor market. In Western Europe, the search for improved flexibility in the labor markets took a variety of forms. In many countries, one of its elements was privatization of traditionally governmental industries and activities. In others, where the power of trade unions was considered excessive and exerting a sclerotic hold on the processes of labor market adjustment, industrial relations law was changed to weaken them (Margaret Thatcher is well-remembered for this effort). In yet other countries, where strong restrictions on discharging employees had been developed, calls were made for relaxation of such restrictions. For example, in France, a variety of consultations with plant councils and labor inspectors were required before "collective economic dismissals" could be imposed, while various restrictions on women's employment and attempts to cushion the effects of terminations by meshing with the social insurance retirement scheme added further costly impediments to labor market adjustment.

The second thrust was based closely on more traditional West European ideologies, particularly those that underlay the policies of those Social Democratic governments responsible for installing many elements of the welfare state throughout the region. This policy, which has received the formal approval of the EU Council of Ministers, has in turn three parts: (1) a policy of high wages, accompanied by high productivity, (2) a policy of high levels of training, to generate the high levels of productivity, and (3) a policy of "high social cohesion" (that is, relatively narrow wage and income differentials), to generate popular support for the whole enterprise. It remains to be seen, of course, whether the new Europe has the economic and political will to deliver on this promise.

EASTERN EUROPE AND THE NEW INDEPENDENT STATES

Although the underlining theme of our discussion of Western Europe was *unification*, the theme of this section is *privatization*. That is, the political upheaval of the late 1980s in the former Soviet Union and countries in Eastern Europe ushered in a new economic era for this region, marked by a transition from control to market economies. At the onset, the appropriate speed and means of privatization were hotly debated. Everyone agreed that the goal was to promote private ownership, yet the prevailing opinion among Eastern Europeans was that the selling off of public enterprises was less important than establishing an environment for the growth of new organizations. Initially, the transition was difficult for many East European countries, with output falling on average more than 20 percent between 1989 and 1993. Since then, however, economic growth has resumed. Indeed 1994 data reveal an average growth rate of about 4 percent—from about 0.2 and 0.8 percent in Bulgaria and Croatia, respectively, to 6 percent in Poland and Slovakia.

Compared with most of the former planned economies of Eastern Europe, Russia experienced an even more severe and protracted drop in officially reported economic output after the collapse of the Soviet Union. The removal of price controls caused a huge escalation in inflation and prices, causing the value of the ruble to plummet and real incomes to fall dramatically. Industrial and agricultural production declined, causing a shortage of consumer goods. Other Commonwealth of Independent States (CIS), including all of the former Soviet republics except the Baltic states of Georgia, Azerbaijan, and Moldova, suffered even worse cuts in output. This is particularly true of the Caucasian and Central Asian Republics, where armed conflicts have destroyed production facilities. The Baltic states have been somewhat more successful in stabilizing and developing their economies. Moreover, Estonia appears to have reached an end to its recession with zero growth (UN/ECE, 1996).

To gain an appreciation of how these economic changes influenced labor markets, a bit of recent political history is in order. Prior to the dissolution of the Soviet Union, the Central Committee of the Communist Party exercised considerable economic control throughout Eastern Europe. This influence was no more evident than in the HRM practices throughout the region. In 1970, for example, the Communist Party stipulated that the main promotion criterion for managers would be loyalty to the communist ideology. As Kubeš and Benkovic (1994) indicate, rather than serving individual organizations, HRM came to serve the requirements of the political ideology. They conclude that the objectives of this ideology took priority over the realities of market forces.

Koubeck (1993) points out that the political environment during this time served to centralize management generally and HRM in particular. Specifically, HRM was divided into several departments, each with a clearly established role. The personnel policy department in each organization was, in effect, the central arm of the Communist Party. This department decided on selection, placement, promotion, training and development, termination, and so on, and applied mainly one principle: the preferment of Communist Party members (Koubek & Brewster, 1995). The role of departments of labor and wages was to administer compensation and work design policies that had been developed by central authorities. Special departments provided training and development opportunities. For the most part, training was based more on expectations of central authorities than on organizational needs. Personnel departments were responsible for personnel record keeping. They provided statistics and information on the labor force to state agencies. Separate departments existed for human resource planning. Finally, many organizations supported departments of employees' care, which administered such benefits as organization-provided housing, nurseries, and recreational activities. Trade unions controlled access to many benefits, notably vacation facilities. During the period of communist rule, the major buyers of labor in East European and Soviet bloc countries were large, state-owned companies. And since full employment was a socialist mandate, labor supply and demand issues were fairly straightforward: government employers were expected to hire the unemployed. Understandably this policy influenced the number and types of people companies hired, producing inefficient labor markets.

The downfall of the Soviet Union and the transition to market economies radically altered the labor market context in this region. Unemployment has become a significant social and economic reality. As Table 2.6 indicates, with the exception of the Czech Republic, East European countries are suffering double-digit unemployment rates. Again, the primary reason is that the transition from centrally planned economies to market-driven systems has substantially reduced state-sponsored employment. To be sure, in some countries, reductions in employment in the state sector have been in part offset by a decline in labor force participation rates. In Poland, Hungry, and the Czech Republic, the private sector has undergone a robust growth, offsetting state-sector declines. The relatively low un-

TABLE 2.6

Labor Market Data

Countries	Population (000s)[1]	Unemployment Rate[2]	Total Employment (000s)[2]	Change[3]
Eastern Europe				
Albania	3,414	18.0	1,161	-19.4
Bos/Herz	3,202	n.a.	n.a.	n.a.
Bulgaria	8,775	10.7	3,242	-25.7
Croatia	4,666	16.5	1,211	- 25.2
Czech Republic	10,433	2.8	4,885	-9.6
Hungary	10,319	10.6	4,045	-26.1
Poland	38,792	15.1	14,475	-14.9
Romania	23,198	9.9	10,012	-8.5
Slovakia	5,432	13.3	2,110	-15.7
Slovenia	2,052	13.4	752	-20.5
Macedonia	2,160	38.0	433	-18.3
Yugoslavia	11,102	24.6	2,413	-13.5
Former Soviet Republics				
Armenia	3,557	6.4	1,500	-5.8
Azerbaijan	7,790	1.0	2,587	-7.5
Belarus	10,437	2.3	4 ,696	-9.7
Estonia	1,625	5.4	662	18.6
Georgia	5,726	3.3	1,778	-34.6
Kazakhstan	17,377	1.4	6,582	-11.9
Kyrgyzstan	4,770	1.9	1,646	-5.4
Latvia	2,763	6.1	1,205	-14.4
Lithuania	3,876	6.0	1,675	-12.0
Moldova	4,490	1.3	1,681	-4.2
Russia	149,909	7.7	68,484	-9.4
Tajikistan	6,155	1.8	1,800	-4.2
Turkmenistan	4,075	n.a.	1,665	11.6
Ukraine	51,868	0.4	23,025	-9.4
Uzbekistan	23,089	0.4	8,150	6.9

[1]U.S. Bureau of the Census, International Data Base (1994 data).
[2]UN/ECE data on registered unemployment for Second quarter, 1995.
[3]Percentage change between 1990 and 1994.

employment rate in the Czech Republic can be attributed to the dissolution of Czechoslovakia. That is, a large share of the older production industries was located in Slovakia. In the resulting Czech Republic, moreover, "small businesses have absorbed many employees who left large state owned enterprises to set up on their own shops, or to reclaim past ownership of them" (Hegewisch, Brewster, & Koubek, 1996, p. 53).

Of particular note is the high rate of unemployment in Yugoslavia and Macedonia, which were part of the Yugoslav state until 1991. Woodward (1995) notes it is odd that this socialist regime was able to survive politically. She finds the answer in the Tito administration itself. In her assessment, Tito's unnatural obsession with acquiring resources abroad for economic growth and national defense provided temporary political support from Yugoslavians, but eventually led to a number of complications, including high unemployment and to the eventual collapse of the post-Tito regime.

By comparison, 1995 rates of unemployment in the CIS countries are very low, averaging 5.0 percent. But these rates must be put in perspective. Prior to the fall of the Soviet Union, low unemployment rates in these countries reflected a mandate for full employment, imposing a macroeconomic policy that caused a large amount of overemployment in large state owned enterprises (UN/ECE, 1996, p. 8). Low unemployment rates after the decline in government-supported employment suggest a lingering effect of the political and cultural history of the CIS countries. That is, the stigma associated with unemployment has given rise to an underreporting of it. A recent account, for example, suggests that for every Russian who is registered as unemployed, there are 2.65 unemployed who are not registered, but claim to be working (A&G Information Services, 1996)

In the past few years, many companies in Western Europe have been lured to Central and East European countries to take advantage of the lower labor costs. Wages and social welfare taxes in these countries have been generally less than half those in Western Europe. But conditions are changing. The sharp deterioration of consumer markets and skyrocketing inflation coupled with greater freedom to leave these countries and to make individual job choices are intensifying competition for quality workers. Accordingly, one of the major HRM challenges in this region is to develop fair, competitive, and motivating compensation systems.

In Russia, for example, a variety of approaches are being used to compensate Russian employees. One of the major governmental actions was to increase the minimum monthly wage from 20,500 rubles (about $5) in 1995 to 63,000 rubles (about $15) a year later. To be sure, this figure is low, but very few workers actually receive the minimum wage. Instead this wage level is used to calculate public sector wages and benefits as well as unemployment benefits and the Excess Wage Tax. Accordingly, an increase in the minimum wage is likely to have a substantive effect on other wages. Indeed in March 1996, the average monthly wage of Russian citizens was about 740,000 rubles, an 8 percent increase from February (ITAR-TASS, 1996). Still, critics of the transition from a command economy to a market economy in Russia argue that the current average wage in Russia buys only three-fifths of what it did immediately prior to price liberalization in January of 1992 and is lower than the 1985 average wage. What this argument ignores is that while wage-price ratios were higher under the old system, there was essentially nothing to buy in the shops, making such ratios meaningless as indicators of quality of life in Russia (Guzda, 1993).

In response to competitive labor markets, other countries in this region are beginning to depart from the centralized nature of determining wages and salaries, particularly those that apply to managers, professionals, and technicians. For example, over 60 percent of the Czech Republic organizations report setting salaries for these occupational categories at the company or division level. By contrast, the determination of clerical and manual wages in private organizations and traditional state institutions (e.g., schools and police departments) still takes place at the national and regional levels. Wages in the Czech Republic are much higher than in many of the other Central and East European countries; consequently, citizens from poorer countries in the region relocate to the Czech Republic, oftentimes illegally. Specifically a large number of Ukrainians are entering the Czech Republic without authorization in an effort to find better paying jobs.

In short, the labor market context in this region is improving. Belobaba (1994), for example, notes that in a recent survey of Western countries, over 40 percent of the respondents indicated that the business environments in the Czech Republic and Hungary are either good or excellent. Even in Russia a few signs indicate that the economy is beginning to grow for the first time in a decade. Russia's vast natural resources and highly educated workforce will enhance the labor market context in the future. However, certain governmental and market institutions necessary to generate long-term investment and entrepreneurship have not yet been firmly established, leading some experts to predict that steady economic growth would be impossible for Russia to sustain.

THE MIDDLE EAST

The labor market context in this region has been the target of conflicting forces in the recent past. For example, the Soviet Union's influence on this region was strongly felt in the 1950s, when a form of state control based on the centrally planned model of the Soviets was imposed on the economies of Egypt, Iraq, Syria, and South Yemen (now part of the Republic of Yemen). In these countries, the governments set economic policy and controlled major industries. They also broke up and redistributed large landholdings, while imposing import controls and foreign exchange rates. At the same time, Western countries were supplying financial, technical, and military aid to such countries as Iran, Israel, Jordan, and Turkey. Elements of these structural components remain in place. Yet with the collapse of the Soviet Union in 1991 and worldwide tendencies toward privatization, some forms of Soviet-style government assistance such as food subsidies and easy access to healthcare, education, and welfare have been greatly reduced. Moreover, there has been a deterioration of Western influence on such countries as Iran, where the 1979 revolution "popularized" an anti-American sentiment.

The economic, financial, and social structures also have been volatile as a result of so-called religious struggles. Yet the conflict between Arabs and Israelis over the land in Palestine is more a product of the Jewish Zionist movement and other recent developments than any age-old hostility between Muslims and Jews. Furthermore, although there have been conflicts between Persians and Arabs in the past, they have been caused by political tensions and border disputes—not by religious disagreements. Islamic militancy, which has produced deadly results in Egypt, Iran, Israel, and Lebanon, is a consequence of problems associated with widespread unemployment, political and socioeconomic turmoil, and an overarching sense of despair rather than a result of any violent or extremist characteristics inherent to Islam.

Although only 14 percent of the land in the Middle East is arable and about 6 percent of it is actually cultivated, a substantial number of people in the Middle East are engaged in agriculture. As Table 2.7 indicates, roughly 60 percent of the men in Afghanistan, Sudan, and Yemen work in agriculture. Over 80 percent of the women workers in Sudan and Turkey as well as nearly 70 percent in Iran and Iraq are employed in agriculture. The major commercial crops consist of cotton (Egypt, Turkey, and Syria), tobacco (Turkey), and coffee (Yemen). Some wheat, barley and rye are produced in the northern countries, while maize, millet, and rice are grown in the southern countries. A variety of fruits (e.g., oranges, grapes, and olives) are produced in the Mediterranean countries. But the limited amount of arable land in this area has forced many Middle East countries to import a substantial amount of food in order to feed their own people.

In recent times, petroleum has been a driving force in the economies of the Middle East. The enormous jump in oil prices during the 1970s fostered rapid economic growth in most of the countries in this region. Indeed over 60 percent of the known petroleum reserves are located in the Middle East, with Saudi Arabia, Kuwait, Iran, and Iraq having about 80 percent of the region's reserves. In 1979, petroleum production peaked in the Middle East, which produced about 40 percent of the world consumption. In response to increased revenue, governments in this region sharply increased their investment spending. A comparison of the period 1970-73 (just prior to oil price increases) with the period 1974-81 reveals that the share of public investments in GDP increased from 8 to 25 percent among Arab countries. Private investment increased as well, especially in Egypt, Jordan, and Saudi Arabia. Following the collapse of oil prices in the 1980s, Arab oil revenues declined substantially, from $213 billion in 1980 to $53 billion in 1986 (Diwan & Squire, 1992). This had a dramatic effect on the economies of this region. As Shaban, Assad, and Al-Qudsi (1995) observe, the growth during the period 1986-90 declined markedly. They note, for example, that "in Egypt, Jordan, Sudan, and the Syrian Arab Republic, GDP growth rates fell to less than a third of what they had been during the boom period" (p. 71). Moreover, in the oil-exporting countries, such as Algeria, Iraq, Saudi Arabia, the United Arab Emirates, growth rates became negative.

Almost all of the governments in the Middle East have attempted to enhance their economies by placing a high priority on greater industrialization. Initially these efforts did not fare very well in the manufacturing sector, primarily because the oil windfall of the 1970s encouraged the importing of manufactured goods. In Algeria, where import-protectionist legislation existed, manufacturing production increased immediately. Eventually, substantial investments of oil revenues in the manufacturing sector were made by many oil-producing countries, particularly Iraq and Saudi Arabia. Today, the production of heavy capital goods is still limited, but major assembly plants now exist for vehicles and machinery in Turkey, Egypt, Iran, and Israel. Iron and steel production is important in Turkey and Egypt, and Turkey is one of the world's leading producers of cement.

TABLE 2.7

Breakdown of Gender Distribution of Employment

	Percentage Distribution of Labor Force					
	Agriculture		Industry		Services	
Country	Female	Male	Female	Male	Female	Male
Afghanistan	3	60	85	10	12	30
Algeria	10	16	21	34	69	51
Bahrain	0	3	4	39	96	58
Egypt	8	42	20	25	71	33
Iran	69	22	15	40	16	38
Iraq	68	18	9	26	23	56
Israel	4	4	17	37	79	59
Jordan	1	11	7	27	92	62
Kuwait	0	2	2	36	97	62
Lebanon	16	6	22	32	62	62
Libya						
Morocco	27	35	46	30	28	34
Oman	12	45	39	25	49	30
Qatar	0	3	0	30	100	67
Saudi Arabia	16	34	6	20	79	46
Sudan	84	60	5	10	11	29
Tunisia	47	25	44	46	10	28
Turkey	84	27	6	30	10	43
United Arab Emirates	0	4	7	40	93	56
Yemen	45	58	6	14	49	28

Sources: U.S. Bureau of Statistics, International Labour Office. Agriculture covers hunting, forestry, and fishing; Industry covers mining, manufacturing, electricity, gas, water, and construction; Services include wholesale and retail trade, restaurant, hotels, transportation, communication, financing, insurance, real estate, business services, and community, social, and personal services.

As Table 2.8 suggests, although unemployment is negligible in the Gulf Cooperation Council (GCC) countries, it is widespread in Algeria (25%), Egypt (20%), Jordan (16%), Sudan (30%), Tunisia (16%), and Yemen (30%). Where high rates of unemployment exist, current workers are not suffering as much as the new job entrants. Indeed a sample of 11 Arab countries reveals that 59 "percent of the unemployed were first-time job seekers. Analysis of age-specific unemployment rates shows that unemployment in the cohorts aged 15-19 and 20-24 is 2.7 and 1.4 times higher, respectively, than the average unemployment rate" (Shaban, et al., 1995, p. 77). Unemployment for women in Arab countries is much higher than for men, with 83 percent of the female, first-time job seekers out of work compared to 55 percent of their male counterparts. These trends have been driven by high population and labor force growth rates, "macroeconomic fluctuations caused by oil price instability, and the pervasive role of the State in the region's

TABLE 2.8

Labor Market Statistics

Country	Unemployment Rates[1] (%)	Labor Force Participation Rates[2] (%)	
		Male	Female
Afghanistan	n.a.	87.5	7.2
Algeria	25.0	76.4	7.8
Bahrain	25.0	88.2	29.2
Egypt	20.0	74.0	23.0
Iran	30.0	79.8	9.9
Iraq	n.a.	74.0	10.3
Israel	6.3	62.8	44.7
Jordan	16.0	72.5	12.7
Kuwait	NEGL.	80.1	34.3
Lebanon	30.0	n.a.	n.a.
Libya	n.a.	n.a.	n.a.
Morocco	16.0	74.9	25.1
Oman	n.a.	84.1	15.8
Qatar	n.a.	61.8	34.2
Saudi Arabia	6.5	78.8	6.9
Sudan	30.0	85.2	31.0
Tunisia	16.2	74.5	20.3
Turkey	10.2	76.5	31.9
United Arab Emirates	NEGL.	92.5	24.2
Yemen	30.0	80.6	1.9

[1]Data from The World Factbook 1996 of the CIA.
[2]Data collected from the Statistics Division of the United Nations Secretariat and ILO.

economic activity " (Shaban et al. 1995, p. 65). Such evidence suggests that any country's specific unemployment policy must address the young, inexperienced job seekers.

The relatively high concentration of employment in services for both men and women is due to a couple of factors (see Table 2.7). First, historically public-sector employment was very high among the Arab countries because the governments wanted a means of control over material incentives—carrots not sticks, thereby fostering citizen loyalty. More recently, public-sector jobs were used to deal with the mid-1980s recession. As was a tradition in the former Soviet Union, government provision for jobs has been taken for granted by certain citizens in Arab countries. In Egypt, for example, programs guaranteeing jobs to graduates from vocational secondary schools and institutions of higher education have produced a public-sector employment level that is one-third of the total employment. Similar programs exist in Morocco (Amerah, 1990). Even Jordan and Tunisia, Arab countries that have not been as committed to government-guaranteed jobs, have sizable public sectors, with 45 and 23 percent, respectively, of their employment located in public jobs.

Another factor that accounts for the high employment rates in services is the concentration of labor in financial institutions. For example, in Bahrain and Qatar, where nearly 100 percent of the women and roughly 60 percent of the men are employed in services, offshore banking is a major industry. Indeed Bahrain has become the Persian Gulf's preeminent financial center, with 60 offshore banks and a stock exchange, along with excellent telecommunication facilities. As a result, these countries have become the home of numerous multinational firms doing business in the Gulf. In part, this explains the large proportion of nondomestic workers in these countries, accounting for about 90 percent of Qatar's labor force.

Labor markets throughout the Middle East have been substantially influenced by recent intraregional migration. One factor that accounted for this migration was the decline in agricultural employment stemming from increased mechanization and capital intensity in agricultural production, as well as the worsening of terms of trade for agricultural products during the oil boom (Tully, 1990). To fully comprehend this shift, it is important to understand that up until the early 1970s, agriculture employed the majority of workers in most of the Arab countries. Yet by the early 1990s, only Sudan and Yemen had labor forces that had more than 50 percent of the workers in agriculture. As Shaban et al. (1995) note, "the most dramatic decline in the importance of agricultural employment occurred in Iraq and Jordan. In Jordan the share of agriculture in total employment declined from 42 percent in the 1960s to less than 7 percent in the early 1990s" (p. 70).

In short, the rise in oil prices provided a catalyst for increased migration to the oil-producing countries in order to complete ambitious development projects that these countries could now afford. This migration tended to tighten the labor markets in the non-oil exporting countries, consequently reducing unemployment and raising the real wages of workers in these countries. By the late 1980s, "expatriate workers in the total labor force was 40 percent in Bahrain, 45 percent in Oman, 81 percent in Qatar, 85 percent in the United Arab Emirates, and 87 percent in Kuwait" (Shaban et al., 1995, p. 74). Data also indicate that the total number of Egyptians working in other Arab countries was about 2 million, with 100,000 of them going to Jordan as replacements for Jordanian emigrants.

Many of the labor-exporting countries were vulnerable to oil prices and political developments in the oil producing countries. For example, oil price reductions and the Gulf War forced many migrants home. Estimates suggest that the total number of returnees during this period was about 2 million people, including 732,000 Yemenis, 700,00 Egyptians, and 300,000 Jordanians. According to Shaban et al. (1995), most of those returning were working in Iraq, Kuwait, or Saudi Arabia. To illustrate, "41 percent of Egyptian returnees had been in Kuwait and 59 percent in Iraq; approximately 82 percent of Jordanian returnees had been in Kuwait; and 92 percent of Yemeni returnees had been in Saudi Arabia" (Shaban et al., 1995, p. 75). Understandably, the wave of returnees had a profound effect on the economies of the counties to which they returned. For example, Sudan's economy experienced negative growth in 1990-91. But the economic pressure on Jordan was offset by the savings of those who returned. Indeed many of the repatriated Jordanians invested their savings in small businesses, thereby creating their own employment in the informal sector. To be sure, initially the unemployment rate in Jordan increased, but as the repatriates began to invest, the economy experienced a mini-boom.

By comparison, the assets of most Yemenis returning from Saudi Arabia were effectively confiscated because they were forced to sell their assets and businesses at substantial discounts before they left. Consequently, Yemen had to reabsorb most unskilled, comparatively poor laborers. Another complicating factor in this country was that although 52 percent of the returnees formally had been agricultural workers prior to migration, fewer than 4 percent of them intended to return to farming—placing a tremendous burden on the labor markets. Once the Gulf War was over, the political realities of the region influenced the feasibility of those migrants returning to work in oil-producing countries. For example, workers from countries or groups perceived to have supported Iraq (Jordan, Sudan, Yemen, and the Palestinians) were typically denied entry in their labor markets. Meanwhile, one million Egyptian workers received work permits from Saudi Arabia as a reward for their government's anti-Iraq position.

As the previous discussion implies, some Arab countries have attempted to regulate their labor markets for either political or economic reasons. One of the main instruments of control for many Arab countries involves setting limits on permits for the entry and work of expatriates. Bahrain, for example, has raised the cost of foreign labor visas in addition to promoting vocational projects for citizens (Nakhoul, 1996). Oman and Saudi Arabia also raised visa fees, but they also have waged public campaigns to expel undocumented foreign workers. For countries like Saudi Arabia, where millions of foreign workers reside, the only way to treat citizen unemployment is to deport at least some of the foreigners. Gause (1997), however, indicates that this solution may be too simple. By expelling foreign workers, Arab countries face the challenge of replacing low-cost foreign laborers. And at "a time when the GCC governments are talking about having the private sector assume a greater role in the economy, it is difficult to impose increased labor costs upon it" (Gause, 1997, p. 150).

The problem with kicking the habit of foreign workers is further illustrated by the Kuwaiti experience. Prior to the outbreak of the Gulf War, foreign workers, in particular Palestinians and South Asians, made up three-fourths of the workforce in Kuwait. Following the Iraqi invasion, large numbers of these workers left Kuwait. After the liberation of Kuwait, the Kuwaiti government undertook a critical review of their dependence on foreign workers and, subsequently, revised their policies toward this supply of labor. Yet by 1994, the composition of the Kuwaiti workforce once again consisted of more than 75 percent foreign laborers, with fewer Palestinians, but many more South Asians (Russell & Al-Ramadhan, 1994).

Up to this point, little has been said about the labor market context in Israel. Israel is far more culturally and economically tied to Europe and the United States than any of the other countries in this region. Consequently, the Israeli economy differs significantly from the other countries in the Middle East. For example, the Israeli GDP now exceeds that of Egypt, Jordan, Syria, and Lebanon combined. Moreover, despite limited natural resources, Israel has developed markedly its agricultural and industrial sectors during the past two decades. But during the period 1990-95, migration of Jews from the former Soviet Union to Israel put a strain on the Israeli government budget, increased unemployment, and intensified housing problems. Still, as Table 2.8 indicates, Israeli unemployment is comparatively low among the Middle East countries. The data also suggest that Israel has the highest labor force participation rate for women in the region. A further breakdown of the labor markets in Israel reveals that although a low percentage of Israeli women are employed in agriculture, over three-quarters of them work in services. The 1999 average hourly compensation cost for production workers in Israel, measured in U.S. dollars, was $11.91 (BLS, 2000). This compares with the U.S. rate of $19.20 and a West European average of $20.31. Further compensation issues for this region in general and for Israel in particular will be discussed in Chapter 5.

CHAPTER SUMMARY

The 1998-99 issue of the International Labour Organization's (ILO) World Employment Report states the situation frankly: The picture we see as we survey the world's labor markets is "grim." In Western Europe, unemployment rates of 12 to 15 percent are common; in Eastern Europe, they are higher. Most countries in the Middle East support double-digit unemployment rates, with a disturbing disregard for the young, new labor market entrants. And, concludes the ILO, the United States' record has not been solely built on *cheap jobs*. The upshot, says the ILO, is that worldwide roughly 1 billion people are either unemployed or underemployed. Formal unemployment as found in the industrialized market economies brings familiar costs (e.g., loss of earnings) which can be met by such social programs as unemployment insurance, but the longer run costs need consideration as well. These include the unemployability of the long-term unemployed and the resulting

social exclusion. The persistence of such levels of unemployment and underemployment poses great threats to the stability of social and political systems. We
have only to recall the Iranian Revolution of 1979, certainly fueled in part by religious zeal, but which drew much of its strength from the clash of elevated expectations, especially on the part of better-educated rural migrants to Tehran, with the
reality of poor or nonexistent jobs which they found. And, of course, social and
political stability are key elements in a favorable climate for business.

There are, however, some positive developments. After years of decline,
the economies in many East European countries are beginning to grow. Indeed the
Czech Republic, Hungary, and Poland are viewed as very promising countries in
which to conduct business. And despite its many failings, the EU has had great
success in developing a culture of collaboration among its member states. What is
at issue here is not whether the EU will survive, but what kind of EU will lead
Europe in the 21st century. Finally, the United States and Canada support very
robust economies that provide a foundation for strong labor market contexts.

CHAPTER 3

Acquiring Human Resources

At the heart of a firm's competitive advantage is the quality of its workforce. Accordingly, successful organizations place a high priority on the acquisition of human resources. The typical acquisition stages involve a process by which organizations anticipate future staffing needs (human resource planning), a program that identifies and attracts a qualified applicant pool (recruiting), and a hiring procedure to fill vacant positions (selecting). As will become evident in what follows, there are extensive intra- and interregional variations in terms of the extent to which organizations engage in these stages.

THE UNITED STATES AND CANADA

Few intraregional differences in almost all HRM practices exist between the United States and Canada, which is not surprising because both countries share similar cultures, educational opportunities, and economic and political systems.

Human Resource Planning

Duane (1996) found that many U.S. and Canadian organizations develop and implement different human resource planning strategies, depending on organizational type. For example, organizations that face relatively predictable environments, with a centralized structure, tend to use more standardized planning methods (e.g., regression analysis to predict human resource demand and Markov analyses to track supply). Other types of organizations approach the planning process with less quantitative fervor, opting for qualitative analyses of labor demand and supply (e.g., Delphi technique).

Recruitment

In most medium and large U.S. and Canadian organizations, HRM professionals do most of the recruiting. These individuals may be HRM generalists who spend all their time performing recruitment activities. Although recruiters may make hiring decisions for some lower-level jobs, they typically find and screen applicants who will eventually be sent to line managers for the selection process. In any event, recruiters must work closely with line managers throughout the recruiting process. Perhaps the most important decision that recruiters and line managers must make is whether the position will be filled internally or externally.

As Table 3.1 suggests, most U.S. and Canadian organizations use a mixture of internal and external recruiting methods. Each type of recruiting has its advantages and disadvantages.

Internal recruitment has the obvious advantage of filling vacancies with individuals who are already known to the organization. Similarly, internal applicants are likely to be more knowledgeable about the organization and the vacancies than external applicants, minimizing misperceptions and unexpected experiences. Another advantage of recruiting internally is that it motivates valued employees; as a result, they are less likely to leave the organization. Finally, it is generally cheaper and faster to fill vacancies internally.

With all these advantages, you might ask why organizations ever resort to external recruitment? External recruitment has several advantages. First, for entry-level positions and for certain specialized needs, there may not be an internal-applicant pool. Second, by relying totally on internal recruitment, an organization may experience considerable disruption due to the ripple effect—vacancies that open up as others positions are filled. Indeed in one organization, 195 vacancies eventually produced 545 job movements. External recruitment prevents such disturbances. Third, bringing in outsiders fosters creativity and flexibility by exposing the organizations to new ideas and new ways of conducting business. It also may be necessary to achieve affirmative action goals and to provide equal employment opportunities (Fisher, Schoenfeldt, & Shaw, 1993). Golbar and Deshpande (1997) observe that Canadian firms agree with their U.S. counterparts that such external sources of recruitment as employment agencies and educational institutions provide a rich pool of talent.

Selection

The selection process follows human resource planning and recruitment. Most organizations use more than one selection method to identify the best-qualified applicants. Indeed virtually all organizations in the United States and Canada use applicant interviews and reference checks (Golbar & Deshpande, 1997; Noe et al., 2000). Other common employee-selection methods are presented in Table 3.2. In terms of the usefulness or validity of these selection methods, much research has been conducted in U.S. and Canadian organizations. A summary of the findings are presented in Table 3.3. Overall research suggests that while structured interviews and work-sample tests are excellent predictors of future job suc-

TABLE 3.1

Sources of Recruitment

Sources	Office/Clerical	Production/Service	Professional/ Technical
Internal Sources			
Promotion from within	94%	86%	88%
Employ referrals	87	83	64
Walk-ins	86	87	64
Advertising			
Newspapers Journals/Magazines	84	77	94
Radio/Television	6	7	54
Direct-mail	3	6	3
Employment Services	4	3	16
U.S. Employment Service	19	20	11
State employment services	66	68	38
Private employment services	28	11	58
Search firms	1	<1	36
Employee leasing firm	16	10	6
Computerized resume services	0	0	4
Outside Referral Sources			
High/trade schools	60	54	16
Technical/Vocational institutes	48	51	47
Colleges/universities	24	15	81
Professional societies	4	1	5
Unions	1	10	1
Community agencies	33	32	20
Special Events			
Career/job fairs	20	16	44
Open houses	10	8	7

TABLE 3.1 (continued)

Sources of Recruitment

Sources	Commissioned Sales	Managers/ Supervisors	All
Internal Sources			
Promotion from within	75%	95%	99%
Employ referrals	76	64	91
Walk-ins	52	46	91
Advertising			
Newspapers	84	85	97
Journals/ Magazines	33	50	64
Radio/Television	3	2	9
Direct-mail	6	8	17
Employment Services			
U.S. Employment Service	7	7	22
State employment services	30	23	72
Private employment services	44	60	72
Search firms	26	63	67
Employee leasing firms	2	<1	20
Computerized resume services	0	2	4
Outside Referral Sources			
High/trade schools	5	2	68
Technical/Vocational institutes	5	8	77
Colleges/universities	38	45	86
Professional societies	19	37	55
Unions	0	1	10
Community agencies	16	10	39
Special Events			
Career/job fairs	19	19	52
Open houses	8	7	22

Source: Casio (1989).

cess, reference checks tend to be problematic. But to conclude that a certain selection method is useful, or valid, for U.S. and Canadian firms, does not necessarily mean that it will be equally so for organizations in different regions of the world. Indeed cultural differences may negate such a transfer.

TABLE 3.2

Selection Methods

Method	All Jobs	Clerical	Production/ Service	Professional/ Technical	Sales	Managers
Skill performance test/work sample	64%	55%	19%	10%	4%	3%
Medical examination	57	43	57	47	46	45
Mental ability test	31	23	10	8	9	9
Job knowledge test	27	14	14	14	3	5
Drug test	26	21	26	22	23	21
Personality test	17	1	2	6	23	13
Assessment center	12	-	1	3	4	10
Physical abilities test	11	1	12	2	1	1
Honesty test	7	4	6	2	4	3
AIDS	1	-	-	1	-	-

Source: Fisher et al. (1993), p. 307.

TABLE 3.3

Evaluation of Selection Methods

Method	Reliability	Validity	Generalizability	Utility
Interviews	Low when unstructured and when assessing nonobservable traits	Low if unstructured and non-behavioral	Low	Low, especially due to expense
Reference Checks	Low, especially when obtained from letters	Low because of lack of range in evaluations	Low	Low, although not expensive to obtain
Biographical Information	High test-retest, especially for verifiable information	High criterion-related validity; low in content validity	Usually job-specific, but have been successfully developed for many jobs types	High; inexpensive way to collect vast amounts of potentially relevant data
Physical ability tests	High	Moderate criterion-related validity; high content validity for some jobs	Low, only pertain to physically demanding jobs	Moderate for some physical jobs
Cognitive ability tests	High	Moderate criterion-related validity	High, predictive for most jobs	High, low cost and wide applications
Personality Inventories	High	Low criterion-related validity	Low, few traits predictive for many jobs	Low, although relatively inexpensive
Work-sample tests	High	High criterion and content validity	Usually job specific, but have been successfully developed for a number of jobs	High, despite the relatively high cost to develop
Drug tests	High	High	High	Expensive

Source: Noe et al. (2000).

WESTERN EUROPE

An interesting pattern exists across Western Europe regarding the extent to which organizations develop an overall HRM strategy, particularly regarding how to acquire the appropriate number and types of employees. For example, more than 70 percent of the firms in Norway, Sweden, and Denmark report having written HRM strategies. This, however, does not mean they implement them. Indeed many of these firms do not translate HRM strategies into work programs and deadlines for their human resource departments. As one moves south, the emphasis on formalized human resource strategy development diminishes. For example, only about 35 percent of the firms in France, Italy, Portugal, and Spain have written strategies. Interestingly, although fewer organizations in the southern and central countries support HRM strategies, those that did were more likely to implement them (PWC, 1991).

Human Resource Planning

As Table 3.4 indicates, almost all West European firms, with or without a formalized HRM strategy, engage in some form of human resource planning. Yet countries differ in how they conduct it. To illustrate, the southern countries tend to utilize relatively short planning periods. The data in Table 3.5 indicate, for example, that 63 percent of the Portuguese firms and 48 percent of the Spanish firms limit their planning periods to one year. By comparison, the northern countries plan farther ahead, with Finnish (51 percent), Danish (28 percent), and Norwegian (24 percent) firms reporting planning periods of two or more years.

With respect to individual human resource planning techniques, it is interesting to note that although recruiting to maintain adequate staffing ratios is widely practiced throughout Western Europe, only 9 percent of the organizations in Finland report doing so. Two explanations seem to account for this phenomenon. First, as noted earlier, the Finnish firms engage in long-term planning, thereby making short-term methods for filling positions less necessary. Another reason is that during the early 1990s, when the data were collected, Finland entered its worst recession in postwar history. Indeed of all the Organization for Economic Cooperation and Development (OECD) countries, Finland experienced the weakest growth of employment, "with total output contracting by 10 percent and unemployment rising from 3.5 percent in 1990 to 15 percent by the end of 1992" (OECD, Finland, 1994, p. 11). Thus, rather than attempting to maintain current staffing levels, many firms were downsizing their workforces.

Recruitment

The recruiting process for firms in the southern countries is highly regulated by their governments. In Italy, for example, employers are required to comply with numerical recruitment (*richiesta numberica*). When this was initially imposed in 1949, selection of employees was based on an ordinal list, without regard to education, training, or skill. Factors that went into the ranking of individuals were an applicant's need, which was determined by the number of dependants and applicant's need, which was determined by the number of dependants and health, and that person's length of time on the list. Professional employees and organizations with fewer than five workers were generally exempt from this practice. These workers were recruited by name (*richiesta nominativa*), which granted employers the right to independently choose an employee (Law 264, Article 14, 29, April 1949).

TABLE 3.4

Human Resource Planning Techniques by Country (Percentage)

Country	Recruit to Maintain Adequate Personnel	Forecast Skills Requirements	Sales/Bus. Forecasts	Analyze Labor Markets	Other
Denmark	83	87	89	45	7
W. Germany	70	92	52	46	9
Spain	74	82	87	60	5
France	65	94	78	37	6
Finland	9	81	68	37	5
Ireland	76	95	71	33	7
Norway	19	80	75	32	6
Netherlands	94	34	63	62	8
Portugal	70	93	74	74	2
Sweden	48	90	87	38	5
Turkey	92	85	90	74	3
UK	63	94	83	59	5

Source: Table 5.3 on page 76, Dany, F., & Torchy, V. (1994) Recruitment and selection in Europe: Policies, practices, and methods. In C. Brewster and A. Hegewisch (Eds.), *Policy and Practice in European Human Resource Management*. Hampshire, UK: ITBP.

Over time, the requirement to comply with *richiesta nominativa* was eased. In 1984, legislation was passed that allowed employers to hire 50 percent of their nonprofessional employees on the basis of qualifications. And a 1991 amendment to Italian law promoted further flexibility in hiring procedures, yet the numerical-recruitment requirement remains a factor in the hiring process. To illustrate, organizations employing more than ten employees must hire 12 percent of their employees on the numerical basis, with preference going to the long-term (2 years or more) unemployed. Although recent Italian labor law changes did deregulate the recruiting process somewhat, the Employment Office, a governmental agency that is divided into regional bureaus, still plays a prominent role in mediating the employment relationship between workers and employers. Indeed regional bureaus are responsible for maintaining the job seekers' list, deciding priority rankings for employee placement, choosing the workers to be placed with employers under the numerical request system, and conducting surveys of the labor market. Although the use of headhunters and private employment agencies for recruiting middle- and top-level managers has just begun to emerge in Italy, the law severely limits their power.

TABLE 3.5

Time Horizons for Human Resource Planning (Percentage)

	No Planning	One Year or Less	Between One and Two Years	More than Two Years
Denmark	11	19	34	28
W. Germany	6	32	38	24
Spain	6	48	30	15
France	7	41	32	19
Finland	0	5	43	51
Ireland	3	57	25	14
Norway	6	34	31	24
Netherlands	9	44	32	11
Portugal	14	63	17	2
Sweden	3	38	37	20
Turkey	11	47	23	20
UK	5	44	27	22

Source: Table 2.14 in Appendix III. In C. Brewster and A. Hegewisch (Eds.), *Policy and Practice in European Human Resource Management.* (1994). Hampshire, UK: ITBP.

Under Greek law, private employment agencies are illegal. Instead, similar to Italy, the government's Employment Office serves as an intermediator between job seekers and employers. Although Spain permits private employment agencies to operate, they must comply with strict governmental rules. Accordingly, unlike the northern and central countries, where employee recruitment tends to be a relatively open operation, with the high use of private employment agencies, the southern countries foster a rather closed staffing process. But even in this region, evidence suggests that it is becoming a more open process. As indicated earlier, legislative reform in Italy has allowed additional employer flexibility in the recruiting process. Furthermore, in 1993, Spain eliminated the requirement that employers use the National Employment Service as the primary source of recruitment (Flolrz-Saborido, Gonzallez-Rendoln, & Alcaide-Castro, 1995).

Data suggest that northern countries seem to experience less difficulty recruiting applicants (see Table 3.6). In part, this tendency may be because managers in this region are long-term planners, which can reduce some of the uncertainties in the staffing process. But even in these countries, recruiting quality managers is a problem. As Table 3.7 indicates, efforts to confront recruitment problems have led many West European firms to lower age requirements, posing a potential child-labor problem. Indeed the southern countries have been particularly negligent in protecting children in the workplace. Reports have been filed, for example, concerning tens of thousands of child laborers in Naples alone, with the leather industry being the most grave offender. Likewise, in Spain more than 100,000 instances of child laborers have been observed (Adkins, 1995). To be sure, most of the southern countries have some form of age restrictions for participation in the workplace. In Italy, for example, the minimum age for starting work is typically 15, 14 for certain types of work, and 18 for jobs covered by special protective regulations (ECHO). But fines for violators are minimal. The EU has taken a first step in standardizing child-labor laws by adopting Council Directive 94-33-EC, which essentially bans the employment of children under the age of 15, except in the case of apprenticeships, certain defined occupations, and "light work" (Addison & Siebert, 1994). (Further discussion of child-labor problems will be covered in Chapter 6.)

Understandably, relocation of the company is the least popular means of recruitment. Many Spanish and Portuguese firms have found it necessary to move at least certain segments of their organizations in order to attract and retain quality employees. But recent improvements in the economic and infrastructure conditions in these countries may make this recruitment alternative less necessary in the future.

Although many central and northern countries use part-time employees to address their problems with recruiting full-time workers, the southern countries are reluctant to do so. In Italy, for example, there is a traditional and firmly rooted commitment to permanent employment. Accordingly, temporary employment has been subject to governmental regulations under the terms of Law 230, which lays out the conditions for hiring part-time workers. In 1987, Italian law was amended so that the parties in some national multi-industry collective bargaining agreements could negotiate a contractual provision that permitted temporary employment contracts for employees over the age of 29.

Selection

Most West European firms use a variety of methods to select employees (see Table 3.8). But the exact combination of selection devices differs not only across this region, but within it as well. For example, regardless of size, almost all organizations in the United Kingdom and Ireland use references. References are also frequently used in Norway, Switzerland, and Sweden—where over 90 percent of the firms use them in making employment decisions. By comparison, the Netherlands, Finland, and the southern countries deemphasized references in reviewing the potential of job applicants. To be sure, 54 percent of the Spanish firms report that they require references, but as Levy-Leboyer (1994) notes, information from them is rarely given much weight. When size of the organization is taken into ac-

TABLE 3.6

Recruiting Problems by Job Categories (Percentage)

Category	Denmark	West Germany	Spain	France	Finland	Ireland	Norway	Netherlands	Portugal	Sweden	United Kingdom
Management	28	24	32	17	22	25	10	17	3	25	13
Qualified Pro.	17	8	13	6	10	14	11	11	11	19	27
Health/Social	25	2	0	7	1	18	51	0	0	16	8
Engineers	5	11	9	14	0	15	7	5	8	13	14
Inform. Tech.	4	5	8	5	0	8	2	5	11	6	12
Technicians	2	5	12	17	0	1	1	15	20	4	5
Admin./Clerical	2	6	2	1	0	1	1	8	3	3	5
Sales/Distri.	7	9	13	11	0	4	5	10	6	1	5
Skilled Manuals	4	18	7	16	12	11	5	20	25	10	7
Manual	3	2	0	1	0	1	2	7	4	1	2
Foreign Lang.	1	1	3	1	0	1	0	0	1	0	0
No Recruitment Problems	24	65	23	28	74	44	44	18	16	60	35

Source: Table 5.4 on page 78, Dany, F., & Torchy, V. (1994) Recruitment and selection in Europe: Policies, practices, and methods. In C. Brewster and A. Hegewisch (Eds.), *Policy and Practice in European Human Resource Management.* Hampshire, UK: ITBP.

TABLE 3.7

Practices to Assist in Recruitment (Percentage)

Category	Denmark	West Germany	Spain	France	Finland	Ireland	Norway	Netherlands	Portugal	Sweden	United Kingdom
Flexible work hours	42	76	26	40	55	28	51	25	25	63	39
Recruiting abroad	13	16	13	16	9	35	27	14	14	15	20
Relaxed age requirements	13	54	52	27	26	25	29	52	48	27	40
Relaxed qualifications	13	12	46	22	16	10	10	26	50	25	21
Relocation of firm	3	3	13	4	5	2	2	2	10	3	7
Retraining programs	49	56	67	38	56	54	53	69	71	53	67
Training programs for new employees	59	58	64	73	59	51	61	71	65	39	68
Part-time employees	31	67	17	30	27	33	45	33	12	30	53
Increased pay and Benefits	32	47	52	37	26	32	35	47	67	23	44
Marketing the firm's image	41	64	37	59	63	33	42	52	50	54	53

Source: Table 5.5 on page 80, Dany, F., & Torchy, V. (1994) Recruitment and selection in Europe: Policies, practices, and methods. In C. Brewster and A. Hegewisch (Eds.), *Policy and Practice in European Human Resource Management.* Hampshire, UK: ITBP.

count, however, two findings are noteworthy. First, in small Greek firms, "friends' recommendations are often granted serious consideration, and such candidates are favored, provided they are equal to, or not significantly worse than, other candidates" (Papalexandris, 1993, p. 168). Second, although most large firms in France use references, data indicate that only 11 percent of the French small- to medium size firms elicit references in selecting managers.

Graphology is the process of deducing personality and behavioral characteristics about individuals through the analysis of their handwriting. Overwhelming evidence discounts graphology as a reliable and valid source of information for making personnel decisions (Smith & Roberston, 1986). And, as the data in Table 3.8 suggest, although this selection device receives little attention in most West European countries, 57 percent of the French firms use it in selecting employees. Levy-Leboyer (1994) argues that one factor that may explain the popularity of graphology in France is its cultural acceptability and perceived legitimacy by employees and employers. To this point, Steiner and Gilliland (1996) found that significantly more French subjects perceived graphology to be a valid tool in the selection process than did their U.S. counterparts. Fetherston (1995) observes that in France, "graphology is seen as a valuable analytic tool. Handwriting is *de rigueur* on any job application: 'If you want to compete in the French job market,' notes one guide to getting a job in France, 'put away your word processor and pull out your pen.'"(p. C03).

The interview is one of the most popular means of selecting employees in Western Europe. Yet there are some differences among countries regarding how it is structured. In their study of organizations in France and the United Kingdom, for example, Shackleton and Newell (1991) found that 93 percent of the French organizations require applicants to undergo more than one interview, compared with 60 percent in the United Kingdom. They explain that inasmuch as French organizations are more inclined to conduct one-on-one interviews, applicants have to endure a number of them in order to be seen by different people. The greater use of more than one interview in France also supports the claim by Hofstede (1984) that the French are less comfortable with uncertainty than are the British. Thus, French managers "seek confirmation of their views of candidates from colleagues, to lessen the uncertainty of having to make the decision themselves" (Shackleton & Newell, 1991, p. 35).

In Spain, 85 percent of the organizations report using interviews. Evidence suggests, however, that in many Spanish firms, the interview carries little weight in making employment decisions. Instead, it is seen as a social situation, where the parties can informally discuss the applicant's aspirations and self-image (Prieto, Blasco, & Quintanilla, 1991). But as Vicente (1993) argues, when structured interviews are used by Spanish firms, the selected employees make greater contributions to profits. Accordingly, he expects that many Spanish firms that are now conducting informal interviews will in the near future adopt a more structured format.

Psychometric tests can be grouped into two broad categories: personality tests and cognitive/aptitude tests. As Table 3.8 indicates, psychometric testing is

TABLE 3.8

Employee Selection Methods (Percentage)

Selection method	Denmark	West Germany	Spain	France	Finland	Ireland	Norway	Netherlands	Portugal	Sweden	United Kingdom
Application form	4	96	87	95	82	91	59	94	83	na	97
Interview panel	99	86	85	92	99	87	78	69	97	.69	71
Bio data	92	20	12	26	48	7	56	20	62	69	8
Psychometric testing	38	6	60	22	74	28	11	31	58	24	46
Graphology	2	8	8	57	2	1	0	2	2	0	1
References	79	66	54	73	63	91	92	47	55	96	92
Aptitude test	17	8	72	28	42	41	19	53	17	14	45
Assessment center	4	13	18	9	16	7	5	27	2	5	18
Group selection methods	8	4	22	10	8	8	1	2	18	3	13
Other	2	3	4	3	2	6	5	6	0	5	4

Source: Table 5.6 on page 81, Dany, F., & Torchy, V. (1994) Recruitment and selection in Europe: Policies, practices, and methods. In C. Brewster and A. Hegewisch (Eds.), *Policy and Practice in European Human Resource Management.* Hampshire, UK: ITBP.

commonly practiced by Finnish, Spanish, and Portuguese organizations. If medium- to large size organizations are isolated, however, it appears to be most popular in French and Belgian organizations (Levy-Leboyer, 1994). To illustrate, Bournois (1993) observed that 62 percent of large French organizations administered personality tests as part of the employee-selection process, 55 percent of them used aptitude tests, and 22 percent administered such tests as the Rorschach. These results are consistent with the study by Steiner and Gilliland (1996), who found that French job applicants perceived personality tests to be more scientifically valid than did their U.S. counterparts. In Belgium, psychometric tests are applied to specific situations. Sparrow and Hiltrop (1994) note one situation involves "graduate recruitment (because of concerns about the gap between theoretical education qualifications and employers' desire to recruit adaptable, mobile and linguistically skilled students)" (p. 345). Belgian organizations also use psychometric tests in evaluating the qualifications of workers who apply for particularly sensitive positions.

Little use of psychometric testing is reported in Germany and in the southern countries. In the case of Germany, psychometric assessments must satisfy three criteria before an organization can use them. First, the tests must have a qualified psychologist administer and interpret their results. Second, evidence of the tests' job-relatedness must be provided. Third, test takers must be notified of the content and nature of the tests and agree to participate in the process (Sparrow & Hiltrop, 1994). With respect to the southern countries, psychometric testing violates many cultural and religious tenets. Specifically, the people in most of these countries are predominately Catholic, and the Catholic Church in the past has disapproved of psychological tests. It is not surprising, therefore, that in 1970 the Italian government passed legislation on worker rights that forbade using most psychometric-assessment tools in the workplace (Shimmin, 1989). Yet a recent survey revealed that large organizations in this region are beginning to incorporate them into their staffing procedures (Filella, 1993).

Although assessment centers tend to be expensive to conduct, they are valid and well-accepted methods for making employment decisions (Noe et al., 2000). Even though the data indicate that only 13 percent of the organizations in Germany use assessment centers, they have a long history there. Specifically, in 1939, the German army conducted assessment centers to identify qualified leaders. Centers were then adopted by the British War Office Selection Board and the U.S. Office of Strategic Services (Sparrow & Hiltrop, 1994).

Despite evidence to the contrary, the French generally perceive assessment centers as an invalid employee-selection method (Steiner and Gilliland, 1996). Still, centers are used in 19 percent of French organizations with more than 500 employees (Shackleton & Newell, 1991). Countries where assessment centers appear to be developing some popularity include the United Kingdom and the Netherlands (Levy-Leboyer, 1994).

EASTERN EUROPE AND THE NEW INDEPENDENT STATES

In the old days, governments in most East European and Soviet countries funneled able-bodied adults into jobs. Blue-collar workers were recruited by advertising vacancies in state-sponsored publications. Although managerial and professional personnel had to have more education, their selection was based in large measure on political loyalty, rather than on their competencies. In either event, however, almost everyone was assured a job.

Human Resource Planning

As a rule, human resource planning was ensured by planning departments located in individual organizations. Yet under the system of central planning and central authorities' tight control over productive factors, including human resources, the role of planning departments was very limited. Individual organizations were allowed to submit requests for human resources during the formation of state plans or to ask for changes once the plans had been developed. Oftentimes the desire to achieve full employment caused the state to force additional workers on organizations, regardless of their needs. And some organizations welcomed the surplus workers in order to get related financial gains. Accordingly, human resource planning during these days resulted in overemployment within individual organizations. From the perspective of individual workers, it fostered a sense of dependence on the state to coordinate their job-hunting activities.

Although some changes in HRM, including human resource planning, have occurred in Russia, developments in the Czech Republic, Hungary, and Poland have been impressive. This is no coincidence inasmuch as these countries are in the early stages of attempting to join the EU. Koubek and Brewster (1995) note that "the division of Czechoslovakia accelerated the transformation process in the Czech Republic and consequently moved it to a leading position in the group" (p. 224). In short, the Czech Republic is establishing HRM patterns that countries like Hungary and Poland are expected to follow. It is not surprising, therefore, that in the Czech Republic, as in Western Europe, the importance of human resource planning is beginning to be acknowledged. Indeed over 85 percent of the Czech Republic organizations report engaging in human resource planning, "a higher figure than for all countries except Finland and West Germany" (p. 235). Moreover, in 1991, roughly half of the organizations in the Czech Republic reported that HRM executives were involved in the development of corporate strategies from the beginning. West European involvement ranged from 32 percent in Ireland to 65 percent in Norway. Moreover, about 90 percent of the Czech organizations reported having HRM strategies, 60 percent reported having written strategies, and the remaining having unwritten strategies (PWC survey, 1994). Finally, personnel managers are beginning to serve on main boards. To illustrate, data indicate that 64 percent of the Czech Republic organizations include personnel managers on their top-level decision making bodies, compared with 84 percent in France, 73 percent in Spain, 54 percent in Sweden, and 49 percent in the United Kingdom.

Recruitment

Employment in this region is no longer guaranteed the way it was in the past. Thus, job hunting has taken on a different strategy. Now on their own, individuals have found job hunting tedious and in some cases demeaning. For example, in Russia "applicants face frustration of cryptic want ads, sexism, and overly blunt bosses. Some aspiring workers even try go-go dancing to gain attention" (Simon, 1996a, p. A-1). Simon (1996a) provides specific accounts of these problems at a recently held job fair:

> Yulia wanted to work as an accountant. So, she pulled on a tight green miniskirt, squeezed into saucy high heels and pranced onto the stage of a hotel ballroom, batting her lashes and swinging her hips as she tried to win a job balancing books. Nearby danced Valeria, hopeful of landing a managerial post. Also Irena, in body-hugging white, her law school courses all but forgotten as she flirted behind a cat-eye mask and dreamed of finding secretarial work.

Although these instances of recruiting may not be widespread, they do point out how comparatively unsophisticated the staffing process is in this region.

The traditional method of getting hired—sitting and waiting for an offer—does not work for most job seekers. As the anecdotal accounts suggest, now people are more or less on their own. Alexander Tkachenko, a demographer who heads the Russian Labor Ministry's population department, notes that many job seekers in Russia are not accustomed to the new staffing process: "Before, everything was well-defined: You got a job when you got out of school. That was our planned economy . . . ." (Simon, 1996b, p. A-2). He adds that the Russians have much to learn about the hiring process under the capitalist system, which requires a good deal of self-promotion. Indeed the only way that people learn about many lower-level jobs is through word of mouth or by reading notices attached to the doors of plants or businesses. A good example of this exists in nearly every Moscow subway car, where "a poster woos potential train drivers with promises of fat pensions and free uniforms. Yet only men ages 18 to 40 may apply—and only if they have served in the army and completed middle school"(Simon, 1996b, p. A-2).

While improving marginally, the help-wanted advertisements in Russian newspapers provide little information. Most of the job vacancies simply say "Work," accompanied by a phone number. Typically there is no description of the job, no salary information, and no clue about location. Other jobs are advertised by being only slightly more descriptive: "Work for young people," "Interesting work," or "We are looking for colleagues." In these cases, the jobs often turn out to be less than glamorous, typically low paying manufacturing or sales jobs (Simon, 1996b).

Some recruiting methods that are beginning to appear include Western-type college job fairs, but there is a virtual lack of career counseling or placement services at Russian universities and colleges. Moreover, the Russian equivalent of *Cosmopolitan* magazine recently published some tips on how to develop a resume. Yet many students still do not know how to write a cover letter (Simon, 1996b).

For some professions (e.g., scientist and economist), the traditional recruiting method involving invitations from government ministries to new graduates is still used. The best students, however, scorn such jobs, opting for work abroad. This has become a particular problem for the former Soviet Union republics; as Landau (1992) observes "the influx of newcomers from republics of the former Soviet Union has changed employment patterns in Israel. The number of engineers has doubled and the number of doctors has risen by 70 percent" (p. PG). In the United States, Russians make up the fastest-growing legal immigrants since the end of the Soviet Union regime in 1991. A Harvard mathematics professor notes that the Russian people have "seen virtually a collapse of the mathematics culture in the former Soviet Union because so many left" (Possehl, 1995). These accounts suggest that the former Soviet republics are having a difficult time recruiting professional employees. In response, their future recruiting efforts must address compensation and working conditions issues. And there is some evidence that they are moving in this direction. Governments of Russia and other former Soviet republics are beginning to offer competitive grants to those scientists who stay (Venkat, 1995).

As in the case of human resource planning, the recruitment process in the Czech Republic is a model in this region. Even during the depths of the recent recession, Western Europe generally experienced problems in recruitment. But only 11 percent of the organizations in the Czech Republic indicated having problems recruiting employees—the lowest figure across Europe. In addition, 72 percent of the Czech organizations target school dropouts when recruiting employees, the highest proportion in Europe with the exception of Portugal. Koubek and Brewster (1995) note further that "a larger number than in most countries have targeted people with disabilities, the long-term unemployed and older people; the Czech Republic is in the top few countries in Europe on each item" (p. 237).

Selection

Little evidence exists regarding the current use of specific selection techniques in this region of the world. What is available, however, suggests that there are some differences between this region and Western countries. For example, there tends to be considerably more pessimism in the application of selection devices. To illustrate, "in a job interview, a Hungarian interviewee response would be to emphasize all of the things that they cannot do—a very unlikely response for a U.S. job candidate. This again comes from a system of avoiding punishment" (Kovach, 1995, p. 93). In a survey of Western companies doing business in Russia, interviews were the most frequently used selection device. And even though transcripts and diplomas were looked at, they were viewed as less important than the perception of whether the applicant was honest, ambitious, hardworking, and able to learn the job responsibilities. Only a few of the organizations required references and used psychological tests to make selection decisions (Fey, Engstrom, & Bjorkman, 1999). Such information suggests that the Westernization of employee selection in this region will take place in the near future, however. Prokopenko

(1994) notes that in these newly formed market economies the most important criteria for selection will be competence, experience, and trainability rather than good connections.

THE MIDDLE EAST

There is a paucity of information on how Middle East organizations acquire employees. Reports suggest that, as with other regions of the world, the process of recruiting and selecting employees in Middle East countries varies widely. Indeed the Arab countries have become an important destination for legal and illegal Indonesian workers since the early 1980s. A substantial number of Indonesian recruits are women who work as domestic servants in the more affluent countries, particularly Saudi Arabia. As a result, in an effort to combat high unemployment the Indonesian government began to promote and formalize the recruitment of workers migrating to oversees destinations, including the Middle East. In 1984, for example, the Center for Overseas Employment (AKAN) was established by the Ministry of Labor to promote, select, and monitor overseas labor. This program has been mildly successful in sending workers to the Middle East, with an annual migrant movement of roughly 50,000 workers (Cremer, 1989). Many migrant recruits who enter Arab countries do so on a Haij or Umroh visa. After staying a period of time, they attempt to find work. Although Arab governments have imposed added provisions in an effort to reduce such illegalities, migrants still manage to find their way to the Middle East—often with the help of employment brokers.

The multinational organizations in Arab countries tend to adopt conventional methods of recruitment and selection. One reason for this trend is heavy recruitment of managers and skilled labor from Western Europe and the United States. For example, separate countries have developed Web pages to attract Western workers. With regard to specific methods of recruitment, the Price Waterhouse Cranfield Survey (PWCS) of 1994 offers some interesting insights into practices in Turkey. Similar to organizations across Western Europe, a considerable proportion (94 percent) of the Turkish organizations used forecasting to determine future skill requirements. But contrary to many West European organizations, while 35 percent of the organizations in Turkey report having no recruitment problems, a substantial number (13 percent) of them had difficulty recruiting individuals with foreign language skills. Similarly, unlike many West European countries that invoke flexible working hours in an attempt to recruit employees, over 60 percent of the Turkish organizations attempt to retain existing employees and/or retrain current employees to fill vacant positions.

Regarding the selection of employees, the PWCS reveals that the application form was used in over 90 percent of the organizations in Turkey, with over 60 percent of the organizations reporting use of interviews and references (Dany & Torchy, 1994). In most Arab countries, informal selection techniques are very common. For example, Cohen and House (1996) note that in the Sudan informal methods of hiring deprive potentially competent workers of employment. Specifically, they argue that businesses rarely resort to advertisements in developing a pool of qualified applicants. Instead they prefer factory-gate recruitment and family or employee referrals. They conclude that large private organizations tend to hire workers because of social connections rather than on training and ability.

Research suggests that in some Arab countries, there is a high incidence of mismatch of graduates from certain college or university programs. For example, a study by Abdel-Halim and Ashour (1995) reveals that a relatively large number of graduates from Kuwait University who were selected for supervisory jobs left their jobs in a short period of time. In acknowledging this disturbing trend, the university is embarking on a program to provide adequate information about jobs and careers to its graduates, which should help them make better job choices. It has been suggested that there is a need for assistance in job-seeking activity and career planning.

Israeli organizations rely on an extensive variety of devices to recruit and select employees. In many instances, recruitment by word-of-mouth referrals or newspaper advertisements limits information to Israeli applicants and/or discourages Arab workers who are citizens of Israel from applying for positions. Moreover, as Wolkinson (1994) notes, when "Israeli Arab workers do succeed in identifying and applying for job vacancies, their chances of employment are disproportionately impaired by intensive employer use of selection factors as the personal interview, experience, residency, and army service requirements" (p. 260). Rafaeli (1999) notes that from the perspective of the educated Israeli applicant, knowledge testing was viewed as more valid and work-related than the personality tests.

CHAPTER SUMMARY

This chapter examined the practices and policies affecting the acquisition of human resources in several regions of the world. Several generalizations can be advanced. First, countries vary widely in the degree of technical sophistication used in the acquisition of human resources. At one extreme, the United States, Canada, and northern Western Europe use comparatively advanced methods. There are, however, countries, located chiefly in Eastern Europe and the Middle East, where the family or a religious group provides the basis for transmission of job and employment information as well as the basis for evaluating a prospective employee's qualifications, notably trustworthiness.

Second, cultural effects may be subtler than the crude "markers" of family or sectarian association. Hofstede (1984) has advanced a number of dimensions on which major cultures have been argued to vary. Such characterizations as a culture's receptivity toward "individualism" or "uncertainty" or its toleration of greater "power distance" will arguably be a part of the criteria for recruiting and acquiring employees.

Finally, the degree of concern for reliability and validity of selection techniques varies considerably throughout the world. Graphology, popular in France, would be laughed out of a U.S. courtroom, which is where employers would quickly find themselves should they try to use it.

A word of caution for those who argue that international standards of selection should be imposed is in order. Elsewhere in this book, it was suggested that International Labor Conventions might be viewed as international standards of best practice—and might present challenges to some U.S. ways of conducting business. In the context of acquiring human resources, it will be instructive to look at one international standard that seems not to have fared very well. International Labor Convention No. 96, the *Fee Charging Employment Agencies Convention (Revised)* of 1949 provides for the progressive abolition of fee-charging agencies (conducted with a view to profit), or their regulation by the ratifying state, depending on the state's preference.

The theory seems to have been that no person should take money away from someone just because he or she finds a job through that agency. Economists, who see information as very important in labor markets and consider it to have a value, will have and have had difficulties accepting the wisdom of abolishing fee-charging employment services. Nevertheless, a number of countries have adopted Convention No. 96—as we saw above, private employment agencies are illegal in Greece, while Italy and Spain (until recently) have required employers to use some form of state system of worker-job matching. In any event, whether it was the arguments of the economists or the general drift toward privatization of many formally public activities, the International Labor Conference in recent years has begun a fundamental revision of Convention 96, to the end that for-profit agencies will soon no longer be pariahs.

CHAPTER 4

Developing Human Resources

Not only do organizations benefit from a well-trained workforce, the countries in which they are located prosper as well. Accordingly, investment in human resource development is not simply the responsibility of individual organizations, but of society as a whole. In this chapter, the role of government in providing opportunities for citizens to receive education and training is addressed. Policies and practices of employee training for individual organizations within countries will also be examined.

THE UNITED STATES AND CANADA

On the surface, literacy data for the United States and Canada are very impressive, with both countries reporting rates of around 99 percent. Moreover, in the 1994 International Adult Literacy Survey (Statistics Canada, 1997), Canada and the United States had the highest percentage of employees with postsecondary education, almost double that of the other countries surveyed: Germany, the Netherlands, Poland, Sweden, and Switzerland. A more detailed analysis, however, is very revealing. Indeed Table 4.1 indicates that over a fifth of the U.S. citizens read at the lowest level of literacy, the worst reported in the survey—with the exception of Poland. Such data bring Carnevale, Gainer, and Meltzer (1990) to conclude that the supply of individuals with the necessary skills and training will not meet the demands for jobs in the U.S. economy. Specifically new jobs in the next decade will require higher levels of reading and writing, particularly in the technical and science areas. Evidence to support the lack of required skills is provided by the educational characteristics of current members of the labor force. One estimate suggests that 27 million adults in the United States do not have the basic writing, reading, and computational skills needed to perform competently in the workplace (Gordon, Ponticell, & Morgan, 1989). In addition, many U.S. organizations report that their employees lack the basic skills in reading, mathematics, and problem solving to be able to handle upgrades in technology, job redesign, and improvements in product quality and customer service. Finally, although the 1998 Global Competitiveness Report acknowledges the surprising strength of the U.S. economy, it identifies as one of its major weaknesses that "technical education at the high-school level appears to lag behind many other countries. Worker and youth training appear to lag behind some competitors. These are points of social weakness, widely recognized." (Sachs & Stone, 1999, p. 7)

TABLE 4.1

Percentage of Adults Scoring on Four Levels of the Prose Literacy Scale

Country	Level 1	Level 2	Level 3	Level 4/5
Canada	16.6	24.8	36.4	22.3
Germany	3.8	35.3	37.3	13.6
Netherlands	10.4	29.4	44.7	15.5
Poland	42.7	34.3	19.2	3.7
Sweden	7.2	20.7	39.8	32.2
Switzerland (French)	18.5	34.3	37.7	9.6
Switzerland (German)	19.5	34.2	37.1	9.3
United States	20.8	24.4	32.8	22.0

Note: Most of the tasks at Level 1 require the reader to locate and match a single piece of information that is identical to or nearly identical to the information given in the text. Level 2 requires the reader to locate one or more pieces of information from the text and to compare and contrast information. Level 3 requires readers to search the text to match information and make low-level inferences. Level 4/5 measures how well readers perform multiple-features matching, use specialized knowledge, and make text-based inferences from more abstract text sources.
Source: Baldi et al. (2000).

Unlike the United States, countries like Denmark, France, and Ireland are actively attempting to support educational and training endeavors for their workforces through payroll taxes and laws requiring companies to invest at least 1 percent of their payrolls in company or government-sponsored training programs. To be sure, the U.S. government passed the Job Training Partnership Act and implemented other federal programs aimed at providing training opportunities. But these programs have had limited success and are primarily designed for helping unemployed people find new jobs, rather than improving the skills and abilities of those already employed. Because the U.S. government has yet to develop a comprehensive basic-skills policy, the burden has fallen on employers to invest in training and development programs.

Training policies in Canada are very comprehensive. For example, in 1992 when Canada experienced a 7.5 percent unemployment rate, the government implemented a labor-force-development strategy, providing employers with technical assistance and financial incentives to assume the responsibility of training in the workplace. Moreover, the Quebec government passed a law in 1995 requiring any business with a payroll of more than $250,000 to invest 1 percent in employee training. Again, no such laws exist in the United States.

Canadian government assistance for retraining and the Federal Job Development program have been effective at offering training opportunities. An evaluation in 1998 by the World Bank revealed that "62.1 percent of the participants were employed or in training after one year and 74 percent of those employed were using the skills they had acquired. In 1991, 52 per cent of participants were employed three months after the completion of training and did not draw unemployment benefits in the subsequent 12 months, while 50 percent were able to move to higher skill levels" (Mitchell, 1998). Canada also provides for skills clinics, whose facilities are located in all municipalities and big businesses. Their primary benefits are to offer intake, assessment, referral, and career counseling all at the same location. This reduces the duplication of these services by multiple providers and significantly reduces the time and effort invested by clients to receive services.

U.S. and Canadian companies that acknowledge their role in providing training for their employees understand the importance of performing a comprehensive *needs analysis*. The purpose of a needs analysis is to identify discrepancies between desired performance levels of employees and their existing skills and abilities. In general, a needs analysis should involve three stages: organizational analysis, job analysis, and employee analysis.

Organizational analysis begins with an evaluation of business strategies and objectives. The strategic plan of an organization should directly determine the budget for training activities as well as the appropriate training employees will receive. Understandably, therefore, an organizational analysis will specifically identify the availability of resources to offer training programs and the managerial support for such activities. To this end, the organization must determine whether it has the budget, time, and facilities to conduct training. For example, an organization may decide it has the expertise and budget to offer in-house programs to train targeted employees. On the other hand, the organization may find out it lacks these resources and, as a result, must follow alternative courses of action, which might involve either hiring training consultants from outside or turning to the selection process to hire employees with the desired skills.

Job analysis entails collecting task-oriented information, including the responsibilities, attitudes, and behaviors that constitute the job. This analysis should also identify person-oriented information, such as the skills, knowledge, and abilities required for successful job performance.

Employee analysis is conducted to determine whether current employees have the necessary person-oriented capabilities to perform their jobs. This analysis should identify discrepancies between the skills and knowledge of employees and those required of them for job performance. When discrepancies exist, one course of action, among many, is to provide training opportunities.

Once the needs analysis is completed, training activities are planned. A number of methods can be used to assist employees in acquiring new skills and knowledge. A survey sponsored by the Employment and Training Administration (Department of Labor, 1996) reveals that smaller organizations provide fewer hours of formal training per employee. Consistent with an earlier observation, even the larger organizations concentrate their training activities on higher or specialized skill building (e.g., professional and technical training) rather than on general skill building. Indeed formal training in job skills accounted for almost 70 percent of total training hours (see Table 4.2) and roughly 50 percent of total participants in training programs. Among the activities designed to enhance job skills, computer training was offered more than any other training type, consuming 20 percent of the total training hours. Yet only 10 percent of the total trainees participated in computer skill building, suggesting that computer training tends to be of longer duration than other formal training activities.

A further breakdown of these data (not presented in Table 4.2) indicates that the industries providing the most hours of formal training were transportation, communications, and public utilities, with 18 hours of training per employee. Finance, insurance, and real estate offered 17 hours, followed by mining, which provided 14 hours. The retail trade and construction industries provided the fewest hours of training, 4 and 5 hours respectively.

Table 4.2 also reveals that only 34 percent of the training hours were spent on general skills. The greatest concentration on formal general skill building was in communications and quality training, with 1.4 hours per employee, and occupational safety, with 1.2 hours. The industry providing the most hours of formal general training was mining, which offered 5.5 hours of training in occupational health and 1.3 hours in communications and quality training. Data also reveal the lack of basic-skills training offered by employers. Lynch and Black (1998) note that this is particularly troublesome in such industries as wholesale and retail trade, hotels, and health services, because these are industries that generally hire unskilled workers who would benefit from this type of training.

In terms of expenditure for formal training in the United States, organizations spend on average 2.1 percent of payroll on training (see Table 4.3). Some organizations like General Electric, U.S. Robotics, W. H. Brady, Texas Instruments, Anderson Consulting, and Federal Express have recently increased their investments in training, which now range from 3 to 5 percent of their payroll (Noe et al., 2000). By comparison, Canadian organizations spend on average 1.6 percent of their payrolls on training. In the United States, organizations with over 50 employees spent on average $139 per employee on wages and salaries of in-house trainers. Although larger organizations spent more per employee on both in-house and outside trainers than smaller organizations (50-99 employees), small organizations tended to rely more on outside trainers than in-house trainers. An analysis of

TABLE 4.2

Percent of Total Training Hours Spent in Various Types of Formal Training by Industry, May-October 1995

Characteristic	Total 50 or more employees	Mining	Construction	Manufacturing Durable	Manufacturing Nondurable	Transportation, communi-cations, and public utilities	Wholesale trade	Retail trade	Finance, insurance, and real estate	Services
Type of formal training:										
Any formal training	100.0	100.0	100.0	100.0	100.0	100.0	100.0	100.0	100.0	100.0
Job skills										
Management training	7.3	1.9	1.5	9.7	4.0	8.5	10.0	9.2	7.6	6.5
Professional and technical training	11.8	7.3	3.4	15.8	7.3	10.9	2.6	1.8	12.5	14.2
Computer training	19.9	15.9	3.5	12.7	7.2	9.7	15.1	11.6	33.5	30.6
Clerical and administrative training	5.1	0.4	0.0	0.2	2.1	9.5	0.7	0.6	8.5	7.6
Sales and customer relations training	7.3	2.8	1.0	3.8	1.3	9.9	14.7	39.5	9.9	3.8
Service related training	5.2	0.0	0.0	0.1	0.7	11.3	0.0	12.8	0.2	8.3
Production and construction training	10.2	11.6	23.5	16.1	18.7	19.5	35.9	8.3	0.0	0.9
General skills										
Basic skills training	1.0	0.0	0.0	2.9	3.0	0.0	0.8	0.0	0.1	0.1
Occupational safety training	11.0	38.0	58.0	13.1	19.1	5.7	6.2	1.3	0.0	11.5
Employee health and wellness training	1.5	4.3	0.3	0.5	0.7	0.6	3.6	0.0	3.7	1.9
Orientation training	5.7	6.0	1.2	2.4	10.8	5.0	2.9	12.9	1.1	6.7
Awareness training	0.5	0.3	0.0	0.2	0.8	0.7	1.0	0.0	1.8	0.1
Communications and quality training	13.2	9.0	7.5	22.4	23.6	8.7	6.4	2.1	20.9	7.2
Other types of formal training	0.4	2.5	0.0	0.1	0.9	0.0	0.3	0.0	0.3	0.7

Source: Bureau of Labor Statistics, May 30 1997. URL: http://stats.bls.gov/news.release

industry differences indicates that transportation, communications, and public utilities spent the most on formal training, with an overall expenditure of $541 per employee. These industries also spent the most on in-house ($334) and outside trainers ($135).

TABLE 4.3

Selected Expenditures per Employee, by Size of Establishment, 1994

Characteristic	Total 50 or more employees	50-99 employees	100-499 employees	500+ employees
Tuition reimbursements	$51	$30	$41	$76
Wages and salaries of in-house trainers	$139	$52	$104	$236
Payments to outside trainers	$98	$63	$86	$135
Contributions to outside training funds	$12	$12	$9	$15
Subsidies for training received from outside sources	$5	$2	$8	$4

Source: Bureau of Labor Statistics, May 30 1997. URL: http://stats.bls.gov/news.release

For this region, the training and educational opportunities are very impressive. This not to say, however, that citizens are taking advantage of them or that such opportunities are ample enough to meet the dynamic needs of these economies. Indeed evidence suggests that for the United States to maintain its dominant standing among the world economies, education and training must be a top priority.

WESTERN EUROPE

The ultimate success of the EU in implementing its social agenda and in enhancing the competitiveness of member counties depends on a well-educated and well-trained workforce. This point was underscored by Jacques Delors, president of the Commission, in a June 1993 address to the European Council, where he pointed out that the EU economies lagged behind those of the United States and Japan partly because of the educational opportunities offered by the latter countries. As a result, he recommended an eight-point plan for recovery, which stressed further investments in training and development programs (Addision & Siebert, 1994). But are his concerns consistent with the facts? West European countries in general have exercised greater control over (through legislation) and support for (through various funds) training activities than the United States (Brewster, 1995). Today, as the data in Table 4.1 suggest, the literacy rates for many countries within this region rival that of the United States and Canada. In terms of education, there is evidence that West European countries are beginning to fare better than the United States and Canada. For example, in 1998, the average time a 5 year old can expect

TABLE 4.4

School Expectancy in Years, 1998

Countries	All levels of education combined	Primary and lower secondary education	Upper secondary education	Higher education
Austria	16.0	8.2	3.7	2.2
Belgium (Fl.)	17.3	8.6	4.8	2.4
Canada	16.7	8.9	3.5	2.8
Denmark	17.5	9.8	3.3	2.4
Finland	17.9	9.1	4.0	3.8
France	16.6	9.5	3.3	2.6
Germany	16.8	10.1	2.9	2.0
Greece	15.5	9.0	2.8	2.4
Iceland	17.7	10.0	4.8	2.0
Ireland	15.9	10.7	2.3	2.3
Italy	15.7	8.2	4.2	2.3
Luxembourg	n.a	n.a.	3.2	n.a.
Netherlands	17.2	10.6	3.3	2.2
Norway	17.7	9.9	3.9	3.0
Portugal	16.9	11.0	3.0	2.2
Spain	17.3	8.8	4.3	2.7
Sweden	19.4	9.8	5.5	2.4
Switzerland	16.2	9.6	3.2	1.6
United Kingdom	17.1	8.9	5.7	2.5
United States	16.8	9.5	2.6	3.5
Country mean (excluding the U.S. and Canada)	17.0	9.5	3.8	2.4

Source: OECD (2000).

to spend in education rose to 17 years for West European countries (see Table 4.4), above the rates for either the United States or Canada. In addition, the number of students enrolled in institutions of higher education in Western Europe grew by more than 20 percent from 1980 to 1998, and in eight countries by more than 50 percent. Thus, on average in this region, a 17 year old can expect to receive 2.4 years of higher education, which may be somewhat lower than the U.S. rate but about the same rate for Canada.

With regard to vocational training, the Social Charter explicitly describes the need for directives and funding for enhancing the skills necessary for persons who are preparing to enter the labor force or who need training or retraining in the technology of their occupation. More recently, Articles 126 and 127 of the Maastricht treaty reinforce the EU's commitment to "implementing a vocational training policy which shall support and supplement the action of the Member States" (Commission of the European Community, Article 127.1). To finance these ventures, the EU established the European Social Fund. The 1994-99 budget for this fund was $59 billion, eight percent of the EU's budget.

Not all of the member countries have been supportive of the Social Fund; in particular, the United Kingdom and Germany have traditionally resisted state-funded job-creation schemes. But even this opposition cannot explain the poor track record of the Social Fund, as revealed in a 1993 report. The findings indicate that despite a tremendous investment in retraining, using fund money to support training programs from 1986 to 1991, employment in all but two regions grew more slowly than average. Of greater concern, however, is that the number of people not working, including those registered as unemployed and those who were not registered, actually increased. Some EU officials attribute these negative results to fiscal irresponsibility. In Ireland, for example, 94 percent of the organizations that received funds report that they would have trained their employees without monetary assistance. In addition, although employment subsidies did create jobs in Ireland, it is unclear whether they lasted much longer than the grants. Even though there is general agreement that the Irish experience reveals flaws in how monies have been administered, they stress the pivotal role of the Social Fund in advancing hope for employment opportunities in Western Europe (Cowen, 1996a).

A phenomenal number of the organizations in some West European countries have no idea how much they spend on training. To illustrate, over 40 percent of the organizations in Germany and Sweden could not specify how much they invested in training their employees. By contrast, only 2 percent of the French firms and 18 percent of the Spanish organizations were unaware of their training expenditures. This is credited largely to the fact that these two countries have legislation that requires organizations to spend a certain percent of their annual salaries and wages on training. When organizations do not comply with this dictate, they are subject to penalties through taxation. Of those organizations that did monitor training expenditures, over half of them spend less than 2 percent of annual wages and salaries on training. France is unique to the extent that 75 percent of the organizations spend more than 2 percent on training (Holden & Livian, 1993).

As was noted in the section on the United States and Canada, the first step in designing any training program is a comprehensive needs assessment. Indeed without such an analysis, there is no guarantee that the right training activities will be put in place, despite the best intentions. Courpasson and Livian (1991) point out, for example, that a large French banking organization recently experienced negative results after a large investment in employee training. Follow-up analysis indicated that the bank had not conducted a sufficient needs assessment. Overall, West European organizations have attempted to determine training needs. Data indicate that 85 percent of the organizations in France conduct some form of needs analysis, compared with 80 percent in the United Kingdom, 79 percent in Italy, 76 percent in Sweden, 74 percent in Switzerland, 72 percent in Spain, 68 percent in the Netherlands, 63 percent in Norway, 56 percent in Denmark, and 55 percent in Germany. As Table 4.5 illustrates, about 40 percent of the French, Italian, Norwegian, and Swedish organizations tie needs assessments to overall business plans. Swiss and German organizations are the least likely to draw this connection. Additional related findings suggest that other than France, countries in this region do not tend to incorporate employee requests into their needs assessments.

In line with training expenditures, a surprising number of organizations do not know how much training per year their organizations offered to various types of employees (see Table 4.6). Of equal concern is the limited amount of training that employees receive in most countries, with the exception of Spain. In particular, although only about 10 percent of the organizations across Western Europe offer ten or more days of training per year for managers, approximately one-third of the Spanish organizations do so. This is consistent with the recruiting data, which indicate that Spain has difficulty recruiting managers. That is, when an organization cannot recruit the quality of employees needed, it is generally forced to train those applicants it hires. Conversely, Sweden, where 60 percent of the organizations report no overall recruitment problems, spends little time on training employees.

When different methods of management development are reviewed, a mixed picture emerges (see Table 4.7). For example, the most popular means of management development is through performance appraisal, where those being appraised are provided feedback regarding how they can improve their performance. In the case of professionals and managers, the specific content of training programs is partially determined through succession planning, resulting in good performers being selected to begin preparation for replacing key personnel, who for whatever reason are expected to leave the organization. Respondents from Switzerland and Germany insist that succession planning is "strategic" in terms of contributing to management stability (Leupold, 1987, p. 52). In Spain, Italy, and the United Kingdom, formal career planning is a standard method for training managers. Countries that report low use of this method of management training are Germany, Denmark, and Norway. As one Norwegian manager indicated, "'we are not growing our own managers,' and that managerial careers are not in general carefully planned" (Price Waterhouse/Cranfield Project, 1991, p. 26).

In the context of management development, the purpose of job rotation is twofold. First, it allows the trainees to acquire new skills and knowledge by working in different jobs throughout the organization. Second, the job rotators can be observed and assessed regarding their potential for future job placement. Only about a quarter of the organizations surveyed opted for job rotation as a means of management development. High-flier management schemes often involve job

TABLE 4.5

Methods of Needs Assessment for Training Programs

Method of Needs Assessment	Switzerland	Denmark	West Germany	Spain	France	Italy	Norway	Netherlands	Sweden	United Kingdom
Analyses of business plans	10	12	27	30	41	39	39	20	36	22
Training audits	19	39	19	8	0	9	1	31	1	16
Line management requests	36	36	44	45	0	35	35	19	18	20
Performance appraisal	21	10	8	8	n/a	13	22	24	38	35
Employee requests	9	3	2	9	31	4	2	7	7	6

Source: Holden, L., & Livian, Y. (1993).

TABLE 4.6

Average Number of Days of Training per Year

Categories	Switzerland	Denmark	West Germany	Spain	France	Italy	Norway	Netherlands	Sweden	United Kingdom
Per Manager										
Less than 5	60	59	51	32	59	56	46	61	57	69
5-10	32	30	38	40	33	37	41	28	35	23
over 10	9	11	11	29	9	8	12	11	8	8
Don't know	22	33	47	30	23	7	47	26	40	36
Per professional/ technical em- ployee										
Less than 5	80	72	55	30	63	55	48	58	61	64
5-10	15	19	34	40	30	35	37	29	32	27
over 10	5	9	11	30	7	10	15	13	7	9
Don't know	25	32	47	28	24	6	47	25	40	38
Per Clerical em- ployee										
Less than 5	93	88	80	57	n/a	82	81	84	91	86
5-10	6	8	15	24	n/a	14	17	14	9	11
over 10	1	4	5	19	n/a	4	2	2	0	3
Don't know	32	38	47	30	n/a	11	50	26	40	38
Per manual em- ployee										
Less than 5	93	87	83	59	74	81	75	75	98	81
5-10	5	9	12	22	20	14	17	17	2	13
over 10	2	4	5	19	6	5	8	8	0	6
Don't know	31	39	47	30	24	14	52	27	40	39

Source: Holden, L., & Livian, Y. (1993).

TABLE 4.7

Methods of Management Development

Method of Manage-ment Development	Switzerland.	Denmark	West Germany	Spain	France	Italy	Norway	Netherlands	Sweden	United Kingdom
Formal career plan	20	12	13	28	7	34	12	24	22	27
Performance appraisal	84	58	29	49	56	76	63	87	90	84
Succession plans	50	48	11	27	17	39	41	17	42	43
Planned job rotation	13	12	23	21	8	32	28	22	24	19
High flier schemes	33	21	28	39	44	28	38	24	41	29

Source: Holden, L., & Livian, Y. (1993).

rotation. Derr (1988) outlines three steps in a typical executive high-flier career development program: (1) they are chosen, (2) they are given test assignments, and (3) they are rotated through various jobs and engage in certain training activities. Although the process is fairly standardized, the criteria for detecting high flyers are not. As Bournois, Chauchat, and Roussillon (1994) observe, countries vary substantially with respect to their concern over who should be piloted as high-flying managers. They comment that this sometimes reflects a cultural difference, where some countries (e.g., France) favor their elite, while others (e.g., Sweden) give equal recognition to all talent.

On average less than 20 percent of the organizations across Western Europe use international assignments as a means of developing their executives. The relatively low emphasis on international experiences is somewhat surprising at a time when European countries are attempting to move toward an economically unified region (Bournois et al., 1994).

Obviously, different methods of training can be used to provide employees with a variety of skills and knowledge. The data in Table 4.8 report those areas in which at least a third of the management employees have received training. The southern countries place the greatest emphasis on foreign language training for their managers, probably because of their need to expand recruiting efforts for managers. Remember, organizations in Spain and Portugal are the most likely to relocate their operations to attract quality workers. It is curious that so few organizations in the central and northern countries provide comparatively little language training for their managers. Tyson (1989) observes that in the United Kingdom, where there has been considerable publicity about growing opportunities in Europe in the aftermath of its unification, lack of interest in foreign language training is a real concern.

According to Table 4.9, organizations report using an assortment of methods to monitor the effectiveness of their training programs. Over 90 percent of the organizations informally assess whether their training programs have been successful. Unfortunately, informal assessments provide little information about the effectiveness of training. As Heneman, Schwab, Fossum, and Dyer (1989) indicate, positive results from informal evaluations of training programs can influence the support from top-level management regarding the contents of the program, but they provide "no solid evidence of whether any learning or behavioral change occurred" (p. 444).

The most informative way to assess the effectiveness of training is through formal evaluation some months after the training has occurred, allowing sufficient time for *transfer*—application of what has been learned on the job. Unfortunately, with the exception of the United Kingdom, France, and Spain, less than half of the companies in West European countries assess the effectiveness of their training programs in this fashion. Although the methods of monitoring training programs listed in Table 4.9 may assist in assessing whether or not employees have acquired skills or knowledge from a particular program, they do not provide a cost-benefit analysis of it. That is, they provide no information about the dollar value of the training. West European countries are not alone; few organizations worldwide perform a thorough utility analysis of their training programs. Noe et al. (2000) re-

TABLE 4.8

Areas in Which at Least a Third of Managers Have Been Trained

Areas of Training	Switzerland	Denmark	West Germany	Spain	France	Italy	Norway	Netherlands	Sweden	United Kingdom
Performance appraisal	69	32	19	31	36	45	64	69	73	70
Staff communication	69	45	43	48	53	49	63	57	64	54
Motivation	76	64	41	44	33	47	59	46	55	47
Delegation	56	42	35	30	22	34	53	35	46	40
Team building	39	25	22	39	25	29	36	39	51	49
Foreign languages	24	27	18	56	28	49	27	27	11	6

Source: Holden, L., & Livian, Y. (1993).

TABLE 4.9

Methods Used to Monitor the Effectiveness of Training Programs

Assessment methods	Switzerland	Denmark	West Germany	Spain	France	Italy	Norway	Netherlands	Sweden	United Kingdom
Tests	48	39	45	52	36	39	19	60	51	45
Formal evaluation immediately after training	90	73	90	80	84	73	71	79	89	89
Formal evaluation some months after training	35	33	49	51	53	44	28	40	47	64
Informal feedback form line managers	93	92	92	92	92	97	99	97	93	97
Informal feedback from trainees	90	92	93	91	92	97	98	98	93	96

Source: Holden, L., & Livian, Y. (1993).

67

commend that such an analysis involve "estimates of the difference in job performance between trained and untrained employees, the number of individuals trained, the length of time a training program is expected to influence performance, and a measure of the variability in the job performance in the untrained group of employees" (p. 249). Other information would include direct and indirect costs, development costs, overhead costs, and compensation for trainees as well as a breakdown of the benefits of the program.

Enhancing the educational and training opportunities in Western Europe is not only the goal of individual countries, but of the EU as a whole. And as the previous discussion suggests, major advancements have been made in terms of increasing the amount of education citizens receive in this region. Moreover, training opportunities are being created and funded by employers, countries, and the EU. According to the 2000 OECD survey, the biggest obstacle to increasing participation of individuals in job-related training programs is lack of interest. The challenge, therefore, is to convince Western Europeans to participate in such opportunities.

EASTERN EUROPE AND THE NEW INDEPENDENT STATES

In this region, the Soviet Union model of education has been dominant during the past century. During this time, Soviet leaders envisioned comprehensive public education as necessary for purposes of economic growth as well as for social modernization and political indoctrination. In 1918 the government took over all private and parochial schools and colleges, abolished fees, and determined that all children ages 8 to 15 were to attend school full time. By the 1980s, compulsory study was lengthened so that most children remained in the classroom from ages 7 to 17. A standardized curriculum stressed language, literature, mathematics, military and physical training, history, manual skills, and natural sciences. The gifted or the children of the politically well connected sometimes studied in special schools dedicated to foreign languages, music, ballet, or art. Outside the school walls, all were exhorted to join youth organizations sanctioned by the Communist Party (CPSU). These included the Young Octoberists for children ages 6 to 9, the Pioneers for ages 10 to 15, and the Komsomol (Communist Youth League) for ages 14 to 28. Pupils were streamed after ninth grade into one of three programs. Students bound for higher education received two years of advanced secondary courses; those bound for industrial trades took "vocational-technical" courses; and those bound for semiprofessional work were sent into "specialized secondary" schooling. The Soviet Union screened schoolchildren to find talented athletes at an early age, sometimes as young as five or six; those selected for competitive sports were sometimes sent to special schools for that purpose. This model of education did a good job of inculcating basic knowledge. The literacy rate, which was 44 percent in 1920, climbed to 87 percent by 1939 and to 99.7 percent by 1970. Of the population aged 15 or older in 1989, 49 percent had graduated from a secondary or vocational school and 11 percent had completed a higher education. The narrow proficiency typically acquired, however, dampened creativity and was often out of step with the labor market.

Higher education followed two channels in the Soviet Union: universities, teaching the pure sciences and humanities; and specialized institutes with a direct connection to a branch of the economy, usually funded by an industrial ministry. Of the 904 institutions of higher learning in 1989, only 69—with 630,000 out of 5.2 million enrolled students—were universities. The most prestigious were in Moscow, Leningrad, Kazan, and other large Russian cities, and in the capitals of the other union republics (Colton, 2000).

Following the collapse of the Soviet regime, no other aspect of life in this region is undergoing a greater transformation than educational and training systems. For example, once banned in the Soviet Union and some East European countries, where education was regimented indoctrination, private schools are now flourishing (Hiatt, 1994). A wide disparity between private and public education is developing in Russia. To illustrate, in a typical public school, overcrowding has caused students to be taught in shifts and standards to decline. By comparison, at Zhukovka Humanities School, one of the most expensive private schools in Moscow, students receive an education comparable to that obtained at the most prestigious educational institutions in the world. Many fear that only the rich will get a quality education (Stanley, 1994). But Education Minister Valdimir Filippov recently vowed to improve the quality of public education in Russia. At a press conference in February 2000, he told reporters that the federal government hopes to introduce a 12-year educational program within the next three to four years. Under this plan, children would start school at age 6 and complete it at 18. He added that greater funds would be targeted to purchase new textbooks and educational facilities. Other East European countries are even beginning to make an honest reappraisal of their histories by allowing students to use textbooks that paint a candid picture of the past.

Although people in this region are among the best educated in the world, they lack the skills and knowledge necessary to make them competitive in a rapidly changing market economy. Thach (1996) observes that the most pressing training needs are in foreign languages, especially English, and computer skills. There is also a need to provide training in marketing and customer services. Other key areas of education in business skills that are needed in this region include teamwork and systems thinking. Employees in East European countries were rarely expected to think about the big picture; instead they were expected simply to carry out their jobs. Thach (1996) comments that the "idea of assisting a coworker in order to help the whole business succeed was foreign, as was the idea of making day-to-day decisions in the larger context of the business as a whole" (p. 35). Likewise, there is a need for training in planning and organizing skills as well as training in Western management skills. Remember, supervisors throughout this region used control or directive approaches to manage their workers. More participative, employee-oriented approaches may not work until everyone in the workplace understands how they should be used.

Little information is available regarding the current training practices for employees. Yet Kiriazov, Sullivan, and Tu (2000) observe that the most popular training method in Eastern Europe is on-the-job. For example, Neftochim, the largest employer in Bulgaria, rotates its managers through all its operations, consisting of 40 manufacturing units. Koubek and Brewster (1995) provide some data concerning training and development in the Czech Republic, perhaps one of the most Westernized countries in this region in terms of training efforts. Consistent with training of managers and professional/technical staff. As Table 4.10 shows, the time devoted to training these employees is longer than it is in any West European country. Specific training programs are generally focused on operating personal computers (64 percent of the organizations offered personal computer training to at least one-third of their managers), foreign languages (62 percent), and marketing and management under a market economy (55 percent). Interestingly, little attention is being giving to personnel skills of management.

TABLE 4.10

Average Days of Training per Year, by Profession (Percentage of Organizations)

Days of training	Professional Managerial	Technical	Clerical	Manual
Less than 3.00	10	18	35	66
3.01-5.00	18	22	32	19
5.01-10.00	29	31	25	12
10.0+	43	30	8	4

Source: Adopted from Koubek, J., and Brewster, C. (1995), pp. 223-247.

A survey of Russian computer organizations revealed that the lack of trained personnel with experience in the development, implementation, or use of modern computer systems has severely limited the growth of the computer market in Russia. In response, Hewlett-Packard (HP) recently opened the Moscow Educational Center (Moskovskii Obrazovatelnyi Tsentr), where courses on the use of HP network equipment, data processing, and other computer related activities are taught weekly for HP associates or corporate clients. Compaq offers a similar program for individuals in most of the former Soviet republics (Moskovskie Novosti, 1996, p. V29).

Some assistance regarding the development of training options is being provided by Western countries. For example, the Office of Citizen Exchanges of the U.S. Information Agency offers grants to design training programs in Albania, Bosnia-Herzegovina, Bulgaria, Croatia, the Czech Republic, Estonia, Hungary, Latvia, Lithuania, Macedonia, Poland, Romania, the Slovak Republic, and Slovenia. Grant proposals must address the growth of democratic institutions and political and economic pluralism, while specifically focusing on local government administration, independent media, or business administration. Moreover, the British government's Know-How Fund, the World Bank, U.S. Educational Aid, the United Nations Economic Development Office, and the EU's TEMPUS and PHARE programs now provide technical and managerial programs for this region (Kiriazov et al., 2000). Even individual Western companies are providing support for training efforts. Poland, for example, recently received a $150,000 grant from the Coca-Cola Company to train workers there (Saporta, 1990).

Political and economic developments in this region have created a more promising business environment. One problem that remains, however, has been characterized as "the Russian paradox." On the one hand, people in this region are very well educated, but on the other hand, their Soviet-era educational systems have ignored such business subjects as finance, strategic planning, marketing, customer relations, and human resources, thereby ill preparing them for global competitiveness. To address these shortcomings, governmental and private-sector efforts are being waged to offer more educational and training opportunities.

THE MIDDLE EAST

There was little difference among country literacy rates in the previous three regions, with most countries having rates in the upper 90th percent. By contrast, there is a wide variation in rates among countries in the Middle East, ranging from 44 percent for Morocco to 95 percent for Israel (see Table 4.11). In terms of formal education, Morocco also ranks last, with a citizen average of 6.9 years of education. The overall educational and training standards in the Middle East fall short of those in the previous three regions. Not surprisingly, therefore, the countries in this region that fare the best tend to have had close ties to Western Europe. Interestingly Israel, with a mean educational level of 12.2 years, falls behind Bahrain, which in part can be explained by Bahrain's historical ties to the United Kingdom and to an impressive expansion of the access for women to educational resources, at all levels. Indeed in several Arab countries (Bahrain, Jordan, Qatar, and United Arab Emirates), the educational levels for women are higher than they are for men. As a result, over 90 percent of the women in these countries are employed in service industries, where formal training and education are more important than in other industries (e.g., agriculture).

With Bahrain's comparatively high commitment to education in this region, it follows that the literacy rate there is the highest in the Arab world. Moreover, Bahrain's higher education system is well developed, consisting of several vocational schools and colleges as well as Bahrain University, which offers several bachelor's degrees along with postgraduate programs and Master's degrees in education, civil engineering, and business. Bahrain's fine formal educational system is supplemented by the Bahrain Training Institute, which successfully prepares young Bahrainis of both sexes for the market. According to Dr. Naji Al-Mahdi, director of the Institute: "We guarantee prospective employers quality training programs. . . . The training facilities are constantly upgraded and our staff is trained according to internationally recognized standards. This young, well-educated workforce will be prepared for quality jobs in business, technical, and service industries" (Arab.net, Bahrain).

Qatar is another Arab state that has long been committed to educating and training its citizens. As with Bahrain, this is in part due to its strong British influence. The average Qatari receives 11.8 years of education, ranking second among the Arab states and third in the region—behind Israel and Bahrain. The government also has invested in training programs. In 1962, for example, the Department

TABLE 4.11

Literacy and Education Data for Countries in the Middle East, 1995

ountry	Literacy rates			Average Years of Education		
	Total	Male	Female	Total	Male	Female
Algeria	62	74	49	10.8	11.4	10.1
Bahrain	85	89	79	12.9	12.5	13.2
Egypt	51	64	39	9.8	10.8	8.8
Iraq	58	71	45	8.3	9.4	7.1
Israel[1]	95	97	93	12.2	12.2	12.2
Jordan	87	93	79	11.0	11.4	11.6
Kuwait	79	82	75	9.0	8.9	9.0
Lebanon	92	95	90	n.a.	n.a.	n.a.
Libya	76	88	63	n.a.	n.a.	n.a.
Morocco	44	57	31	6.9	8.0	5.7
Qatar	79	79	80	11.8	11.4	12.4
Saudi Arabia	63	72	50	9.2	9.5	8.8
Syrian Arab Republic	71	86	56	9.5	10.2	8.7
Tunisia	67	79	55	10.3	10.9	9.7
United Arab Emirates	79	79	80	11.2	10.7	11.7

Source: UNESCO Institute for Statistics, (2000) World Education Indicators, New York: United Nations Organization for Education. Collect July 3, 2000 from http://unescostat.unesco.org/uisen/stats/stats0.htm.
[1]*Source:* Statistical abstract of Israel 1996, Israel Census Bureau of Statistics.

of Training and Vocational Education was established in response to the country's need for skilled and semiskilled labor. This government agency consists of several training centers and a regional training center that was set up in1970 with the assistance of the United Nations Development Program. The specific responsibility of the regional center is to offer special workshops and training opportunities in the following fields: mechanics, air-conditioning and refrigeration, welding and industrialization, carpentry and decoration, filing and turnery, power-generation and water distillation, and sanitary and electrical installation (Arab.net, Qatar).

The educational system in Israel is unique in the region. Indeed school attendance in Israel is mandatory from ages 6 to 16 and free to the age of 18. The structure of the Israeli formal education system consists of four groups: state schools, attended by the majority of students; state religious schools, where Jewish studies are emphasized; Arab and Druze schools, which focus on Arab and Druze history, religion, and culture; and private schools, with instruction from a variety of religious and cultural perspectives. The majority of secondary schools offer curricula in the sciences and humanities, leading to a matriculation certificate for those intending to pursue higher education. Some secondary schools provide specialized education. For example, technological schools train engineers and technicians, some of whom simply want to obtain the practical skills. Other students, however, use the training in preparation for higher education. Agricultural schools supplement a traditional curriculum with subjects related to agronomy. Military preparatory schools offer training for students who intend to take up a career in the Israel Defense Forces. Finally, Yeshiva high schools complement their secular curricula with intensive religious studies that promote observance of the traditional Jewish way of life.

Youths choosing not to attend any of the above schools are subject to the Apprenticeship Law, which requires them to study at an approved vocational school. This law also requires the Ministry of Labor to provide apprenticeship programs in schools affiliated with vocational networks. These programs, which last three to four years, consist of two years of classroom learning, followed by one to two years of study and work in their chosen trades ranging from hairstyling and cooking to mechanics and word processing. The Ministry of Education and the Ministry of Labor also sponsor a wide variety of courses for individuals interested in learning Hebrew language as well as those interested in upgrading basic educational or vocational skills (Israel Ministry of Foreign Affairs).

As the data in Table 4.11 suggest, many countries in this region suffer from undereducated and untrained populations. For example, the educational and literacy attainments in Morocco are profoundly inadequate to support the country's desired pace of economic development. The government, however, is planning to launch some education and training reforms, including an adult literacy campaign (Lavy & Spratt, 1997). Moreover, Abdalla and Al-Homound (1995) observe that the Kuwaiti basic educational and training systems are not only inferior—even by regional comparisons—but are also tragically deficient in covering management methods that ensure more efficient and productive business operations. They note further that management development at all levels consists primarily of on-the-job and short-term training programs.

Another problematic country is Saudi Arabia, where the average citizen receives only 9.2 years of formal education. Not only is the amount of education comparatively low, the typical curriculum lacks skills-oriented studies, with much of the learning focused on Islamic texts. A couple of factors suggest a change in the policy toward human resource development. First, the government is increasing its budgets for education and training. Second, industrial diversification programs coupled with workforce policies indicate that education and training of all kinds will be in great demand by Saudi nationals and organizations, especially in the area of technical training. What does remain in Saudi Arabia is a clear gender difference regarding educational and training opportunities. The Saudi system of segregated education separates educational facilities for boys and girls. But UNESCO reports that while most facilities are duplicated, those for girls tend to be markedly inferior. Regarding higher education, women were not admitted to universities until 1962. Today, Saudi women are still limited in their choice of higher-education institutions. Indeed the best Saudi universities do not admit women. Saudi Arabia has 7 universities, 78 colleges, and 11 female colleges. Only 5 universities accept both males and females. Moreover, even though the Saudi government committed itself in 1985 to expanding the areas of study for women, their education and training remain restricted to areas where, once they are employed, they will deal exclusively with women. As a result women enroll primarily in medical schools, social sciences, and teacher preparation. Professions such as engineering, architecture, and pharmacy remain limited to men (Saudhouse, 2000).

        In short, for some countries (e.g., Iraq, Morocco, Saudi Arabia) in this region, serious shortfalls remain in providing their citizens with basic learning opportunities, including access to primary and secondary education. Filling the gaps will be a challenge for these countries. The countries in this region, even Bahrain, Qatar, and Israel, suffer from two fundamental problems concerning the development of human resources. First, even where education is provided, its quality is generally poor, as reflected in the learning performance of students. Second, the countries and organizations in this region have been unwilling to amply invest in training programs aimed at enhancing the work-related skills of individuals. Global competitiveness will eventually demand that these problems be addressed by policymakers both at the governmental and corporate levels.

CHAPTER SUMMARY

        This chapter has focused on several interlinking themes in the development of human resources, but the overall thrust has been on the centrality of human resource development to success in the competitive, globalizing economy. This has been seen in a number of geographical and historical contexts: In North America, where the conception of compulsory and free primary education was developed; in Western Europe, where the human capital of German people accounted for the country's rebound from the devastation of World War II; in Eastern Europe and the former Soviet states, where education appreciated but where it is undergoing substantive change in light of the Soviet demise; and in the Middle East, where the educational starvation of some populations is all too commonplace.

        The prospective importance of human resource development policies is perhaps nowhere seen more clearly than in the case of the European Union. The announced intention of the EU is to build a European society based on three pillars: high wages, high solidarity, and high human resource development. High wages are essential so that Europeans may continue to enjoy the standard of living they have attained, even if, as we saw in Chapter 2, those high wages may come at a cost in unemployment levels. High solidarity means a relatively even distribution of incomes in European society to generate the political support needed for a three-pillar policy. Finally, in recognition of the need to earn one's way in the world of trade, the feasibility of the whole policy will be based on high levels of effective and cutting-edge human resources development programs.

Implications for the EU's human resource policy are neither obvious nor necessarily uniform. If we consider the alternative models of production discerned by Applebaum and Batt (1994), each may have different implicit human resource development policies. For what they call the "Swedish socio-technical systems" model, job skills are attained through public education and training, and cross training is quite high. For the Italian "flexible specialization" model, a combination of formal training and on-the-job training is needed, with cross training achieved by worker movement among firms. For the German "diversified quality production" model, training is acquired through apprenticeship with cross training limited to the craft involved. These three models of industrial production (and others to be sure) will appear throughout Europe, each bringing its characteristic human resource development needs. The simple mantra "high wages-high solidarity-high human resource development" turns out to be not so simple. But even if the human resource development implications are more complex than first would appear to be the case, they are nonetheless central.

The nuts and bolts of the chapter show many ways in which human resource development polices may be achieved: indirectly, through taxes, credits, and other incentives to employers and employees, or directly through establishment of public, private, or mixed training institutions. The most appropriate means of training will depend in many cases on the nature of the training.

CHAPTER 5

Rewarding Human Resources

Organizations exist throughout the world to accomplish specific goals. Likewise, individuals work for these organizations in order to satisfy their own needs. One of their needs is for direct compensation or money, which allows them to purchase goods and services in the marketplace. Another is indirect compensation that provides them with benefits in the form of health-care coverage and pensions as well as time off, including vacation and sick days. Taken together, both types of compensation are designed to attract the talent an organization needs, to reward employees, and to motivate them in terms of developing and utilizing the skills and abilities they need. In the international arena, cultural, economic, and social differences play a central role in shaping compensation systems. These differences are particularly reflected in compensation legislation and in pay and benefits systems. Thus, these differences serve as principles for a comparative analysis of compensation systems. But inasmuch as performance appraisal is so closely tied to compensation, the chapter will begin with a brief discussion of how workers are evaluated, with some attention given to regional trends.

PERFORMANCE APPRAISAL

Performance appraisal is the process of evaluating how well employees do their jobs in relation to a set of standards. Although it is useful in such HR practices as employee development, the performance appraisal is a critical component in an effective compensation system, by rewarding those who perform well or imposing organizational sanctions (e.g., demotion or discharge) on those who do not. Several different approaches can be adopted to appraise the performance of employees: comparative, attribute, behavioral, and results-oriented.

The comparative approach to appraisal assesses the overall work performance of employees so that rankings can be generated. An example of this type of performance appraisal is *forced distribution,* where the evaluator assigns certain percentages of employees to predetermined categories. Categories might be set up so that 10 percent of the employees must be slotted into the unsatisfactory category, 15 percent in the fair category, 50 percent in the average category, 15 percent in the good category, and 10 percent in the excellent category. Another comparative method is *ranking,* which simply involves directly comparing employees against each other. Thus, the best employee is identified first, then the best of the remaining group, and so on until the worst employee is assigned the lowest ranking. Although comparative methods are easy to use, assist in making merit pay decisions, and control many of the rater biases, they provide little information about specific job-related behavior.

Instead of comparing an employee's overall performance with that of a fellow worker, the attribute method focuses on certain characteristics or traits believed to be important for the organization's success. The most popular method used in the attribute approach is *graphic rating scales.* With this method, the evaluator assesses an employee on each of several performance dimensions using a continuum consisting of clearly defined scaled points. Common examples of performance dimensions include knowledge, quality of work, quantity of work, and attendance. Attribute-approach methods of performance appraisal are relatively easy to develop and are generalizable across a variety of jobs. And if care is taken to identify relevant job-related characteristics and to carefully define them on the rating scale(s), these methods can be reliable and valid evaluation tools. In general, however, such care is not taken in developing these methods, which accounts for the skepticism they have received, at least by researchers in the area.

The behavioral approach to performance appraisal attempts to specify behaviors employees must exhibit in doing their jobs. The *critical incidents* method falls within this category, and requires the evaluator to keep a log for each employee that describes effective and ineffective performance. The following provides hypothetical examples of critical incidents for a college professor that a department chair might generate:

> During the class lectures I observed, professor X was very effective in responding to student questions. In a very nonjudgmental fashion, he would have the student think through the issue, and then he would ask the student a series of questions that eventually led to an answer to the initial question.
>
> In response to student complaints, I have compared the syllabus for Professor Y's course with the tests that he gave. Clearly he is testing over material that is not specified in the syllabus.

Behavioral-approach methods can be very effective in linking the organization's strategy with specific behaviors necessary for implementing it. But obviously, they are very time-consuming for evaluators, and they may be hard to quantify when used for compensation purposes (Noe et al., 2000).

Finally, the results-oriented approach attempts to capture the outcomes of job performance; in so doing, it focuses on objective, measurable phenomena. The best example of a results-oriented method is *management by objectives (MBO),* which typically has four components. First, evaluators meet with employees individually to set goals with them. To be effective, these goals must be mutually acceptable, clear, specific, and measurable. Second, employees, either on their own or with the assistance of their evaluators, then develop action plans that describe in detail what measures will be taken to achieve these goals. Third, after an established period of time has elapsed, the evaluators and employees meet to discuss and review the progress that was made. Finally, corrective action is taken in the form of either changing action plans or setting different goals (Duane, 1996). Clearly, the advantage of this approach to performance appraisal minimizes the subjectivity that often biases the evaluation process. At the same time, the objective measures can be contaminated by circumstances beyond the control of those being evaluated.

From a global perspective, the obvious question is: What's the best approach? It would be simple if there were a best way to evaluate the work behavior of employees, but the most effective approach depends on the situation. Although there is little information regarding the use of performance appraisals in the Middle East and North Africa, some observations can be made about the other regions. In terms of general comments about Western Europe, for example, IBM/Towers Perrin (1992) estimated that by the year 2000, 55 percent in Germany, 57 percent in the UK, and 78 percent in France would make performance appraisal a top priority. More specifically, Rojot (1990) reports that MBO is fast becoming a popular means of evaluating the performance of managers in France. In support of this, a Hay Group study (1987) sampled 220 French organizations and found that 91 percent of them set objectives for managers and 81 percent evaluated their performance on the basis of these objectives. Moreover, 87 percent of these organizations actually held annual performance reviews for their managers (Sparrow & Hiltrop, 1994).

The southern countries in Western Europe generally lag behind in adopting formal performance appraisal systems. A study by the Centre for Research on Business Organizations in Milan, for example, found that 39 percent of the organizations did not evaluate their employees at all. Hinterhuber and Stumpf (1990) note that this low emphasis on performance appraisal reflects the desire of Italians to retain a high degree of flexibility concerning such personnel matters. Similarly, although large foreign-owned multinationals in Greece employed relatively systematic and objective performance appraisal systems, methods of appraisal in domestic organizations were very informal and subjective. Papalexandris (1993) observes that "while formal appraisal was not considered justifiable in smaller, family-type firms, the rather limited use of formal appraisal in larger Greek firms is due to the existence of close personal relationships and the difficulty in setting precise targets, as a result of frequent changes in the external environment of firms" (p. 170).

During the Soviet regime, a characteristic feature of HRM across Eastern Europe and the Soviet Union was a lack of objective performance appraisal systems. As Koubek and Brewster (1995) note:

> There existed formal systems of "political reliability appraisal", which included very general characteristics related to the performance, capability, and potential of individuals . . . The absence of any objective performance appraisal had three sources: socialist egalitarianism resulting in wage and salary leveling; full (i.e., social) employment policy (implying that nobody was concerned about a negative appraisal, since

implying that nobody was concerned about a negative appraisal, since salaries could not vary much and there was no danger of underemployment); and the scarcity of labour in poorly planned and managed economies (organizations had to fulfill the labour plan and therefore they didn't take risks with job vacancies—an employee with poor performance was better than a vacant job). (p. 227)

Pearce (1991) attributes the neglect of formal employee performance appraisals in Hungary to a lack of cooperation on the part of personnel directors and line managers. Employees of organizations in this region report that they found the experience tedious and all too often found no relationship between appraisal and other personnel decisions, including pay increases and promotion.

Within the past few years, these countries have made some headway in adopting Western style methods of evaluating the performance of employees. To a large degree, however, these advances have taken place in multinational organizations, with little change in domestic organizations. Kovach (1995) explains that in Central and Eastern Europe, a cultural factor contributes to disregarding the performance-appraisal process as an important administrative responsibility. He notes that for many supervisors, the transition from command to market conditions represents the first time they have been in control of evaluating their employees. His conclusion is that, at least initially, these supervisors are expected to differ considerably from their U.S. counterparts in terms of their HRM functions, including performance appraisals. But eventually they will come to recognize the importance of evaluating more formally the work behavior of their subordinates.

Part of this learning experience must take place with those being evaluated. In the past, these employees generally have been uncomfortable with the "American type" performance appraisal process. This attitude stems back to the Soviet regime, under which there was a distrust of supervisors—a view that "what is up is bad (Feher, 1991). Employees also tend to avoid standing out from their co-workers, an attitude that was derived from the socialist conception of fairness. Kovach (1995) notes that "some managers have even remarked that 'Americans are overly concerned with performance, while we Europeans are more concerned with the process of management" (p. 88). The high degree of pessimism concerning performance appraisal is well illustrated by Feher (1991). He indicates that in response to a performance appraisal, an American employee might say, "Next month, I'll do better." In contrast, a Central or East European employee might say, "Next month, I'll try."

One factor that has been a critical determinant of how employees are evaluated in the United States and Canada is the legal environment. In discrimination suits, for example, the plaintiff often alleges that the organization's performance appraisal systems are unfairly biased against a particular protected class (e.g., gender, race). In light of the potential costs of these lawsuits, Noe et al. (2000) offer the following guides for developing appraisal systems that will withstand legal scrutiny in this region of the world:

1. The system should be developed using valid job analysis information.
2. The system should be based on either behaviors or results; evaluations of ambiguous traits should be avoided.
3. Evaluators should undergo training in how to use the system.
4. There should be an appeal mechanism available to employees who feel that they have been unfairly evaluated.
5. Some form of performance counseling or corrective guidance should be available to poor performers to assist them in improving their work behaviors.
6. When possible, multiple evaluators should be used.

At least in the very near future, organizations in the other regions are not expected to be quite as legally sensitive concerning their performance-appraisal systems. Even in Germany, which is highly legalistic and bureaucratic, one does not find such careful attention to developing performance-appraisal systems. In fact, Sparrow and Hiltrop (1994) observe that "none of the academic reviews of German HRM practices, or European management guides to pay, benefits, training and development make any specific mention of performance management or appraisal" (p. 557).

THE UNITED STATES AND CANADA

Compensation Levels

Compensation laws in the United States and Canada are very similar. For example, both countries have laws that require equal pay for performing essentially equal work, regardless of gender. Although both countries have minimum wage laws, they are administered somewhat differently. Minimum wage rates in Canada are set in each province and territory. According to Canada Online (2000), the following are the current minimum wages by Canadian province or territory:

Province	Wage
Alberta	$5.90
British Columbia	$7.15
Manitoba	$6.00
New Brunswick	$5.75
Newfoundland	$5.50
North West Territory	$6.50
Nova Scotia	$5.60
Nunavut	$6.50
Ontario	$6.85
Prince Edward Island	$5.60
Quebec	$6.90
Saskatchewan	$6.00
Yukon	$7.20

In the United States, the Fair Labor Standards Act establishes a minimum wage for all states and municipalities. In 1997, the minimum wage was set at $5.15, with many exceptions (e.g., participants in apprenticeship programs). The law, which covers almost all public- and private-sector employers, also requires overtime payment for nonexempt employees (i.e., typically nonprofessionals and nonmanagers) who work more than 40 hours per week.

Compensation systems used to generate salaries and wages in U. S. and Canadian organizations are perhaps the most sophisticated in the world. That is, they attempt to address both internal and external equity issues. *Internal equity* refers to the comparable value of jobs within an organization. To illustrate, employees expect the chief executive officer to be valued more than a vice president, who in turn is valued more than a plant manager, and so on. Consequently, these individuals should receive different levels of compensation. In determining internal equity, most U.S. and Canadian organizations conduct a job evaluation. The most common form is the *point method*, which consists of three steps: selecting compensable factors, establishing factor scales, and deriving factor weights.

Compensable factors are job characteristics an organization values because they assist it in achieving its goals and objectives. Classic compensable factors include skill, effort, responsibility, and working conditions. Yet many organizations adopt factors that more accurately define their individual needs. For example, in evaluating computer technical jobs, an organization used experience, education, and complexity as compensable factors. The downside of custom-tailored factors is that they are both time-consuming and expensive to develop, because they at least require a thorough analysis of the jobs being evaluated. However, the factors that are produced from this extra effort are likely to be more work-related and more acceptable to the employees involved. After the compensable factors have been selected, they are scaled to reflect different degrees within each of them. For example, *high school diploma* may serve as the first (lowest) degree of an education compensable factor, whereas a job that required a *college degree* might fall at the third degree for this factor. Finally, factors are assigned weights commensurate with their perceived value to the organization. For the computer technical jobs, for example, it might be determined that out of 400 points, *experience* should receive 200 points (50 % weight), while the other two factors should be equally weighted at 100 points a piece. Initially only a few jobs are evaluated to test the newly developed evaluation device. After some fine-tuning, the rest of the jobs to be covered by the point plan are compared and slotted into the hierarchy.

In establishing external equity, an organization makes comparisons of how much other organizations pay for those jobs under consideration. In other words, an attempt is made to determine what the going rates are among its competitors in particular labor markets, so the organization can make a judgment of how much it wishes to pay. External equity is important in that rates must be high enough to attract and retain quality employees. At the same time, labor costs must be set at a level that will make the organization competitive in producing goods and services. The natural tendency is to *match* the market, or pay the going rate. Some organizations choose to *lead* the market by paying above the market rates. Mathis and Jackson (1997) note that one "transportation firm that pays about 10% to 15 % above the local market medians for clerical employees consistently has a waiting list for qualified word-processing and other office workers. By paying above market, the firm feels that it deters efforts of its office workers to unionize" (p. 389). On the other hand, in an attempt to keep labor costs down, some organizations *lag* the market rates. This pay policy, however, can result in higher turnover rates or in hiring less-qualified workers.

The key methods an organization uses to determine external equity are wage and salary surveys. Many different surveys are available from a variety of sources. Surveys are sponsored by national trade associations (e.g., Society of Human Resource Management, American Management Association) and by the Chamber of Commerce in many localities. Wage and salary survey information can also be obtained from private firms, such as the Hay Group. National sources of wage and salary data for many jobs and industries are available from Statistics-Canada and the U.S. Bureau of Labor Statistics. For example, according to a February 2000 survey by Statistics Canada, the average Canadian employee earned $622.42 per week before taxes. That is a 2.8 percent increase over last year and just a touch larger than the 2.7 percent increase in the inflation rate. Workers in the mining and oil industries were the best paid, on average, at $1,133.10 per week, while service-sector employees had the worst pay. The average retail employee made only $373.89 weekly. Among the 16 industry groups that StatsCan tracks, workers in forestry enjoyed the largest earnings increase—0.7 percent. Salaries fell in only two sectors: wholesale trade and the real estate and insurance agency group (Maclean's, 2000).

According to the National Compensation Survey conducted by the Bureau of Labor Statistics (1999), the 1998 average earnings for all private-and public-sector employees in the United States was $15.72 per hour, excluding pay for overtime, vacations, holidays, nonproduction bonuses, and tips. Average hourly wages for state and local workers ($18.95 per hour) were higher than that of private industry workers ($14.95 per hour). In part, this difference is due to the industrial and occupational compositions of these two sectors. That is, professional and technical specialties are proportionately more prevalent in state and local governments than they are in private industry. In terms of worker characteristics, white-collar pay, with an average of $19.39 per hour, was higher than the blue-collar pay average ($12.90). Among occupations, average hourly pay ranged from $27.78 for executive, administrative, and managerial workers to $9.52 for service workers. Pay also remained higher for union workers ($17.76 per hour) than for nonunion workers ($15.19 per hour).

In recent years, international competition and global restructuring have required organizations throughout the world and in the United States and Canada in particular to become more productive. As a result, traditional methods of addressing internal and external equity have had to be supplemented by variable pay programs. Examples of these programs include annual bonuses, company wide incentive plans, stock options, gainsharing, as well as other individual and group incentive-based pay. For these programs to be successful, Ivancevich (1995) insists that they must be based on clear goals, unambiguous measurements, and be visibly linked to employee performance. They must also include the following factors:

1. Management support—line managers must demonstrate a commitment to these programs.
2. Employee acceptance—employees must view the programs as just and fair.
3. Supportive organizational culture—the organization's culture must be based on teamwork, trust, and employee involvement at all levels when setting performance goals.
4. Timing—the programs must be introduced when there is minimal risk of economic downturns that would affect the size of awards.

In reporting on the results of a survey of variable pay programs in the United States, Zitaner (1992) notes that the annual bonus plan is still the variable compensation program that most organizations (84.6%) use, following by spot awards (30.3%), individual incentives (22.9%), current cash profits sharing (16.6%), gainsharing (9.1%), small group incentives (8.6%), skill-/knowledge-based pay (8.0%) and key contributor (4.0%).

Benefits

Both the United States and Canada have comparable legally required social security systems, which have been crafted to provide retirees with an income that is dependent on, among other things, their average working earnings. These benefits have traditionally been supplemented by employer-sponsored pensions, by individual savings, and, to a growing degree, by part-time employment of the retiree. In the United States, the Social Security Act (1935) not only addresses retirement-income issues, but it also provides for disability insurance, supplementary medical insurance, and survivor benefits. This act also established a system of unemployment compensation insurance, which grants benefits to out-of-work employees at a rate of 50 to 80 percent of their normal pay. In addition, all states have some form of worker's compensation, offering workers reasonable and prompt benefits when injured on the job, regardless of fault. Across the border, the Canada Pension Plan supplies retirement and disability income and survivors' benefits to older workers. It is supplemented by the Old Age Security Act (1957), which includes the basic Old Age Security pension, the Guaranteed Income Supplement, and the Spouse's Allowance. According to Human Resources Development Canada (2000) recent amendments include the following:

- drop in age of eligibility from 70 to 65 (1965);
- establishment of the Guaranteed Income Supplement (1967);
- introduction of full annual cost-of-living indexation (1972);
- quarterly indexation (1973);
- establishment of the Spouse's Allowance (1975);
- payment of partial pensions based on years of residence in Canada (1977);
- inclusion of Old Age Security in international social security agreements (ongoing); and the extension of the Spouse's Allowance to all low-income widows and widowers aged 60 to 64 (1985);

- maximum of one year of retroactive benefits (1995);
- ability for an individual to request that their benefits be cancelled (1995).

Legislative differences between the two countries are nowhere more evident than with health care coverage. In Canada, a national system of health coverage was established with the Medical Care Act of 1966, committing the federal government to contribute about half the cost of the Medical Care Insurance Program (Medicare), with the respective province contributing the remainder. This program is administered by Health and Welfare Canada and stipulates the following regulations: (1) comprehensive coverage, to cover all medically required services rendered by physicians and surgeons; (2) universal availability to all residents; (3) portability, to cover temporary or permanent change in residence to another province or territory; and (4) nonprofit operation. In the face of mounting public debt, Ottawa has reduced its share of the funding, but the basic system remains intact. Private health insurance companies also operate in Canada, providing coverage for services beyond the regular system, such as ambulance fees and private hospital rooms. In the United States, the major government health care provisions are aimed at the aged (Medicare) and the needy (Medicaid). But as Levy (1990) notes "what the U.S. federal government does not do for benefits directly, it does indirectly by granting a wide range of tax incentives to encourage" (p. 21).

In terms of benefits provided by organizations, Table 5.1 indicates that 84 percent of full-time U.S. employees working in goods-producing industries receive medical benefits; this compares with 72 percent of those working in service related industries. Within this category, three basic types of benefits are generally covered: hospital expenses, surgical expenses, and physicians' visits. Other health-care benefits offered by some employers include dental care, vision care, and outpatient prescription drug coverage. Closely related to health-care benefits are disability benefits. Although only 38 percent of the goods-producing employers offer paid-sick leave, 67 percent of the service-producing employers do so. The number of sick days is often determined by how long an employee has worked in an organization or in a particular position (e.g., one day per month not to exceed 26 weeks). Short-term disability plans typically provide benefits up to six months, at which time long-term benefits, if provided, take over. Under these plans, employees typically receive from 50 to 70 percent of their salaries, although short-term plans sometimes provide higher percentages. Noe et al. (2000) point out that for these benefits "there are often caps on the amount that can be paid each month. Federal income taxation of disability benefits depends on the funding method. Where employee contributions completely fund the plan, there is no federal tax. Benefits based on employer contributions are taxed. Finally, disability benefits, especially long-term ones, need to be coordinated with other programs, such as social security disability benefits" (p. 457). Other benefits that are sometimes offered in this category consist of life insurance, accidental death and dismemberment, as well as survivor benefits and survivor income benefits.

To be sure, vacation and other forms of part-time-off benefits are costly to an organization. It can be argued, however, that they are a good investment in attracting and retaining quality employees. Unlike Western Europe, where many countries require organizations to provide a minimum number of vacation days for even new employees, there are no mandated vacations in the United States and Canada, with the exception of provinces like Ontario, which requires two weeks' vacation with pay. Still as the data in Table 5.1 suggest, almost all employers provide their workers with holidays and vacations. Similarly, most employees receive funeral leave, jury duty leave, and military leave with pay. Finally, although family leave with pay is a unique benefit, unpaid family leave is very common. Indeed

TABLE 5.1

Participation in Selected Benefits for Full-time Employees in Goods-producing Industries, 1997 (Percentage)

Benefit	All Employees	Professional	Clerical	Blue-Collar and Service Workers
Part time off:				
Holidays	96	98	100	95
Vacations	96	99	99	94
Personal leave	14	17	26	11
Funeral leave	85	86	87	84
Jury duty leave	90	95	91	88
Military leave	57	76	57	50
Family leave	1	2	1	1
Unpaid family leave	95	96	98	94
Disability benefits				
Paid sick leave	38	68	66	24
Short-term disability	71	68	58	74
Long-term disability	37	58	51	28
Survivor benefits				
Life insurance	91	95	94	90
Accidental death and Dismemberment	74	74	76	74
Survivor income benefits	9	9	5	9
Health care benefits				
Medical care	84	82	81	85
Dental care	65	74	67	62
Vision care	25	31	21	24
Outpatient prescription drug coverage	82	81	80	82

TABLE 5.1 (Continued)

Participation in Selected Benefits for Full-time Employees in Goods-producing Industries, 1997 (Percentage)

Benefit	All Employees	Professional	Clerical	Blue-Collar and Service Workers
Retirement income benefits				
All retirement	88	93	84	86
Defined benefit	62	61	57	63
Defined contribution	62	79	62	56
Savings and thrift	43	63	47	35
Deferred profit sharing	16	15	16	16
Employee stock ownership	5	9	3	4
Money purchase pension	6	7	5	5
Stock bonus	1	<.05	3	1
Cash or deferred arrangement: With employer contribution	55	71	56	49
Salary reduction	49	69	54	41
Savings and thrift	43	63	47	35
No employer contribution	9	9	11	8

Source: Bureau of Labor Statistics (1999).

in 1993, the Family and Medical Leave Act was passed in the United States, requiring organizations with 50 or more employees to provide at least 12 weeks of unpaid leave to everyone but key employees for the following conditions: childbirth or adoptions; care for seriously ill child, spouse, or parent; or an employee's own serious illness. In Canada, laws requiring such leave vary among the provinces. But an example of standards is set out in the Ontario Employment Standards Act (OESA), which mandates a pregnancy leave of 17 weeks for women followed by a parental leave of 18 weeks for both parents. At the end of a leave, an employee is assured of reinstatement in the same job or its equivalent.

As mentioned earlier, the United States and Canada have legally required retirement income for the elderly. Such income is often supplemented by benefits offered by a retiree's organization—even though the federal governments in each country do not legally obligate them to do so. As Table 5.1 indicates, the most common type of retirement plan is the defined benefit. With this type of retirement program, a specified retirement benefit level is guaranteed ("defined") to employees, based generally on a combination of years of service, age, and the employee's level of earnings. By comparison, defined contribution plans, offered by 62 percent of the goods-producing organizations and 53 percent of the service-oriented organizations, do not guarantee a specific benefit level for employees when they retire. Instead, an account is established for each employee with a defined size of contribution. From the perspective of employers, defined-contributions programs shift some of the risk to employees and involve less administrative cost, because there is no need to calculate payments based on age and service.

WESTERN EUROPE

Compensation Levels

Unlike the United States and Canada, few countries in Western Europe have minimum wages that are unilaterally set by governments. Government-mandated minimum wages do exist in France, the Netherlands, Portugal, Spain, and the United Kingdom. France has a relatively high minimum wage, which is revised whenever the cost-of-living index rises by two percentage points. In July 1999, the minimum wage was set at $6.57 (40.72 francs). In the Netherlands, a U.S. State Department report (2000) states:

> The minimum wage for adults is established by law and can be adjusted every 6 months to changes in the cost-of-living index. Over the last few years, the statutory minimum wage has been pegged to the average wage in collective labor contracts. The gross minimum wage is about $1,172 (2,345 guilders) per month. For workers earning the minimum wage, employers currently pay $3,750 a year (6,000 guilders) in premiums for social security benefits, which includes medical insurance. Only 3 percent of workers earn the minimum wage because collective bargaining agreements, which normally are extended across a sector, usually set a minimum wage well above the legislated minimum. The Government, unions, and employers have taken measures to increase the number of minimum wage jobs and to decrease employers' social payments in order to lower the cost of hiring new workers and to create more jobs, especially for the long-term unemployed. A reduced minimum wage applies to young people under the age of 23—one of the demographic groups with the highest rate of unemployment—intended to provide incentives for their employment. This wage ranges from 34.5 percent of the adult minimum wage for workers 16 years of age to 85 percent for those 22 years of age. The legislated minimum wage and social benefits available to all minimum wage earners provide an adequate standard of living for workers and their families.

Minimum wages in Portugal [approximately $326 (61,300 escudos) per month] and Spain [$14.16 (2,356 pesetas) per day or $424.80 (70,680 pesetas) per month] provide a basic standard of living for workers and their families.

The first minimum wage in the United Kingdom went into effect on April 1, 1999. Under the basic provisions of the National Minimum Wage (NMW), rates vary according to age: the rate of pay for adults aged 22 and over is £3.60 per hour, the rate of pay for 18-21 year olds is £3 per hour, 16 and 17 year olds are exempt from the NMW. There is also a special rate of £3.20 for individuals aged 22 and older, who are in the first six months of a new job and are participating in an authorized training program. Inasmuch as some firms are taking advantage of the regulations and paying lower wages to workers under the age of 22, the Low Pay Commission is now evaluating the regulations to determine whether the £3.60 minimum should apply to 21 year olds.

Although the West European labor movements will be covered in the next section, it is crucial at this point to acknowledge the role unions play in determining compensation levels, including minimum wages, in this region. In Germany, wages and salaries are set either by collective bargaining agreements between unions and employer federations or by individual union-employer contracts. These agreements set minimum pay rates for roughly 90 percent of all employees and are legally enforceable. Similarly, collective bargaining between the Confederation of Greek Workers (GSEE) and the Employers' Association in Greece determines a nationwide minimum wage. The Ministry of Labor routinely ratifies this minimum wage, which has the force of law and applies to all workers. In recent years, however, there has been a movement away from centralized bargaining in establishing wage levels. In Sweden, for example, multiemployer bargaining continues to predominate, yet the newly elected conservative government would like to dissolve the employers' associations (Soderstrom, 1992). Moreover, industrywide negotiations in Sweden only establish wage floors, rather than specific wage rate. Ahlen (1989) points out that several "blue collar workers in private industry and commerce earn more through the combination of local agreement excesses and individual wage supplements, collectively known as wage drift, than they do as a result of central agreements" (p. 337). In Denmark, the combination of a conservative government and high unemployment also has weakened the central bargaining structure (Hegewisch, 1993). Moreover, Purcell (1991) explains that in the last decade, the United Kingdom has dramatically altered its approach to determining employee compensation, which can only be described as "the culmination of a process of collapse of multi-employer bargaining" (p. 37). France has also undergone a decentralization of determining compensation policies. To illustrate, in order to encourage company-level negotiations, the CNPF, the French employers' federation, has refused to issue central pay guidelines since 1984. In 1987, the French engineering employers' federation, UIMM, followed suit by not setting a national wage rate. Oddly enough, support for local bargaining has not reached the managerial staff, "where UIMM continues to provide reference points for salary scales and increments" (Hegewisch, 1993).

In 1975 the European Community issued an Equal Pay Directive, stating that Article 119 of the Treaty of Rome implied a requirement for equal pay for work of equal value, regardless of gender. To be sure, many countries in Western Europe have laws that require equal pay for men and women. But such laws have typically fallen short. For example, the United Kingdom passed the Equal Pay Act in 1970 covering comparisons between men and women undertaking the same or broadly similar work, or work that was rated as equivalent under a job evaluation plan. But soon after the Equal Pay Directive was issued, the European Court of Justice (ECJ) held that the United Kingdom was in breach insofar as women had no entitlement to equal pay for work of equal value unless their employer had chosen to implement a job evaluation scheme. In response, the United Kingdom amended the Equal Pay Act in 1983 to incorporate the case where a woman could show the work she did was of equal value to that of a man employed by the same organization in terms of effort, skill, and decision-making. But the procedures for bringing complaints have turned out to be cumbersome, long-winded, and ineffective (Sloane & Mackay, 1997). As a result, the Equal Opportunities Commission reported in March of 2000 that women are paid an average of 20 percent less than men, with a gap of 55 percent in the financial sector.

Other countries with laws mandating equal pay for equal work include Denmark, France, Greece, Spain, and Sweden, although in Denmark wage inequality still exists. The requirements of the French legislation are often not the reality. Reports by various governmental and nongovernmental organizations indicate that men continue to earn more than women. For example, a report released on September 2, 1999 by National Assembly Deputy Catherine Genisson indicates that in the 5,000 largest French firms, the average difference in salary between men and women is 27 percent. Greek women enjoy broad constitutional and legal protections, including equal pay for equal work. The National Statistical Service's most recent data (the second quarter of 1998) show that women's salaries in manufacturing were 70.8 percent of those of men in comparable positions; in retail sales, women's salaries were 88 percent of those of men in comparable positions. Moreover, although the law in Spain mandates equal pay for equal work, a 1997 report by the Economic and Social Affairs Council shows that women's salaries still remain 27 percent lower than those of their male counterparts. Sweden, however, has perhaps made the most headway in this region. According to Statistics Sweden, women's salaries were 83 percent of men's salaries in 1997. When such factors as age, education, and occupational groups were held constant, the women's adjusted salaries were on average 93 percent of men's salaries (U.S. State Department Report, 1999).

Table 5.2 presents wage data for production workers in West European countries and the United States. Total compensation costs include pay for time worked, bonuses, and vacation and holiday pay as well other legally required insurance programs and contractual and private benefit plans. When measured in U.S. dollars, the average hourly compensation costs for production workers are higher in nine West European countries than they were in the United States. Indeed European hourly compensation costs are 11 percent higher than those in the United States. According to the Bureau of Labor Services (BLS) (2000) data, compensation costs in Europe rose at a historically low rate of only 2.6 percent. The slowest growth occurred in Spain and Switzerland, although compensation costs in national currency actually declined in Italy. The decline in Italy was attributable in large part to the substantial reduction of employer contributions to legally required social insurance programs. The data also indicate that hourly compensation costs in Western Europe rebounded in 1998, following a dramatic decline in 1997. Indeed the United Kingdom was the only West European country that recorded an increase in costs in 1997. In 1998, however, the picture looked very different. Compensation costs in all of the West European countries rose, and in Denmark and the United Kingdom, the percentage increase was higher than that in the United States.

Drawing comparisons using the data in Table 5.2 must be done with extreme caution. For example, if the data are taken at face value, the obvious course of action for manufacturers is to move their operations to Portugal or Greece. But

TABLE 5.2

Comparative Hourly Compensation Costs

Country	Average Hourly Compensation for Production Workers, in U.S. Dollars			Percentage Change in Hourly Compensation Costs for Production Workers, in National Currency (1997-1998)
	1996	1997	1998	
Austria	24.80	21.91	22.16	2.6
Belgium	25.89	22.82	23.11	2.7
Denmark	24.11	22.03	22.69	4.5
Finland	23.56	21.37	21.57	3.9
France	19.93	17.99	18.28	2.7
Germany	30.26	26.90	27.20	2.6
Greece	9.59	9.20	8.91	4.7
Ireland	13.85	13.55	13.33	4.7
Italy	17.75	17.57	17.11	-.8
Netherlands	23.08	20.61	20.57	1.4
Norway	25.05	23.72	23.70	6.5
Portugal	5.58	5.38	5.48	4.7
Spain	13.51	12.24	12.14	1.2
Sweden	24.37	22.23	22.03	3.1
Switzerland	28.34	24.19	24.38	.8
United Kingdom	14.09	15.47	16.43	5.0
United States	17.70	18.21	18.56	1.9

Source: Bureau of Labor Statistics (1999).

other factors such as productivity come into play. Indeed although the United States has a relatively high average hourly compensation rate, robust productivity levels there translate into lower unit labor costs than in West European countries (Sparks & Greiner, 1997). When data are converted into U.S. dollars, they may be used as gross measures for comparing levels of employer labor costs, but they do not indicate relative living standards of workers or the purchasing power of their incomes.

Table 5.3 provides comparative indexes of gross annual salaries for three different management positions in various countries. After adjusting for purchasing power, Germany offers the highest average wages, although most of the northern countries fall below average. In part, this finding is due to the tax rates and the cost of customer products. Spanish and Portuguese managerial incomes are relatively high, again suggesting that companies in these countries must offer competitive salaries to attract and retain managers.

TABLE 5.3

1992 Average Wages in Representative Professions (Netherlands = 100), Adjusted for Purchasing Power

Country	Junior Middle Management	Senior Middle Management	Senior Executive Management
Germany	154	164	217
Spain	154	159	195
Italy	114	157	201
Austria	133	155	195
Portugal	126	144	178
United States	127	136	185
France	126	132	164
Switzerland	126	130	165
United Kingdom	106	113	150
Greece	99	110	130
Belgium	108	107	133
Netherlands	100	100	100
Ireland	95	97	121
Norway	·87	75	82
Finland	75	71	87
Denmark	58	68	89
Sweden	66	68	80

Source: Logger et al. (1995).

In addition to the traditional wage and salary structures, employers in this region also are pushing for greater flexibility in putting together variable-pay programs. Variable pay is attractive to countries that have difficulty in employee recruitment. Indeed approximately three-quarters of the employers in southern countries have had to be more creative in designing their compensation systems to attract and retain a quality workforce. But variable-pay options have not been limited to just the southern countries; they have begun to appear in almost all countries in this region. Sparrow and Hiltrop (1994) note that the increase in variable pay has been greatest in the retail and distribution sector. Over three-quarters of Spanish organizations in this sector and nearly two-thirds of German, French, and British organizations indicated they have made variable pay a more important part of their reward structure from 1988-91" (pp. 524-525).

Statistics on the utilization of specific variable-pay options are presented in Table 5.4. Employee-sharing programs generally involve some form of ownership of the organization by employees. Although there are a variety of such programs (e.g., cooperatives), one of the latest programs to appear in Western Europe is Employee Share Ownership Plans (ESOPs). Under an ESOP, shares of stock are

TABLE 5.4

Variable Pay Programs in West European Countries (Percentage)

Occupation/ Program	Denmark	West Germany	Spain	France	Finland	Ireland	Norway	Netherlands	Portugal	Sweden	United Kingdom
Managers											
Employee share	n/a	11	11	12	13	28	14	18	8	10	37
Profit sharing	6	60	17	70	14	15	5	38	29	18	26
Group bonus	7	3	9	34	13	16	10	7	11	12	25
Individual bonus	20	48	36	44	36	28	12	59	18	18	32
Technical/professional											
Employee share	n/a	9	5	3	11	16	13	12	7	7	29
Profit sharing	3	20	11	68	18	12	4	38	22	12	21
Group bonus	6	7	5	30	27	15	13	9	12	11	18
Individual bonus	16	67	32	34	29	22	10	59	19	3	27
Clerical											
Employee share	n/a	8	5	3	11	10	13	10	5	8	26
Profit sharing	3	11	9	68	17	12	4	32	20	16	19
Group bonus	4	6	2	n/a	33	12	11	6	7	12	14
Individual bonus	6	52	4	n/a	13	11	3	36	7	1	7
Manual											
Employee share	n/a	7	4	4	10	10	13	10	5	7	23
Profit sharing	2	10	8	57	16	11	4	31	19	13	17
Group bonus	18	14	3	25	43	17	15	7	10	27	25
Individual bonus	9	30	3	17	8	13	7	35	10	6	17

Source: Developed from Tables 4.3 a-d in Appendix III. In C. Brewster and A. Hegewisch (Eds.), *Policy and Practice in European Human Resource Management.* (1994). London: Routledge.

transferred to employees by either the issuance of new stock or by purchasing stock currently on the market. An organization typically will establish a trust that purchases the shares and then distributes them to employees. Perhaps because of their recent introduction, employee ownerships generally and ESOP in particular have not experienced tremendous support in Western Europe. An exception is the UK, where the trend is to place an "emphasis on employee share ownership schemes, including ESOPs. By August 1991, the ESOP Centre in London estimated that there were more than 50 British companies with ESOPs that were specifically designed to benefit a majority of each company's employees" (Thompson, 1993, p. 825).

Profit sharing is similar to employee share in some key respects, such as providing a direct economic incentive for employees to focus on the organization's success. In France, profit sharing is widely used in all job categories. The major reason for this is that companies with more than 50 employees are legally obligated to sponsor such incentives. In Germany, profit sharing is a preferred incentive program for managers, yet rarely applied to other job categories. As with variable-pay programs in general, profit sharing tends to be unpopular in the northern countries, even for managers.

Use of individual bonuses is relatively common across Western Europe as part of the compensation packages for mangers. By comparison, bonuses are quite rare for clerical and manual workers, with the exception of Germany, where 52 percent of the employers offer them to clerical workers and 30 percent have extended these benefits to their manual workers. Housemann (1995) adds that 13-month salaries and Christmas bonuses are standard in Germany.

Interest in individual bonus plans have, at best, leveled out in the United Kingdom. It is suggested that some companies there believe that individual incentive programs encourage employees to value quantity over quality, resulting in considerable consumer concerns (Filella & Hegewisch, 1994). In their place, group or team incentive programs appear to be gaining acceptance. As Sparrow and Hiltrop (1994) observe, in the United Kingdom "group bonuses are regularly used in retailing (47 percent of organizations), in banking (36 percent), and in transport and communications (37 percent). In Sweden and France, group bonuses are particularly popular in the extraction and chemical industry (52 percent and 36 percent respectively)" (pp. 528, 530). But German and Spanish organizations are less inclined to provide group incentives.

Employers also are tying pay to employee performance based on merit. The major distinctions between merit pay and other incentive programs are that the former is based on an individual's performance appraisal and is applied to base salary, whereas the latter programs are directed more at group or organization performance. Merit pay is fast becoming a means of compensating managers and professionals in France, Italy, Switzerland, and the United Kingdom, but has not caught on in the northern countries.

Some countries also have experimented with merit pay for other job categories. According to Brewster, Hegewisch, & Mayne (1994), for example, approximately 58 percent of the Portuguese organizations use merit-based pay for manual and clerical workers. Moreover, in 1990, 41 percent of the French organizations offered merit-pay programs for manual workers. By comparison, only 10 percent of organizations in Norway base pay for these workers on their performance.

In general, variable-pay options have been associated with private industry in the United States, but in Western Europe the reverse is true. In point of fact, although 32 percent of the private-sector organizations in Denmark offered variable pay programs, 85 percent of them in the public sector did so. Furthermore, in the United Kingdom, where variable pay has received little support from the private sector, 63 percent of the public-sector employers offered some form of variable pay to managers and 23 percent extended this practice to clerical workers. As Hegewisch (1993) notes, in "this area the UK has developed much faster than France where in 1989-90 only 21 percent of public sector employers had introduced merit/performance pay" for managers (p. 96).

Benefits

Virtually all countries in Western Europe provide universal or near-universal health care to residents, who receive benefits whether they are employed or not. The primary sources of funding for this service are the government and contributions made by employers and employees. For example, in the United Kingdom general taxation pays for 82 percent of the system's cost, and the national insurance payment—money that employers and employees contribute—takes care of 18 percent. In large measure due to costs, almost every country is undergoing changes in their health care systems. To illustrate, the United Kingdom passed the controversial National Heath Service (NHS) and Community Care Act of 1990, with the intent to make health care more efficient and less costly by encouraging competition within the health care industry. According to Kishlansky and Weisser (2000), the act permits hospitals and other health care professionals to become trusts that directly control the funds they receive from the government. They are now able to determine their own human resources needs, salaries, and service fees, things previously determined by local health authorities, who controlled their funds. Under this act, local health authorities, which are responsible for providing health care to the public with government money, "purchase" health care for patients from these trusts. Moreover, general practitioners (GPs), or ordinary family doctors, are encouraged to become fund holders or directly manage the NHS funds allotted for their patients. The new health care arrangements were designed to bring competitive market forces to bear upon health care, with the trusts competing to become the facility chosen by local health authorities and GPs to provide health care to patients.

Countries like Luxembourg approach health care somewhat differently, as the following example from Osborn (2000) illustrates.

> Lara Collins, an Englishwoman, was a bit surprised when she was asked to climb onto the operating table to have her appendix removed at a Luxembourg hospital. "It was as if I'd asked to have my toenails cut," she recalls. This no-frills, workman like approach to hospital care is a characteristic of the Luxembourg health service. It is not to be confused

with penny-pinching. Lara paid the equivalent of about 810 francs a day for her hospital stay, and she had a room to herself all the time she was there. For the operation itself, she paid 20 percent of the hospital and surgeon's fees.

No, Luxembourg does not have a national health service as it is known in some other countries, where every medical need is paid for out of central government funds. Lara's fees were met by the caisse—or sickness insurance fund—to which her father was a paying subscriber.

Luxembourg's health care system works by combining government overall control with monies supplied by quasi-private insurance funds that in turn draw their revenues from worker premiums, which are fixed at a percentage of income. Recently the percentage was raised to about 4.7 and is tax deductible. Unemployed people or others who may not be able to pay the premiums can claim assistance from social security. In general, the caisses will provide up to 80 percent of all medical care a doctor judges necessary. This coverage includes all equipment and all prescriptions for drugs, apart from "lifestyle drugs" like Viagra, Rogaine, and antismoking treatments. Vitamins also are excluded (Osborn, 2000).

The birthplace of modern-day retirement programs is Western Europe. That is, pensions for the elderly first appeared in France and the United Kingdom in the early 19th century and were instituted in Germany in 1873. The establishment of pensions spread to many other European countries in the first decade of the 20th century and later spread to other countries, including the United States. Today, all West European countries have government-run systems to support people in their old age, often supplemented with mandatory private schemes. European taxpayers pay an average of 10 percent of the GDP toward pension bills, though Italians pay 14 percent; in the United States, taxpayers pay just 5 percent of GDP. Due to the high cost of pensions in this region, most countries are undergoing pension reform. Currently there is a wide variation among the countries in the delivery of old-age income-support schemes. Most national pension systems involve one or more of the following pillars:

- basic pensions of a fixed amount to all individuals,
- earnings-related pensions, whereby people contribute to the system during their working life in exchange for earnings-related benefits in retirement,
- contribution-based pensions, where benefits are directly linked to past contributions to pension funds and returns on their investments.

The age at which people become entitled to pensions differs among the countries in this region. The standard retirement age for males is 65 in about half of them, and ranges from as low as 60 in a few countries (e.g., Belgium, France) to 67 in some Nordic countries. In most countries, the entitlement age is lower for females. More important, the standard entitlement age has been falling since the 1960s, with predictable effects according to when people choose to retire. In Belgium, France, and to a lesser extent in Ireland and Sweden, for example, it has led to substantial drops in labor-force participation rates among older people (55-64 years of age); the higher standard ages of retirement in Denmark, Iceland, and Norway, instructively, have helped maintain high participation rates. Indeed there are few incentives for remaining in the labor force after the standard age of retirement. Continuing to work for an additional year often means simply that a year of pensions is forgone with often little or no increase in eventual pensions in exchange. Two countries, Portugal and Spain, make entitlements to old-age pensions beyond the standard age conditional on complete withdrawal from the labor market. And some countries (Finland and France, for example) will grant public pensions only if individuals stop working with their current employer, a qualification that can be a de facto restriction on work in view of the difficulty older workers can have in finding new jobs. Moreover; in countries where there are no direct or indirect restrictions on work beyond the standard entitlement age, the means-testing of pension benefits tends to discourage work; because pensions are reduced as earnings increase beyond a certain point, work becomes unprofitable (Blondal & Scarpetta, 1998).

Most countries in this region have government regulations that guarantee workers generous paid leaves, including holidays and vacations. For example, government regulations mandate six weeks of vacation for all employees in Austria and Denmark. In Finland, France, and Sweden, the law provides all employees with a minimum of five weeks of paid annual leave; labor contracts often provide more, particularly for higher ranking private-sector employees and older public service workers. Norwegian law grants 25 working days of paid leave per year, 31 days for those over the age of 60. Workers in Spain enjoy 12 paid holidays a year and a month's paid vacation. Across the border in Portugal, employees typically receive 14 months' pay for 11 months' work—the extra three months' pay are for a Christmas bonus, a vacation subsidy, and 22 days of annual leave. Although the United Kingdom does not mandate vacation time beyond the eight bank holidays, the average British vacation is 22 days a year. By comparison, the average length of vacation in the United States is 10 days, none of which is mandated by law (Peak, 1995).

In addition to traditional fringe benefits, other indirect compensation such as company cars, credit cards, school-fee allowances, and low mortgages are becoming common in many West European countries. Employers in Spain, where labor markets are tight, have had to be fairly creative in their employee benefits. For example, over 70 percent of a sample of Spanish organizations across industries offered employees 20 different types of fringe benefits: life insurance, accident insurance, gifts, supplements to the social security in case of illness, clothing allowance, company car, loans, meal allowances, job transfer allowances, parking subsidies, and study allowances (Flolrez-Sabirdo et al., 1995). In the past, private pensions were a rarity for Spanish employees, yet many organizations are beginning to offer such benefits.

EASTERN EUROPE AND THE NEW INDEPENDENT STATES

Compensation Levels

In the past few years, many companies in Western Europe have been lured to Central and East European countries to take advantage of the lower labor costs. Wages and social welfare taxes in these countries have been generally less than half those in Western Europe. Conditions are changing, however. The sharp deterioration of consumer markets and skyrocketing inflation coupled with greater freedom to leave these countries and to make individual job choices are intensifying competition for quality workers. Accordingly, one of the major HRM challenges in this region is to develop fair, competitive, and motivating compensation systems. In Russia, for example, a variety of approaches are being used to compensate Russian employees. One of the major governmental initiatives was to increase the minimum monthly wage from about $5 (20,500 rubles) in 1995 to roughly about $15 (63,000 rubles) a year later. Yet in 1998, this amount had declined to $3.33 (83 rubles), which is well below the living wage of $38 (950 rubles)—note that at the beginning of 1998, the Russian government replaced the ruble with a denomination 1,000 times smaller (1,000 old rubles = 1 new ruble). This is insufficient to provide a decent standard of living for a worker and family. In August, 37.7 percent of the population had incomes below this survival minimum, compared with 21.8 percent one year earlier. Examples of other countries in this region that have obscenely low monthly minimum wages include the Ukraine, $16.37 (73.7 hryvnia); Azerbaijan, $3.00 (12,500 manat); Bulgaria, $37 (67 lev); and Armenia, which in October 1998 quintupled the national minimum wage to less than $10 (5,000 drams).

Although the Central European countries generally have higher minimum wages than other countries in this region, they do not provide a decent standard of living for employees and their families—perhaps with the exception of Slovenia, with a minimum wage of $325 (59,150 tolars) per month. In Hungary, for example, the National Labor Affairs Council establishes the legal minimum wage, which is subsequently administered by the Ministry of Social and Family Affairs. The minimum wage is $95 (22,500 HUF) per month, which does not afford a decent standard of living for a worker and family. Consequently, many workers supplement their primary employment with second jobs, and there are reports that many citizens, while officially earning the minimum wage, actually make more. Reporting the minimum wage is a way for both employer and employee to avoid paying higher taxes. The Czech Republic also sets minimum wage standards. In July 1999, the government increased the minimum wage from approximately $108 (3,250 CZK) per month to $115 (3,600 CZK). And although this was the second raise in six months, the minimum wage still provides a sparse standard of living for a worker and family, even though allowances are available to families with children. In Poland, the Ministry of Labor, the unions, and employers' organizations negotiate a revised national minimum wage every three months. The minimum monthly wage in state-owned enterprises is approximately $162.50 (650 PLN), which constitutes no real increase over the 1998 amount. This amount was insufficient to provide a worker and family with a decent standard of living in view of rising prices. A large percentage of construction workers and seasonal agricultural laborers from the former Soviet Union earn less than the minimum wage. The large size of the informal economy and the small number of state labor inspectors make enforcement of the minimum wage very difficult (U.S. State Department, 2000).

Unlike the previous two regions of the world, virtually no country in this region has adopted and enforced equal pay legislation. Indeed women are openly discriminated against in the workplace. Russian women, for example, continue to report cases in which they are paid less for the same work that male colleagues perform. Furthermore, the situation for workingwomen has worsened after the 1998 financial crisis, as women were more likely to be let go first. Even the Czech Republic, Hungary, and Poland, which are now associate members of the EU and are expected to become full members within the next few years, have problems with gender equality. Although gender discrimination will be discussed in more detail in the next chapter, a couple of compensation-related examples are in order here. The Czech Republic passed an employment law in 1991 that bans discrimination based on gender. In practice, however, employers continue to consider gender, age, or even attractiveness when making employment decisions. This does not necessarily constitute "discrimination" under current legal interpretation. The median wages for women in the Czech Republic lag behind those of men by roughly 25 percent; the upside is that this gap is narrowing. Poland's constitution provides for equal rights regardless of gender, granting women equal rights with men in all areas of family, political, social, and economic life, including equal compensation for work of similar value. In practice, however, women frequently are paid less for equivalent work, mainly hold lower level positions, are discharged more quickly, and are less likely to be promoted than men (U.S. State Department, 2000).

Critics of the transition from command economies to market economies in this region argue that the standard of living in many countries is now worse. They point out that the post-Soviet period has been marked by a dramatic drop in the standard of living for the majority of the people in this region. Wages have been distributed erratically and have not kept pace with the rising cost of living. Food supplies, though plentiful in some countries, are priced beyond the reach of many. In 1995, for example, the prices of essential commodities in Kazakhstan rose sharply, while wages decreased. Moreover, the current average wage in Russia buys only three-fifths of what it did immediately prior to price liberalization in January of 1992 and is lower than the 1985 average wage. Despite the merits of this argument, it ignores the fact that although wage-price ratios were higher under the old system, there was essentially nothing to buy in the shops, making such ratios meaningless as indicators of the quality of life in Russia (Guzda, 1993).

Although limited data are available concerning wages in this region, Table 5.5 presents some comparisons. Again, these data should be used only as gross indicators because they do not take into account such factors as purchasing power. What they do suggest is that wages in the Central European countries tend to be higher than those in the East European countries and in the new independent states. These observations are consistent with the notion that the central countries in general are making the transition from controlled economies to market-oriented ones with less difficulty. Indeed some organizations in lower paying countries have had to be creative in their compensation systems. For example, a survey of Russian organizations revealed that although some organizations paid workers strictly in rubles, others paid them in more valued currencies (see Table 5.6). To be sure, seven of the 18 organizations paid bonuses in rubles, ranging from 50 to 200 percent of base pay. Six of the organizations used hard currency for bonuses, which typically totaled several hundred dollars. Two organizations combined the currency in their bonus plans, with the remaining three organizations opting for no employee bonuses.

TABLE 5.5

Monthly Average Wages for Workers in Eastern Europe, in U.S. Dollars

Countries	1993	1994
Albania	30.2	50.4
Bulgaria	115.0	86.0
Czech Republic	200.0	240.0
Hungary	296.0	317.0
Poland	221.0	241.0
Russia	63.0	96.0
Slovakia	175.0	196.0
Ukraine	15.0	30.0

Source: Muco, M. (1996).

Variable pay as part of the total compensation package is also beginning to appear in this region. Since 1992, variable pay increased in 60 percent of the organizations in the Czech Republic (Koubek & Brewster, 1995). Today, as Table 5.7 indicates, profit sharing for managers has been adopted by close to 70 percent of the organizations. Merit/performance-related pay programs are offered to clerical and manual workers in 70 and 77 percent of the organizations, respectively (see Table 5.7). In Hungary, many of the former communist enterprises have retained a complex monetary bonus system. Similar to Russian bonus plans, this system grants bonuses ranging from zero to 200 percent of an employee's base pay. Although the bulk of the high-ended bonuses go to managers, even low-level employees have grown to expect bonuses as high as 40 percent of their wages. In most cases, bonuses are administered at the discretion of supervisors, often with little relationship to the actual performance of those receiving them (Pearce, 1991).

Benefits

In this region of the world, a comprehensive welfare system was established in the immediate postwar period as an explicitly social objective in its own right (and became the major source of régime legitimization for some time), includng not only universal health and education, but also housing, transport, and food subsidies. Despite the failure to adequately provide these basic needs, and the undoubted discrimination in access to them (i.e., through Party membership), they were legal entitlements of all citizens. Moreover, citizens had the constitutional right to employment.

TABLE 5.6

Base Salaries Paid to Russian Employees , 1992

Training House (fully U.S. owned)	
Sales Manager	U.S. $30,000 (annual)
Sales Force	U.S. $6,000
Training House (joint venture, Russian/Italian)	
Sales Manager	U.S. $12,000 (annual)
Sales Force	U.S. $6,000
Hotel (fully German owned)	
Shift Manager	Deutsche Mark 12,000 (U.S. $7,500) (annual)
Maid	Deutsche Mark 6,000 (U.S. $3,750)
Hotel (fully French owned)	
Shift Manager	Rubles 20,000 (per month, U.S. $55) plus
	French Francs 14,000 (annual U.S. $2,600)
Maid	Rubles 7,000 (U.S. $18) plus
	French Francs 10,000 (U.S. $1,850)
Manufacturing Company (joint venture Russian/U.S.)	
General Manager	Rubles 48,000 (monthly, U.S. $140)
Marketing Manager	Rubles 32,000 ($90)
Mechanic	Rubles 7,500 ($21)
Manufacturing Company (joint venture, Russian/U.S.)	
Senior Managers	Rubles 16,333 (monthly, $65)
Factory	
Supervisors	Rubles 5,863 ($23)
Factory Workers	Rubles 6,437 ($26)

Source: Puffer, S. (1994).

Today, the funding and delivery of these services is undergoing profound change. For example, Poles now have to pay much more directly for health care and other welfare provisions. When the Czech Republic became independent in 1993, the government announced plans to gradually privatize the health-care system. Under the communists, rudimentary health care was free for the entire Alban-

TABLE 5.7

Incentive Programs in the Czech Republic (Percentage)

Incentive	Professional/ Managerial	Technical	Manual	Clerical
Employee share option	6	5	5	5
Profit sharing	68	48	39	35
Group bonus	2	10	11	15
Individual bonus	16	24	21	17
Merit/performance Related pay	43	68	70	77

Source: Kubeš, M., & Benkovic, P. (1994).

ian population, and although all medical services are still offered free of charge, the system suffers from outdated equipment, inadequate hospitals, and a severe shortage of drugs. In Russia, illnesses have increased as the quality and availability of health care have declined. Similarly, Romania is experiencing significantly poorer health conditions. Indeed in the mid-1990s Romania had one of the highest infant mortality rates in Europe. As a result, the World Bank has granted loans to the Romanian government to help improve the country's health care system.

The countries in this region are also having difficulty promoting economic growth while imposing high tax rates needed to finance rapidly growing expenditures on pension benefits. These countries have been spending much more on pensions than their incomes or demographics would predict. In many of them, pension expenditures are the largest single item in the government budget, accounting for about 15 percent of GDP in Poland and Slovenia and 10 percent in Bulgaria, Hungary, Latvia, and Slovakia. For these countries to meet their populations' needs for income security, the World Bank recommended a few years ago that they adopt a multipillar pension system. According to this system, there would be a mandatory pay-as-you-go public pension system, a mandatory privately managed and funded pension system, and a voluntary system (Fox, 1995). In response to this suggestion, Hungary introduced just such a system with a mandatory funded pillar. The existing pay-as-you-go system remains. The second pillar is a separate mandatory funded account at 8 percent of payroll. Employers make the contribution, but get tax and other credits in return. The third pillar is a voluntary plan like a mutual insurance company, with all benefits going to members. Kazakhstan is introducing a formula that allows for full recognition of past service in a frozen pay-as-you-go formula. Fully funded accounts paid for by 10 percent of payroll with a top-up guarantee form the second pillar. Poland has the third most advanced reform in process, but it is stuck in a legislative gridlock. A law providing for reform of a second-pillar pension system is now being developed, but this depends on legislation being passed to reform the current first pillar.

Other mandated worker benefits in this region are not as generous as were observed in Western Europe. In fact, although overtime pay exists in theory for workers in countries like the Ukraine, it is not always paid. Still, in the Czech Republic workers are guaranteed three to four weeks of leave annually. The Latvian labor code requires four weeks of annual vacation for all workers and a program of assistance to working mothers with small children. In Romania, paid holidays must range from 18 to 24 days annually, depending on the employee's length of service. Overtime pay up to a maximum of eight hours per week and 150 hours per year are required of all state enterprises in Slovakia; they are also required to provide their employees with five weeks of annual leave. Romanian law also requires employers to pay additional benefits and allowances to workers engaged in particularly dangerous or difficult occupations. Similarly, the Russian labor code grants workers the right to remove themselves from hazardous or life-threatening work situations without endangering their continued employment and entitlements to such compensations as shorter hours, increased vacations, extra pay, and pension benefits for working under such conditions. In Poland, the law requires overtime payment for hours in excess of the standard 42-hour workweek (U.S. State Department, 2000).

TABLE 5.8

Employee Benefits in Russian Organizations, by Profession

Benefits	General Managers	Managers	Rank/File
Holidays/Vacations	+	+	+
Cars/Drivers	+/+	+/-	-/-
Western Goods	+	+	0
Meals Support	+	+	0
Medical Care	+	0	-
Clothing Allowance	+	+	0
Life Insurance	0	-	-

+ Generally provided, 0 provided to some employees, -generally not provided.
Source: Puffer, S. (1994).

With respect to other employee benefits, there is considerable overlap between the old system and the new one. A major reason for this is the well-entrenched attitude that although societal norms permitted little wage variations, benefits were different. Indeed they served as important symbols of status and prestige. Moreover, the loose benefits system in Russia permitted managers to manipulate it. As Table 5.8 illustrates, benefits differ according to employee position. Top-level managers still enjoy extensive benefits, including chauffeured cars—the most popular being the midsize Volvos. Provisions are frequently made for gas, insurance, and servicing—contingencies that are quite complicated and expensive in Russia. They also are provided with entertainment and travel budgets, with amounts varying across organizations. Interestingly, only a few organizations provide life insurance for their top-level managers, and virtually none of them do so with regard to other employees. The number of mid- and lower-level Russian managers that are provided with cars, usually without drivers, is much larger than in other Western countries. This benefit originated as a way of compensating them when hard currency payments were illegal. Now it has become an integral component of competitive compensation packages. Unlike top-level executives, these managers have few opportunities for foreign travel or entertainment.

A major perk for all Russian employees is company-supplied Western goods. To illustrate, one organization surveyed "gives employees an annual hard currency allowance ranging from 10,000 to 25,000 French francs, depending on their ruble salary, and provides a catalog from which they can choose consumer goods. The goods are purchased by the company and delivered to employees" (Puffer, 1994, p. 39). Some rank/file employees receive clothing, transportation, and meals allowances. But they are rarely provided with medical-care support.

Given the experience of the Czech Republic, one benefit that is likely to be offered to employees in other Central and East European countries is recreation grants to parents for their children, currently offered by 80 percent of the Czech Republic organizations. To stay competitive in the labor markets, organizations are also expected to offer other child-care-related benefits, including holiday camps for children (offered by two-thirds of the Czech Republic organizations) and child-care facilities at work, which are provided by one-quarter of these organizations.

Finally, a benefit that is touted as uniquely Eastern European is *Management by Special Favors*. Under this practice, managers ignore their employees' breaking the rules, allowing them to use organizational resources for their own purposes and to be absent. According to Pearce (1991), a "way in which managers can reward their best employees is by condoning these small illegitimate activities" (p. 82). He notes further that the acceptance of this practice stems from the political environment in these countries. Specifically, the elevation of political prisoners to high governmental positions in such countries as Poland helped sanction rule breaking at the work place.

THE MIDDLE EAST

Compensation Levels

With the exception of the oil producing countries and Israel, workers in the Middle East earn less than what would be considered a living wage. According to Ziskind (1990), even within well-to-do countries, there are substrata of underpaid workers. To be sure, many countries in this region have provisions in their constitutions that make reference to wage standards. Jordan's constitution, for example, calls for laws that "every workman shall receive wages commensurate with the quantity and quality of his work." The Syrian constitution guarantees all citizens "the right to earn his wage according to the nature and yield of work." The fact that individual constitutions make statements regarding some form of livable wage standards does not mean that the governments necessarily implement them. To illustrate, the Iraqi constitution asserts that the government must "promote standards of living" and "provide the means of enjoying the achievements of modern civilization for the masses of the people."

Regarding specific compensation legislation, according to U.S. State Department (2000), a few countries in this region do not have minimum-wage laws, including Saudi Arabia, the United Arab Emirates, Yemen, and effectively Qatar, where the minimum wage is that which "His Highness the Ruler may deem fit to determine." Where such legislation exists, there is a wide variation in its coverage and scope. In some countries, minimum wages apply only to public-sector employees. The minimum wage in Bahrain is set by government decree for public sector employees and generally affords an acceptable standard of living for a worker and family; today the minimum wage for the public is $278.25 (105 dinars) a month. In Kuwait, there is no legal minimum wage in the private sector, but the public-sector law draws a distinction according to citizenship. The effective minimum wage for public-sector employees is approximately $742 (226 dinars) a month for citizens and approximately $296 (90 dinars) a month for noncitizens. The Lebanese government sets a legal minimum wage, currently about $200 (300,000 Lebanese pounds) per month. Although the trade unions attempt to ensure the payment of the minimum wage in both the public sector and the large-scale private sector, the law is not enforced effectively in the private sector. The Syrian minimum wage is $42 (2,115 Syrian pounds) per month in the public sector, plus other compensation (for example, meals, uniforms, and transportation), while the private-sector minimum wage is $39 (1,940 Syrian pounds) per month in urban areas and $36 (1,790 Syrian pounds) in the countryside. In either case, the minimum wages have not been adjusted since 1994 and do not provide a decent standard of living for a worker and family.

On October 2, 1999, the Jordanian government implemented a national minimum wage of $114 (80 dinars) per month for all workers except domestic servants and those in the agricultural sector. Moreover, the Iranian Labor Code empowers the Supreme Labor Council to set annual minimum wage levels for each industrial sector and region. Although the law stipulates that the minimum wage should be sufficient to meet the living expenses of a family and should take inflation into account, the daily minimum wage, which was raised in March 1997 to $2.80 (8,500 rials), is not sufficient to provide a decent standard of living for a worker and family. In Algeria, the minimum wage is $90 (6,000 dinars) per month, which is insufficient to provide a decent standard of living. In July 1998, the government of Oman raised the minimum wage for workers to about $260 (100 rials) per month, plus $52 (20 rials) for transportation and housing. Yet this law does not apply to a variety of occupational categories, including small businesses that employ fewer than five persons, the self-employed, domestic servants, dependent family members working for a family firm, and some categories of manual labor. As a result, many workers take additional jobs or are supported by their extended families. Israel supports one of the highest minimum wages in the region. Indeed the Israeli Knesset Labor and Social Affairs Committee in February 2000 approved a law to raise the minimum wage from $700 to $1,000 per month, providing workers and their families with a decent standard of living.

Most countries in this region do not have laws that promote equal pay for women. Indeed although the Bahrain government encourages the hiring of women, there is discrimination in the workplace, including inequality of wages and denial of opportunity for advancement. Even though the Syrian constitution provides for equality between men and women and equal pay for equal work, the government has not yet changed personal status retirement and social security laws that discriminate against women. In Egypt, labor laws require equal rates of pay for equal work for men and women, but only in the public sector. Even in Israel, despite 1996 legislation that requires employers to provide equal pay for equal work, including important side benefits and allowances, women's rights advocates charged that deep gaps remain (U.S. State Department, 2000).

Specific data regarding wages and salaries in this region are limited. What is known, however, is that the average gross monthly wage in Israel increased by nearly 2.2 percent in 1999, reaching $1,716. The highest average gross wage ($3,225) was earned by employees working in the utilities industry, followed by employees in the banking, insurance, and financial industries ($2,877). These findings are due in large measure to the fact that all utilities, most banks, and some of the insurance industry are owned by the Israeli government and some are monopolies. The lowest paid employees ($889) work in the food industry. The average wage in the education sector fell by one percent during 1999 to $1,265 (*Israel Business Today*, 2000).

With regard to comparable data, Table 5.9 presents World Bank data on average annual wage for workers in manufacturing. This indicator is the ratio of total wage to the number of workers in the manufacturing sector, expressed in U.S. dollars. Wage in this case includes direct wages, salaries, and other remuneration paid directly by employers, plus all contributions by employers to social security programs on behalf of their employees. Although this statistic is often used as a means to assess international competitiveness, it should only be used as a gross comparative indicator of wage levels. As the data indicate, only Israel has a comparable wage with such Western countries as Canada, the United States, and the United Kingdom. Not surprisingly, the countries with the lowest average wage are Jordan and Yemen. The statistic for Iraq is a bit misleading in that besides petroleum and natural gas, manufacturing is not well developed there.

Benefits

Many countries in this region provide essentially free health care. Yet the comprehensiveness and quality of such services vary widely among the Middle Eastern countries. In Israel, for example, the National Health Insurance Law provides for medical services, including hospitalization, for all residents. Medical services are supplied by the country's four comprehensive health insurance schemes, which must accept all applicants regardless of age or state of health. The main sources of funding are a monthly health insurance tax of up to 4.8 percent of income, collected by the National Insurance Institute, and employer participation in the cost of insurance for their employees. The insurance schemes are reimbursed according to a weighted average number of insured persons, calculated by age, distance of home from a health facility, and other criteria determined by the Ministry of Health (JSOURCE, 2000). Israelis should have no complaints about the quality of their health services. More than 8 percent of their gross national product is allocated to health, just slightly lower than that in the United States. They have the highest number of doctors per head in the world, 1 for approximately every 365 persons (U.S. 1 in 700). Hospital clinics are less than 20 minutes away from 90 percent of the population. Israeli doctors boast an internationally recognized level of professional expertise.

TABLE 5.9

Average Annual Wage in Manufacturing, in U.S. Dollars

Countries	Average Annual Wage
Egypt	5,976[2]
Iran	9,739[3]
Iraq	13,288[2]
Israel	26,635[1]
Jordan	2,082[1]
Kuwait	10,281[3]
Saudi Arabia	9,814[3]
Syria	4,338[2]
Tunisia	3,599[2]
United Arab Emirates	6,968[3]
Yemen	1,291[1]
Canada	28,424[2]
United States	28,907[2]
United Kingdom	23, 843[2]

[1] 1995-1999 data
[2] 1990-1994 data
[2] 1980-1984 data
Source: www.worldbank.org

For decades now, health care in Kuwait, from outpatient visits to open-heart surgery, have been free for both Kuwaitis and foreign residents in the country. In attempt to reduce spending, the government began to charge nominal fees for medical care given to non-Kuwaitis.

Among the countries that offer free health care, but that have obvious problems, is Iraq, as the following letter from a Iraqi surgeon illustrates:

Sir: Many people probably do not know the horrible health situation in Iraq under the United Nations sanctions. The health service has come to a halt. During operations, many surgeons find that items are missing, especially the appropriate sutures and instruments. On many occasions, I have sutured the abdominal wall with catgut or silk instead of nylon.

Would anyone believe that sometimes we reuse the nasogastric tubes and surgical blades. Actually, we no longer use a scrubbing brush before surgery and use only cheap soap and water.

On the wards, the situation is worse where no painkillers are available most of the time. The choice of vital medications and antibiotics is so limited that sometimes only porcine penicillin is available for intramuscular injection and nothing is available for patients who are allergic to penicillin. Unfortunately, the situation has not changed much after the Memorandum of Understanding and doctors and patients continue to suffer. The world should realize the depth of this disaster and do something to rescue the patients of Iraq. (*Lancet*, 1999).

Indeed poor sanitary conditions and many endemic diseases abound in Iraq, where the average life expectancy at birth is 58 years; the infant mortality rate was estimated at 62 per 1,000 live births in 1998. Iraq has 1 physician for every 1,700 people and 1 hospital bed for every 603 people.

Since 1974, medical care has been provided free to all citizens in Algeria. The country is currently engaged in an effort to eliminate epidemic diseases such as malaria and tuberculosis. Other health problems that are widespread include malnutrition and eye ailments such as trachoma. On the positive side, however, cholera has been brought under control.

Pension provisions also differ widely in this region. To illustrate, there are countries like Kuwait, where no corporate pensions are required, but where a number of firms offer them, such as an end-of-service allowance by means of special insurance plans. Social security in Israel does not provide a livable pension and many workers, needing their full monthly wage, never join a pension plan. Accordingly, most Israeli employees, both from the public and private sectors, would like to see the government pass a mandatory pension law that would provide workers with livable pensions. Israel's neighbor, Lebanon, introduced an old-age pension bill in July 2000. The bill provides for the payment of a monthly pension equal to 2 percent of the pensioner's last salary multiplied by the number of years of work, up to a maximum of 80 percent of the latest salary. For individuals who have been employed at more than one place of work, all periods of employment are to be added together for the purpose of calculating their pension rights. Pensions are normally payable from the age of 65, but a special application may be made for payment from the age of 60. Employers are to contribute a monthly sum equal to 8.5 percent of the employee's pay for retirement insurance; the portion contributed by the employee has been set at 3 percent (IPR Strategic Business Information Database, July 30, 2000). Finally, the Iranian government, funded by a special tax on wages and salaries, provides pensions for retired public sector employees and some private sector employees.

As Table 5.10 indicates, overtime provisions exist in more than half of the countries in the region. Shift-worker differentials are considered only in Bahrain, Iran, Iraq, Qatar, Syria, and the United Arab Emirates. Holiday premiums are paid in Bahrain, Iran, Iraq, Kuwait, Oman, Qatar, Saudi Arabia, the United Arab Emirates, and Yemen. Finally, day-of-rest premiums are paid in Bahrain, Iran, Iraq, Israel, Kuwait, Qatar, Saudi Arabia, the United Arab Emirates, and Yemen.

TABLE 5.10

Premium Pay Options in Middle East Countries

Country	Overtime	Shift Work	Holidays	Day of Rest
Afghanistan				
Algeria				
Bahrain	X	X	X	X
Egypt				
Iran	X	X	X	X
Iraq	X	X	X	X
Israel	X			X
Jordan				
Kuwait	X		X	X
Lebanon	X			
Libya				
Morocco				
Oman	X		X	
Qatar	X	X	X	X
Saudi Arabia	X		X	X
Sudan				
Syria	X	X	X	
Tunisia				
Turkey				
United Arab Emirates	X	X	X	X
Yemen	X		X	X

Source: Table was constructed out of information presented in Ziskind, D. (1990).

The labor codes in several Middle East countries provide for severance pay. Ziskind (1990) indicates that:

> The amounts generally range from 15 days' pay for each of the first 3 or 5 years of employment to one month's pay for each succeeding year (Bahrain, Iran, Lebanon, Oman, Saudi Arabia, Syria, and Yemen). Qatar provides 3 weeks' pay plus a cost of living allowance for each of the first 5 years of continuous service and up to six weeks' pay for each year of continuous service over twenty years. (p. 154)

He also asserts that lesser amounts are paid to piece workers (Jordan), to retirees (the United Arab Emirates), and to workers who quit (Bahrain, Saudi Arabia). In Israel, although nonsalaried employees have a right to severance pay of two weeks for each year of continuous service, salaried employees receive one-month payment for the same service.

CHAPTER SUMMARY

In this chapter, a comparison of compensation practices was presented. As was noted, performance appraisal is an essential component of developing an effective compensation program. From a comparative viewpoint, organizations in the United States and Canada tend to place the greatest emphasis on formal performance appraisal practices, often due to the legal ramifications associated with such decisions as dismissals or reprimands. Some West European countries are beginning to recognize the importance of a performance appraisal, though many southern countries in this region and most East European countries still lag behind. What little evidence exists for organizations in the Middle East suggests a lack of objective performance appraisal systems in this region.

Most countries have legislation that addresses minimum-wage and, to a lesser extent, equal-pay issues. In terms of minimum-wage laws, there are substantial differences in their adequacy and in how they are administered. Countries like the United States, Canada, France, Israel, and the Netherlands have comparatively high minimum wages, and although they provide the basics, they fall short of providing workers and their families with a solid standard of living. Even though most countries in Eastern Europe and the Middle East mandate minimum wages, they tend to be so low that they do not provide an adequate standard of living for workers. Equal pay legislation is strongest in the United States and Canada. Although many West European countries have adopted and enforce equal-pay laws, women are far less protected in Eastern Europe and the Middle East.

As repeatedly noted, comparisons of wages and salaries across countries are difficult for a variety of reasons. Accordingly, a summary of such information is not straightforward. Yet what can be concluded is that overall wages in Eastern Europe and the former Soviet Union as well as most countries in the Middle East are comparatively low. Moreover, although wages for production workers in the United States are somewhat higher than those of Canadian workers, they are substantially lower than for workers in Germany, Switzerland, Belgium, and Norway.

In terms of benefits, health care is perhaps the most controversial. Although many countries offer national health care programs (e.g., the United Kingdom), others have opted for private insurance programs (e.g., United States). In both cases, however, the problem is to manage the cost of health. Retirement benefits also differ among the various countries. In many countries, pensions are commonplace—even mandated, yet in others, retired workers must fend for themselves. Regarding holidays and paid leaves, Western Europe tends to be the most generous, with countries like Austria and Denmark mandating six weeks of vacation for all employees.

CHAPTER 6

Protecting Human Resources

The labor force throughout the world is composed of individuals of different races, genders, ages, cultural backgrounds, and national origins. This diversity has both positive and negative aspects. On the positive side, it provides organizations with a pool of applicants that have a range of abilities, experiences, and ideas. On the negative side, diversity may lead to increased tensions and conflicts in the workplace, including objections to hiring people with different backgrounds or characteristics. As a result, governments have had to impose laws and regulations to protect certain groups of individuals in the employment relationship. This chapter covers a wide range of issues aimed at preventing discrimination against *protected classes*, which typically include such characteristics as race, gender, national origin, age, and religion. Other issues that are addressed include child-labor laws as well as workplace regulations.

THE UNITED STATES AND CANADA

The United States and Canada have the most comprehensive laws in the world that protect job applicants and employees. In almost every respect, each country's employment laws mirror the other.

Discrimination Laws

The Equal Employment Opportunity Commission (EEOC) administers the primary U.S. federal laws that prohibit job discrimination: Equal Pay Act (1963), Title VII of the Civil Rights Act (1964), Age Discrimination in Employment Act (1967), Americans with Disability Act (1990), and Civil Rights Act (1991). The Equal Pay Act protects men and women who perform substantially equal work in the same establishment from sex-based wage discrimination. The act defines *equal* in terms of skill, effort, responsibility, and working conditions. It does, of course, provide for exceptions. For example, pay differences can occur when there are variations in seniority or when there is a disparity in quality or quantity of work performed.

Title VII of the Civil Rights Act, the major federal antidiscrimination law in the United States, further protects the rights of women in the workplace, particularly in the areas of employment decisions and harassment. It similarly prohibits discrimination based on other protected-class characteristics. Specifically, this law states that it is an unlawful practice for employers "(1) to fail or refuse to hire or discharge any individual, or otherwise to discriminate against any individual with respect to his compensation, terms, condition, or privileges of employment, because of such individual's race, color, religion, sex, or national origin; or (2) to limit, segregate, or classify his employees in any way which would deprive or tend to deprive any individual of employment opportunities or otherwise adversely affect his status as an employee because of such individual's race, color, religion, sex or national origin" (Civil Rights Act of 1964, Title VII, Section 103a). The law applies to organizations with 15 or more employees working 20 or more weeks annually that are involved in interstate commerce as well as to local and state governments, employment agencies, and labor organizations.

The Age Discrimination in Employment Act (ADEA) is designed to protect the older, and thus often more expensive, employees who are often the target of payoffs in order to reduce labor costs. Indeed the act specifically protects the employment rights of workers over the age of 40. Recently, firms have offered early retirement incentives to older workers. Such programs do not violate the ADEA if employees are not forced to participate in them, the programs are presented to the employees in an understandable way, and the employees are given enough time to make a decision. Age-discrimination complaints constitute a large percentage of the cases heard by the EEOC. In 1991, 31,000 age-discrimination cases were filed, and the number continues to grow (Noe et al., 2000).

The Americans with Disability Act (ADA) prohibits discrimination against an individual who has either a "serious disability" (e.g., blindness, deafness), a "history of a disability" (e.g., history of cancer or mental illness), or is "regarded as having a disability" (e.g., severely disfigured). Furthermore the act requires employers to make "reasonable accommodation" for the disabled by making existing facilities (e.g., bathrooms, elevators) readily accessible, restructuring jobs, modifying equipment, or providing readers or interpreters. Of course, employers are not required to make such accommodations if employees do not request them or if by making them, they would impose an undue hardship on the employers.

Finally, the Civil Rights Act of 1991 (CRA 1991) amended the 1964 Civil Rights Act as well as ADEA and ADA. Before CRA 1991, Title VII limited damage claims to such equitable relief as back pay and attorney's fees. CRA 1991 added compensatory and punitive damages for intentional or reckless discrimination. These damages range from $50,000 to $300,000 per violation, depending on the size of the organization. There have been two immediate effects of the CRA 1991. First, given the enhanced payoff opportunities, it has increased the number of discrimination suits filed against organizations. Second, to protect themselves from such suits, more organizations are now establishing equal-employment and affirmative-action programs.

The major federal employment antidiscrimination law in Canada is the Canadian Charter of Rights and Freedoms (1982). This law looks very similar to the U.S. legislation, as the following provision suggests: "Every individual is equal before and under the law and has the right to the equal protection and equal benefit of the law without discrimination and, in particular, without discrimination based on race, national or ethnic origin, colour, religion, sex, age or mental or physical disability." With regard to affirmative-action programs, this law "does not preclude any law, program or activity that has as its object the amelioration of conditions of disadvantaged individuals or groups including those that are disadvantaged because of race, national or ethnic origin, colour, religion, sex, age or mental or physical disability." Similar to the legal environment in the United States, Canadian federal law provides a framework for the laws passed in the provinces (states). Accordingly, the provincial laws may be more comprehensive than federal statutes. For example, the Ontario Employment Standards Act includes sexual orientation, age, record of offenses, marital status, and family status among the classes protected against employment discrimination. The act also stipulates that "every person who is an employee has a right to freedom from harassment in the workplace because of sex by his or her employer or agent of the employer or by another employee."

Child Labor Laws

The United States and Canada have comparatively rigid laws that protect the exploitation of children in the workplace. In the United States, the Fair Labor Standards Act (FLSA) of 1938 sets the minimum age for employment without restrictions on hours at 16 years of age. For hazardous occupations, the minimum age is 18 years. Children aged 14 and 15 may work outside school hours, but they cannot work more than three hours on a school day, 18 hours in a school week, 8 hours on a nonschool day, or 40 hours in a nonschool week. Work for them may not begin before 7 a.m. or extend longer than 7 p.m., except during the summer when 9 p.m. is the required ending time. Child-labor legislation in Canada varies from province to province. Still, most provinces prohibit children under the age 15 from working without parental consent, at night, or in any hazardous employment. The federal government does not employ youths under the age of 17 during school days. These prohibitions are enforced effectively through inspections conducted by federal and provincial labor ministries.

Workplace Regulations

Regarding limits on the hours of work, the Fair Labor Standards Act (1936), which applies to private and public employers in the United States, requires overtime payment for work over 40 hours a week. In Canada, standard work hours vary by province, from 40 to 48 hours a week, with at least 24 hours of rest. The Ontario Employment Standards Act, for example, limits the hours of work to 48 hours per week, 8 hours per day. Overtime (1.5 times the employee's regular wage rate) is required after the employee has worked 44 hours in a week.

Although it is assumed that concern for worker safety would be a universal priority, the U.S. federal government did not pass the Occupational Safety and Health Act (OSHA) until 1970. OSHA authorized the federal government to establish health and safety regulations for businesses engaged in interstate commerce. All states, however, have passed health and safety laws that apply to employers within their boundaries. Workers in the United States have the right to refuse to work under the following conditions:

1. The employee's fear is objectively reasonable.
2. The employee has tried to get the dangerous condition corrected.
3. Using normal procedures to solve the problem has not worked.

The effectiveness of OSHA, and related state laws, has been questioned. To be sure, such regulations have made employers more aware of health and safety considerations. Although some studies have shown that OSHA has had an impact on reducing death and accident rates, others suggest that it has had little impact (Mathis & Jackson, 1997).

The structure of the health and safety regulations in Canada is very similar to that of the United States. Indeed federal law provides safety and health standards for employees under federal jurisdiction, while provincial and territorial legislation provides for all other employees. Federal and provincial labor departments monitor and enforce these standards. Federal, provincial, and territorial laws protect the right of workers with "reasonable cause" to refuse dangerous work (U.S. State Department, 2000).

WESTERN EUROPE

Other than the United States and Canada, no region in the world has been more responsive to social and political demands for equal employment opportunity than Western Europe. Indeed one motivation behind a United Europe was to "ensure and subsequently maintain the application of the principle that men and women should receive equal pay for equal work" (Treaty of Rome, Article 119). Against objections from the United Kingdom, the European Commission recently introduced draft legislation that would make it easier for women to file and prove instances of gender discrimination in the workplace. At the same time, however, the European Court of Justice delivered a landmark ruling in October 1995 that prohibits the imposition of quotas that would give women preference for jobs and promotion. So there are some overall standards being developed in Western Europe concerning employment law, but major differences in legislation among individual countries remain.

Discrimination Laws

All West European countries have laws or regulations aimed at preventing gender discrimination in the workplace. Over the past few years, claims of gender discrimination have increased dramatically across Europe, suggesting greater knowledge of legal rights. For example, the U.K. Equal Opportunities Commission processed more than 13,300 cases of gender discrimination in the workplace in 1992, an increase of 47 percent from 1991 (Travis, 1993). Interestingly, 1995 statistics indicate that for the first time more men than women filed employment discrimination based on gender (Quinn, 1996). As in the United States, pregnancy and gender discrimination are inextricably linked in the United Kingdom. Accordingly, irrespective of hours worked or length of service, legislation in the United Kingdom grants 14 weeks of maternity leave. Moreover, when employees return to work, they now can demand part-time work, unless employers can provide evidence that full-time workers are necessary (Watson, 1996).

The northern countries in Western Europe tend to have the most rigid laws protecting the rights of women in the workplace. Swedish law, for example, requires employers to treat men and women alike in hiring, promotion, and pay, including equal pay for comparable work. According to Statistics Sweden, women's salaries were 83 percent of men's salaries in 1997. Controlling for such factors as age, education, and occupational groups between men and women, the adjusted result is on average 93 percent of men's salaries. In 1998, the law was amended to address sexual harassment. Specifically, it mandated employer responsibility to prevent and, if applicable, to investigate sexual harassment in the workplace and to formulate and post a specific policy and guidelines for the workplace. Those employers who do not investigate and intervene in the case of such harassment may be required to pay damages to the victim. To address gender discrimination in the longer term, the Equal Opportunities Act requires all employers, in both the public and private sectors, to actively promote equal opportunities for women and men in the workplace. Employers with a minimum of 10 employees must prepare an annual equal opportunities plan. By contrast, the southern countries tend to have the most lax gender-discrimination laws. In Spain, for instance, the law prohibits sexual harassment in the workplace, but very few cases have been brought to trial under this law. Moreover, discrimination in the workplace and in hiring practices continues to be a problem (U.S. State Department, 2000).

In response to gender discrimination complaints, many organizations throughout Western Europe have begun to monitor gender data in connection with HRM decisions (see Table 6.1). Brewster et al. (1994), for example, found that more than half of the organizations in the United Kingdom and roughly a third in Germany, the Netherlands, Sweden, and Switzerland monitor the share of women in recruitment, and even though the numbers are smaller in all countries, around a third of organizations also monitor the gender distribution of training and promotion. They also note that the monitoring of these activities is far less pronounced in southern countries and France than in other West European countries.

Western Europe has devoted little attention to employment discrimination based on race or ethnicity. This is reflected in the conspicuous lack of explicit legislation and policy commitments concerning the equality of blacks and ethic minorities in labor markets. This deficiency coexists with the fact that these groups have not been universally accepted in the workplace. As a result, countries such as

TABLE 6.1

Organizations Monitoring Equal Opportunity in Employment Activities, by Group (Percentages)

Activity/Group	Denmark	West Germany	Spain	France	Finland	Ireland	Norway	Netherlands	Portugal	Sweden	United Kingdom
Recruitment											
Disabled	8	39	14	34	11	28	6	28	8	8	60
Gender	15	35	25	22	18	40	38	33	33	41	53
Ethnic minority	4	21	3	0	4	3	5	25	7	6	53
Training											
Disabled	1	10	6	12	18	11	6	21	2	4	17
Gender	11	19	15	20	14	28	26	21	19	34	25
Ethnic minority	1	7	2	0	3	1	4	17	3	3	18
Promotion											
Disabled	0	5	3	6	2	7	1	8	1	2	17
Gender	15	14	17	21	13	33	27	20	18	35	34
Ethnic minority	3	3	1	0	2	1	1	11	3	1	24

Source: Table 2.13, Appendix III. In C. Brewster and A. Hegewisch (Eds.), *Policy and Practice in European Human Resource Management* (1994). Hampshire, UK: ITBP.

the United Kingdom and the Netherlands have come under pressure to address the underutilization of minorities. Consequently, over 50 percent of the organizations in the UK and about 25 percent of those in the Netherlands now monitor their recruitment programs. Organizations in these countries, however, generally do not monitor other employment decisions, with less than 25 percent of them tracking blacks and ethnic minorities with regard to training programs and promotion (Brewster et al., 1994). One problem with interpreting the data in Table 6.1 is with the definition of "ethnic minority." As Hegewisch and Mayne (1994) note, the phrase "is so far only readily accepted in the United Kingdom and the Netherlands; in the survey the closest commonly recognized translation of the term 'ethnic minority' into German is Auslander, or foreigner" (p. 201). Thus, the amount of employment-data monitoring for ethnic minorities may suggest nothing about the status of racial discrimination. Indeed Wieviorka (1996) insists that racism is a "rising tide" in Western Europe. He notes that "a number of studies and surveys have shown that racial discrimination in employment and housing has become widespread in the United Kingdom" (p. 10). His conclusion is that the rise of right-wing movements throughout Europe has worsened racial relations.

Discrimination based on religion has received comparatively little attention from West European countries, with the obvious exception of Ireland. Ever since Northern Ireland was separated in 1921, the Roman Catholics have complained of employment discrimination. In 1973, the Northern Ireland Parliament was de facto suspended, reverting full responsibility of government to the United Kingdom. That same year, the U.K. Parliament undertook an investigation of employment discrimination. One outcome of the group's efforts was the Fair Employment (Northern Ireland) Act of 1976. This act prohibits employment discrimination based on religion or political opinion in both the public and private sectors (Cradden, 1993). By 1985, however, it became evident that the law was ineffective. Even a study conducted by the government of Northern Ireland found that the "Catholic disadvantage remained both quantitative and qualitative. . . . The unemployment rate of Catholics remained double that of Protestants. . . . Catholics also have a greater experience of long term unemployment" (DED, 1986, p. 5).

Accordingly, international pressure from politicians in Northern Ireland and Irish-American groups in the United States as well as the EU itself was applied to change the law. Proposed amendments to the law include:

> affirmative action in the declaration from private sector employers by which they [Catholics] were entitled to be placed on the FEA's list of 'fair employer'; the acceptance of tenders for public contracts only from companies on this list (contract compliance); the withholding of public funding from those that were not on the list (grant denial); and a statutory duty on public sector employers to abide by the same declaration. (Cradden, 1993, p. 482)

As a result, the Fair Employment (Northern Ireland) Act was amended in 1989 to prohibit even unintentional or indirect discrimination in the workplace. Thus the act makes it illegal for an employer to use a criterion for recruitment or promotion that has the effect of disadvantaging members of one community over another, where that criterion was not job-related. Employers are also required to monitor their employment practices at least once every three years in order to determine whether action is needed to achieve fair participation. Employers who do not meet their statutory obligations can be removed from the Fair Employment Commission's register, making them ineligible for government grants or for public-sector tenders. Although critics of the law have insisted that its targets and timetables are too imprecise, most leaders of the Catholic community regard it as a positive step.

Even though an objective of the EU Social Charter is the integration of people with disabilities into the workplace, legislation resembling that found in the United States has yet to appear in the form of EU directives. From the perspective of individual countries, the United Kingdom has been a leader in this area, with 60 percent of the organizations tracking the recruitment of people with disabilities. Yet other than the 1995 People with Disabilities Discrimination Act that outlaws discrimination against disabled persons in terms of access to public facilities, the United Kingdom does not have provisions to guard against employment discrimination of the disabled. Countries that have laws intended to protect the disabled in the workplace include France, Germany, and the Netherlands. The relatively low tracking records suggest minor penalties for compliance. Despite their commitment to equity and social justice in terms of health care, the northern countries provide virtually no affirmative action measures for the disabled (Hegewisch & Mayne, 1994). Indeed in Sweden, there has been a negative trend toward the employment of people with disabilities (Bureau Development, 1991).

Monitoring the results of recruitment efforts of the disabled is an important first step toward providing equal opportunity for them. A more profound commitment will involve the development of affirmative-action programs that not only cover hiring practices, but also promote the fair treatment of disabled in promotion and training opportunities. According to Table 6.1, surprisingly few organizations throughout Western Europe monitor their promotion rates and training programs to ensure fair representation of the disabled. Indeed no organizations in Denmark reported tracking promotion rates. Even in the United Kingdom, where the level of monitoring recruitment is very high, only 17 percent of employers track promotion and training rates.

Laws that protect older workers in the workplace are rare throughout this region of the world. In fact, no country in Western Europe protects the older worker from employment discrimination as much as the United States and Canada. For that matter, the only country that has incorporated specific protection against age discrimination is Spain. To be sure, France has a law that prohibits publicizing age requirements in job advertisements, but it is widely acknowledged to be ineffective. As evidence, a poll of the EU revealed that "80% of respondents—of all ages—believed that older workers were discriminated against in job recruitment" (Cowen, 1996b; p. 5).

Within the EU, Sweden suffers least from age discrimination in employment decisions. In part, this can be attributed to Sweden's experimentation with gradual retirement. Under this policy, flexible arrangements are made for older workers, including partial retirement (Cowen, 1996b). Another reason may be that country's innovative age-based approach to termination notices, under which employees are guaranteed at least a one-month notice (increasing at ages 25, 30, and 45 up to six months) before being terminated (Sparrow & Hiltrop, 1994).

Child Labor Laws

Other than the United States and Canada, no other region of the world has as extensive child labor laws as does Western Europe. Indeed virtually all of the countries in this region have these laws, but more important, they effectively enforce them. To underscore this commitment, Ireland passed the Protection of Young Persons Act in 1997, prohibiting employers from hiring those under the age of 16 in a regular full-time job. Employers, however, may hire 14 or 15 year olds for light work on school holidays, as part of an approved work experience or educational program, or on a part-time basis during the school year (for children over the age of 15 only). In the United Kingdom and France, children under the age of 16 may not be employed, except those enrolled in certain apprenticeship programs or working in the entertainment industry. Individuals under the age of 18 are generally barred from work considered hazardous or work between the hours of 10 p.m. and 5 a.m. In both countries, laws prohibiting child employment are enforced effectively through periodic checks by labor inspectors, who have the authority to take employers to court for noncompliance with the law.

Some problems with child labor have occurred in Spain, where laws prohibit employing children under the age of 16 and where the government has been fairly effective at enforcing them in major industries and the service sectors. But problems remain on small farms and family businesses. The U.S. State Department (2000) notes that in August of 1998, the United Nations Children's Fund demanded an investigation of child labor on tomato farms in Badajoz. Apparently, Red Cross personnel providing assistance to migrant farm workers there observed over 200 children under the age of 16, many of whom were younger than 10 years old, working 10-hour days and earning less than $14 (pesetas 2,000) per day.

Workplace Regulations

The purpose of many EU directives is to create standards that will provide workers with safe and acceptable working conditions. Yet there are still differences among countries regarding the range of regulations. When compared with other countries in Western Europe, France, Sweden, Denmark, and Greece have fairly comprehensive laws that govern working conditions. In mid-1998, the French president signed legislation lowering the legal workweek to 35 hours for firms with more than 20 employees effective January 1, 2000. Firms with fewer than 20 employees are to have until January 2002 to comply with the new law. Under this law, overtime work is restricted to nine hours per week. The Ministry of Labor has overall responsibility for policing occupational health and safety laws. Standards are high and effectively enforced. Workers have the right to remove themselves from dangerous work situations. The law requires each enterprise with 50 or more employees to establish an occupational health and safety committee. Over 75 percent of all enterprises, covering more than 75 percent of all employees, have fully functioning health and safety committees. In Sweden, the law requires a rest period, which in practice is usually 30 minutes, after five hours of work. Swedish law is also one of the more rigorous in terms of health and safety. Its standards are very high, making workplaces both safe and healthy. Safety ombudsmen have the authority to stop unsafe activity immediately and to call in an inspector. An individual also has the right to halt work in dangerous situations in order to consult a supervisor or safety representative. The current focus of concern regarding health and safety is on the psychosocial aspect (U.S. State Department, 2000).

Although almost all countries endorse EU directives that require employers to provide safe working conditions, some countries lack the resources to enforce these provisions. To illustrate, the General Directorate of Hygiene and Labor Security in Portugal has adopted working condition standards consistent with EU standards, but the Inspectorate lacks sufficient funds and inspectors to combat the problem of work accidents effectively. The highest incidence of accidents is in the construction industry, but poor environmental controls in textile production are also in need of attention. It is expected that EU funds will be made available to the Portuguese government in the hope of addressing these problems.

EASTERN EUROPE AND THE NEW INDEPENDENT STATES

Employment laws protecting the rights of job applicants and employees are uncommon in Eastern Europe and the new independent states (see Table 6.2). Even where they do exist, such laws are rarely enforced.

Discrimination Laws

In Russia, laws that guarantee equal opportunity in employment have done little to protect women from discrimination in the workplace. Indeed in March 1994, the Women's Rights Project of Human Rights Watch sent a contingent to Russia to investigate widespread complaints of government involvement in illegal discrimination against women. The findings of the group are reflected in the following portion of a press release:

> The Human Rights Watch Women's Rights Project charges that government employers discriminate against women workers by firing them in disproportionate numbers and by refusing to employ women because of their sex. Far from attacking such practices, the government has failed to enforce its own laws prohibiting sex discrimination. (George, 1995, p. 29)

The group found that the political and economic changes have not improved respect for women's rights. Official statistics indicated that in Russia overall, 66 percent of the unemployed are women, and in many regions, close to 9 of out 10 unemployed are women. Gender discrimination is firmly rooted in the labor laws passed during the Soviet era, when women were barred from working in many occupations. Today government employers openly express their preference for hiring men. Even government employment offices advertise jobs for men only and reject applicants based on their gender (George, 1995). More surprising is the blatant discriminatory attitude of government officials. In a recent report issued by the World Bank, Russia's labor minister is quoted as saying: "It's better that men work and women take care of children and do housework" (InterPress, 1996).

Even in the more modernized countries such as the Czech Republic, Hungary, and Poland, gender discrimination, although denied by their respective governments, is widely accepted. To illustrate, a 1991 law in the Czech Republic prohibits discrimination based on gender, religion, and national origin. However, in practice employers remain free to consider these factors (and even "attractiveness") when making hiring decisions, because this does not necessarily constitute "discrimination" under current legal interpretation. Moreover, the U.S. State Department (2000) reports that legally women have the same rights as men in Hungary. Although women are heavily represented in the judiciary and in the medical and teaching professions, their numbers in middle or upper managerial positions in business and government are low. Of particular concern, but quite typical in the region, is the fact that Hungarian law does not prohibit sexual harassment in the work place. The consequences are summarized in a 1995 report prepared by the United Nations that termed sexual harassment in the workplace as "virtually epidemic." Women's groups report that there is little support for efforts to criminalize sexual harassment and that harassment is tolerated by women who fear unemployment more than harassment. But it is expected that change, albeit slow, will take place in this region. Anecdotal evidence exists that supports this. Indeed in the first case of its kind in Hungary, a woman won her court case after suing a potential employer for sex discrimination after the employer advertised for men only.

As Table 6.2 indicates, no country in this region has legislation that specifically protects and promotes the rights of racial and ethic minority groups. This may be because ethnic differences, based to a large degree on religious differences, have been at the heart of a number of skirmishes. Outright international conflicts remain a powerful social force in this region. Indeed in countries like Bosnia and Herzegovina, Croatia, and Serbia some ethnic groups are struggling just to survive, let alone making a case for equality in the workplace. With regard to other countries in the region, it is noteworthy that race discrimination in Russia appears to be on the rise. Henderson (1996) notes that almost all of Moscow's blacks agree that Russian racism is pervasive and particularly troublesome in the workplace. They report that the fall of communism only liberated attitudes of hate and discrimination against them.

In Eastern Europe, the Gypsies suffer tremendous discrimination. Human rights officials are concerned about the rise of expressed hatred of Europe's largest ethnic minority. As in the case of blacks, discrimination against Gypsies once suppressed under the communist regime is now openly practiced across Central and Eastern Europe. The Czech Republic government has gone so far as to codify

TABLE 6.2

Employment Laws in Eastern Europe and the New Independent States

Country	Gender	Race/ National Origin	Disabled	Child Labor	Workplace Regulations
Albania				X	X
Armenia	X			X	X
Azerbaijan				X	X
Belarus				X	X
Bosnia and Herzegovina			X	X	
Bulgaria				X	X
Croatia				X	X
Czech Republic	X			X	X
Estonia				X	X
Georgia				X	X
Hungary			X	X	X
Kazakhstan			X	X	X
Latvia	X		X	X	X
Lithuania	X		X	X	X
Poland			X	X	X
Romania	X			X	X
Russia			X	X	X
Serbia-Montenegro			X	X	X
Slovenia	X		X	X	X
Ukraine	X		X	X	X
Uzbekistan				X	X

Source: U.S. State Department (2000), Country Reports on Human Rights Practices.

discrimination against Gypsies in a restrictive citizenship law. Under this law, residents of the Czech Republic must reapply for citizenship. Generally, only those who can prove that they have lived in the Czech Republic for at least two years and who have not been convicted of a crime in the last five years will be granted citizenship. Although many international officials decry this process to be contrary to human rights standards, roughly 100,000 Gypsies have been denied citizenship since the law was passed in 1993. Those Gypsies who are granted citizenship are typically the targets of discrimination in the workplace. Indeed although the unemployment rate in the Czech Republic is relatively low, about 3 percent, unemployment for Gypsies is about 65 percent.

The disabled also suffer from employment discrimination in this region. As in the case of women, sham laws aimed at protecting the civil rights of the disabled have been passed by the Russian government. Indeed businesses with more than 30 employees are required to set aside at least 3 percent of their jobs for disabled Russians. Organizations that do not comply with this quota are supposed to pay a fine that goes into a government fund to create employment opportunities, yet this remedy is rarely applied. Economic conditions are often used to explain lack of enforcement. Alexander Lomakin, chair of the All-Russian Society of the Disabled, is quoted as saying: "Tell me when we'll get out of the economic crisis, and I'll tell you when the law will be implemented" (Simon, 1996b, p. A-2).

Most other countries also have done little to support the employment of people with disabilities. In the Czech Republic, for example, the disabled suffer disproportionately from unemployment, and the physically disabled experience difficulty in obtaining access to buildings and public transport. Although the Polish constitution provides for aid to disabled persons "to ensure their subsistence, professional training, and social communication," and a number of laws protect the rights of the disabled, implementation falls short. To date, public buildings and transportation generally are not accessible to the disabled. Current law provides only that buildings *should be* accessible."

Recent developments in Hungary, however, provide the disabled with a glimmer of hope. In early 1998, a law was passed that requires all public buildings to be accessible to the disabled within 10 years. Furthermore, a 1997 decree mandates that all companies employing over 20 persons reserve 5 percent of their jobs for the physically or mentally disabled, with fines of up to 75 percent of the average monthly salary for noncompliance (U.S. State Department, 2000).

Child Labor Laws

Most countries in this region have laws that prohibit the exploitation of children in the workplace. Providing representative child-labor provisions in this region, Russia's law limits the employment of children under the age of 16. It also regulates the working conditions of children under the age of 18, preventing them from working in dangerous occupations as well as in jobs that require nighttime or overtime work. Some children can be found selling goods on street corners, yet social norms and the availability of adult workers at low wage rates combine to prevent widespread abuse of child labor legislation. Even though there is some

speculation that the transition to market economies may cause an increase in inci-
dences of child-labor abuses, there has not yet been a noticeable problem in this
area.

Workplace Regulations

Overall, the working conditions in Eastern Europe and the new independent states are poor—although again many of the countries have laws that address
these conditions. This may change soon, however, as many countries in the region,
even Russia, have expressed an interest in becoming members of the EU. Considerable improvements must be made to meet the basic standards required by the EU.
For example, Russian law prescribes minimal conditions of workplace safety and
worker health, even though these standards are not enforced effectively. As the U.S.
State Department (2000) notes, "workers wear little protective equipment in facto-
ries, enterprises store hazardous materials in open areas, and smoking is permitted
near containers of flammable substances. As economic activity continued to decline
during the year [1999], funds were not available for safety and health in the workplace. The pressure for economic survival displaced concern for safety." Furthermore, employers repeatedly violate the labor code, which mandates a 40-hour
workweek, with at least one 24-hour rest period. Understandably, even these conditions do not compare with the dismal plight of workers in Serbia, where virtually
no priority is given to the enforcement of nominal occupational safety and health
regulations.

Recent improvements in working conditions have occurred in the Czech
Republic, again at least partially in response to a desire to become a EU member.
Czech law mandates a standard 42-hour workweek, requires work breaks of at least
30 minutes during the typical 12-hour workday, and prohibits employers from or-
dering overtime in excess of 150 hours per year or 8 hours per week, although local
employment offices may allow exceptions to these overtime limits. Moreover, the
law grants workers a vacation of three to four weeks each year. These standards are
enforced by the Labor Ministry. Health and safety standards, including the right to
refuse to work under unsafe conditions, are administered by the Office of Labor
Safety. Both agencies have become more effective over the past few years; at the
same time, some sectors of heavy industry remain problematic.

THE MIDDLE EAST

Even in the prosperous oil countries, where employment opportunities
abound, violations of human rights in general and employment discrimination in
particular are pervasive. At the same time, laws that protect the worker vary
widely, not only in their content and coverage (see Table 6.3), but also in their degree of enforcement.

Discrimination Laws

The stereotypical perception of all Middle East women dressed in a black robe and a veil is dated. But women are still openly discriminated against, particularly in the workplace. For example, in Egypt and Kuwait, where women have employment opportunities in government, medicine, law, academia, the arts, and to some degree in business, there are no women state prosecutors or judges. Even though no law prohibits female judges, societal and cultural norms appear to limit women's access to such professions. To illustrate, in 1993, an Egyptian woman under consideration for promotion to magistrate was denied the position based on gender. Some countries in this region have laws that prohibit gender discrimination in the workplace, but discrimination is effectively allowed by nonenforcement of them. Although the 1990 Algerian labor law bans sexual discrimination in the workplace, violations are commonplace. In Libya, we encounter disconformities between the vision of the Green Book and the reality of civil law. According to the Guide of the Jamahiriya Col. Ghaddafi, it is unjust to impose men's heavy, degrading or disgusting work on women. By contrast, the labor law provides for complete equality between the sexes. In reality, the overall trend among the more traditional Muslim countries is restricting the rights of females in labor market activity altogether. A further example is Morocco, where single and married women may freely contract for employment; however, the husbands of women may go to court to have these contracts voided. In these cases, the judge's decision is to be based on the welfare of the family. Night work is also forbidden for women and for minor children.

There is some evidence that discrimination against women may be getting worse in some countries. In Saudi Arabia, for example, women make up only 5 percent of the workforce. Where they are employed, women are segregated from male workers, with contact between the genders limited to telephone or facsimile machine. In 1995, the Ministry of Commerce decided to no longer issue business licenses allowing women to work in fields that might require them to supervise foreign workers, interact with male clients, or deal on a regular basis with government officials. Moreover, the Yemen Constitution has long stated that "no discrimination shall be practiced due to sex, color, racial origin, language, occupation, social status, or religious beliefs." In a 1994 amendment, the constitutional language became much more general by simply declaring that "all citizens are equal in general rights and duties." The more general, and consequently more ambiguous, language has increased instances of discrimination based on race, gender, and disability.

The good news is that some countries in this region are at least attempting to improve the economic conditions of women. The government in Bahrain has encouraged the hiring of women and recently passed special laws to promote entry of women into the workforce. Yet even here labor law does not recognize equal pay for equal work, resulting in less pay for women than for men. In Israel, where women also have routinely received lower wages for equal work, recent amendments to labor law not only require employers to pay male and female workers equal wages for equal work, but cover important side benefits as well. Moreover, the law now allows for class action suits against violators. While Kuwait still restricts women from working in "dangerous industries" and jobs "harmful" to health, recent legislation promises a woman remuneration equal to that of a man provided she does the same work. Evidence so far suggests that employers are complying with this legislation.

TABLE 6.3

Employment Laws in the Middle East

Country	Gender	Race/ National Origin	Disabled	Child Labor	Workplace Regulations
Algeria	X		X	X	X
Bahrain	X		X	X	X
Egypt	X		X	X	X
Iran				X	X
Iraq				X	X
Israel	X			X	X
Jordan	X		X	X	X
Kuwait			X	X	X
Lebanon				X	X
Libya				X	X
Morocco				X	X
Oman	X			X	X
Qatar				X	X
Saudi Arabia			X	X	X
Syria				X	X
Tunisia				X	X
United Arab Emirates				X	X
Yemen				X	X

Source: U.S. State Department (2000), Country Reports on Human Rights Practices.

Many countries in the Middle East are infamous not only for their lack of laws that protect people from discrimination based on race or national origin, but for the fact that discrimination is built into their systems of government. Perhaps no other people in the world have received more public attention to their human-rights plight than have the Palestinians. Allegations have been aimed at two countries: Israel and Lebanon. In fact, since the 1970s, the Israeli economy has demanded an increase in Palestinian workers. Although there were requirements for worker registration, authorities tended to ignore the employers' legal obligations in this matter. In 1990, however, the Israeli government imposed substantial limits on the number of Palestinians working in Israel by introducing a new system of compulsory work permits for Palestinians. By 1993, only 84,000 Palestinians worked in Israel and the number has declined constantly since then. In place of this source of labor, Israel has recruited workers from Romania and Thailand (Palestinian National Authority, 1998). Concerns regarding discrimination against Palestinian workers have recently been expressed both within and outside of Israel. For example, only five Arab workers are employed in the National Electricity Company, one of Israel's largest employers with over 130,000 workers. A common explanation for such practice is to ensure Israeli security. In a letter to the State Comptroller and the State Legal Advisor in Israel, "the Justice Committee stated that the interference of the Israeli intelligence system in the employment of Arabs in the Company impinges on and jeopardizes the rights of the Arab individual and the equal employment opportunity; considering the fact that the conditions of accepting or rejecting employment at this company are vague" (Assennara, 1998). Criticisms of how Palestinians are being treated have even come from Israel's allies, including the United States. Accordingly, the Israeli government has taken some steps toward improving its policy toward Palestinian workers. For example, in response to a recent visit by U.S. Secretary of State Madeleine Albright, the Israeli government eased its limits on the number of Palestinian workers coming from Judea, Samaria, and Gaza. Over a quarter of a million Palestinians live in Lebanon. Even though the Lebanese government ended the practice of denying Palestinians work permits in 1991, they still encounter job discrimination. When they are employed, Palestinian workers are typically funneled into unskilled, low-paying jobs.

Palestinians are, however, not alone. Discrimination against the Kurds in all aspects of life remains in many north Middle East countries. Even in Syria, where the government contends there is no discrimination against the Kurdish population, Kurds are unable to own land and are denied the right to vote and to be employed by the government. The Bidoon in Kuwait and Bahrain also suffer many of the problems experienced by the Kurds. Many of the Bidoon are second- or third-generation residents whose ancestors emigrated from Iran. A Bidoon is not only denied citizenship in these countries but employment opportunities as well. The Berbers, descendants of the aboriginal inhabitants of North Africa and located primarily in Algeria, Libya, and Morocco, have suffered similar discriminatory problems. Conditions for them seem to be improving. In Algeria, for example, they made some headway when the Algerian government instituted a council in 1995 to promote Amazigh, a Berber language. Finally, members of the Baha'i faith are prohibited from government employment in Iran. A 1993 law even forbids government workers from participation in any group that denies the "divine religions," terminology the government uses to label members of the Baha'i faith. The law also imposes penalties for government workers who do not observe "Islamic principles and rules." (U.S. State Department, 2000)

Many countries in this region have made some improvements concerning the rights of the disabled in the workplace. In Saudi Arabia, for example, government social services efforts have increasingly brought the disabled into the public domain. Furthermore, joint efforts by the Saudi government and private charities have enhanced the educational and employment opportunities for the disabled. More important, Saudi labor law provides for a hiring quota for those with disabilities. Similar quotas are required in Bahrain (2%), Egypt (5%), Jordan (2%), Syria (2%), and Tunisia (1%).

Although the Israeli government does provide a wide range of benefits (e.g., income maintenance, housing subsidies, and transportation support) for the disabled, it has been surprisingly silent regarding the workplace rights for these citizens. Indeed antidiscrimination laws do not prohibit employment discrimination based on disability. Even a law that requires access for the disabled to public buildings is not widely enforced.

Child Labor Laws

As Table 6.3 suggests, almost all countries in the Middle East have laws establishing a minimum age for employment. They are comparatively permissive relative to laws found in the other regions examined so far. Indeed child labor is prohibited under the age of 8 (Lebanon), 12 (Egypt, Morocco, Qatar, Syria, Yemen), 13 (Jordan, Oman, Saudi Arabia), 14 (Bahrain, Iraq, Israel, Kuwait), 15 (Iran, Tunisia, the United Arab Emirates), 16 (Algeria), and 18 (Libya). Overtime for children less than 17 is prohibited in Bahrain, Iran, Iraq, Oman, Qatar, Syria, the United Arab Emirates, and Yemen. Granted these laws are on the books, but they are often violated. For example, in Morocco, where the law prohibits the employment of children under the age of 12, children are often apprenticed before age 12—particularly in the handicraft industry. Young children also are often employed informally as domestic workers and usually receive little if any pay for their efforts. Moreover, although the minimum age for employment is 13 in Saudi Arabia, this requirement may be waived by the Ministry of Labor with the consent of the child's guardian. There is no minimum age requirement for workers in family-oriented businesses or in businesses that may be construed as extensions of the household, such as farmers, herdsmen, or domestic servants. Similarly in Syria, the minimum age for employment is 15 in the public sector and 12 in the private sector, with parental permission required for children under the age of 16 in either case. The law prohibits children from working at night, but all these laws apply only to salaried workers. Thus, those children who work in family businesses, thereby not technically paid a salary, do not fall under the law. Even in Lebanon, where the age minimum is 8 years old, violations occur—especially after the civil war when the

Labor Ministry was left with few resources and a demoralized and sometimes corrupt staff (U.S. State Department, 2000).

Workplace Regulations

The typical workweek in this region runs from 42 to 48 hours, with a mandated 24-hour rest period. Moreover, as Table 6.3 indicates, all countries in this region have laws that protect the health and safety of workers. In Tunisia, for example, the Ministry of Social Affairs is responsible for enforcing health and safety standards in the workplace. Special government regulations cover such hazardous occupations as mining, petroleum engineering, and construction. Working conditions for organizations serving domestic markets tend to be worse than those associated with organizations that are export oriented. Workers are free to remove themselves from dangerous situations without jeopardizing their employment, and they may take legal action against employers who retaliate against them for exercising this right. Bahrain's labor law, enforced by the Ministry of Labor and Social Affairs, mandates acceptable conditions of work for all adult workers, including adequate standards regarding hours of work (maximum 48 hours per week) and occupational safety and health. Periodic inspections are conducted and fines are routinely imposed on violators. Once a complaint has been lodged by a worker, the Ministry of Labor opens an investigation and often takes remedial action. The Fourth High Court has jurisdiction over cases involving alleged violations of the labor law. Complaints that cannot be settled through arbitration must, by law, be referred to the court within 15 days. In practice, most employers prefer to settle such disputes through arbitration, particularly because the court and labor law generally are considered to favor the employee. Workers in Bahrain also have the right to remove themselves from dangerous work situations without jeopardy to their continued employment.

In Oman, all employers are required to provide first-aid facilities. Work sites with over 100 employees must have medical personnel. Employees covered under the labor law may recover compensation for injury or illness sustained on the job through employer-provided medical insurance. The health and safety standard codes are enforced by inspectors from the Department of Health and Safety of the Directorate of Labor. As required by law, they make on-site inspections (U.S. State Department, 2000).

Some countries do not have laws that provide acceptable working conditions for workers. For example, although workers in Jordan, Lebanon, Saudi Arabia, Israel, and the United Arab Emirates are protected in varying degrees against unsafe workplace conditions, they risk losing employment if they remove themselves from hazardous work conditions. In 1998 the International Labor Organization reported that Syria's law, permitting employers to require their workers to stay on the job as many as 11 hours a day, might lead to abuse. At least on paper, workers in Yemen have the right to remove themselves from unsafe working conditions, but enforcement of occupational safety and health standards in general is nonexistent. Indeed many workers are regularly exposed to toxic industrial products, resulting in the development of respiratory illnesses. It is also common for acceptable working standards not to apply to foreign workers. The Kuwaiti government, for example, has issued occupational health and safety standards, yet compliance and enforcement are poor, especially with respect to unskilled foreign laborers (U.S. State Department, 2000).

CHAPTER SUMMARY

This chapter has surveyed the kinds and degrees of protection afforded to human resources in several broad areas: protections against several types of labor market and workplace discrimination and against the exploitative employment of children and youth. A wide range of formal policies exists, along with an even wider range of actual policy implementation and enforcement. In the area of employment discrimination, the United States and Canada appear to lead the world in both legal and effective policy, with Western Europe close behind. The East European countries do not fare as well in terms of protecting women's rights in the workplace, but they are better than those countries in the Middle East.

By an even larger margin, the U. S. and Canadian governments lead in their commitments to provide protection in the workplace for the disabled as well as for individuals with other protected-class attributes. To be sure, many countries have laws protecting people against discrimination in the workplace; other than in the United States and Canada, however, enforcement has generally been a problem. Almost every country in the world has laws that prevent the exploitation of children. Again outside of the United States and Canada, and to some degree Western Europe, problems in this area persist.

It is recognized that policies aimed at protecting human resources are and always have been controversial. The growth of industrialism in Britain was accompanied by extremely long hours of work—often governed more by the length of available daylight than anything else. Twelve-hour days were very common, and even longer hours on occasion, which leaves little time for the other business of life, especially the rearing and nurturing of children. As a result, one of the early proposed reforms took the form of the Ten Hour Bill—as the name implies, a proposal to limit the workday to no more than 10 hours. Arguments against the bill took the form that profits in English industry were running at a rate of about 20 percent—meaning that they are produced in the 11th and 12th hours of the 12-hour day. Reduce the workday to 10 hours and profits will fall to zero, because they are the source of accumulation (investment), economic growth in turn will end. The fallacy of this argument should be obvious to the readers. Today, even in the Middle East, limits have been placed on the number of hours an organization can require employees to work, ranging from 40 to 48 hours a week, with a mandated rest period of at least 24 hours. Most countries also have made progress at ensuring worker-protection against unsafe or unhealthy working conditions. Much work in this area remains, however, particularly in some East European and Middle East countries.

CHAPTER 7

Managing Labor Relations

In the 1950s, John Dunlop (1958) introduced a conceptual framework that can be used to analyze the similarities and differences that exist in industrial relations practices among firms, industries, and countries. This framework spells out how individuals and institutions relate to each other, how the terms of employment are determined, and how labor problems are handled. Elaborating on the Dunlop framework, Mills (1989) notes that the industrial relations systems of a society may be seen as overlapping with other social systems, including "important aspects of the social, economic, and legal systems of a country as they relate to the industrial workforce and the relationship among employees and managers" (pp. 8-9). In this chapter, the industrial relations systems of the various regions are examined regarding their legal frameworks as well as the structure of their collective-bargaining processes and labor-management cooperation. Accordingly, there is a focus on the role of unions in the industrial relations systems.

THE UNITED STATES AND CANADA

Union-management relations in the United States are very formalized. The legal framework provides constraints regarding the structure of unions and the manner by which unions and management interact. The National Labor Relations Act (NLRA), which applies to almost all private sector employers (except those covered by the Railway Labor Act) overtly supports union organizations and collective bargaining as sound public policy. Section 7 of the NLRA outlines the rights of labor and management: "Employees have the right to self-organize, to form, join, or assist labor organizations, to bargain collectively through representatives of their own choosing, and to engage in other concerted activities for the purpose of collective bargaining." Some pubic-sector employees are allowed to organize and bargain collectively, but these activities are regulated by state and local laws. Certain states, particularly those located in the south, grant workers "right-to-work" privileges, thereby allowing them not to join unions even where a bargaining unit has been established.

The National Labor Relations Board (NLRB), which was established by the NLRA, performs three major responsibilities. First, it determines the appropriate bargaining unit or the eligibility of employees to belong to a single unit for the purpose of bargaining collectively with management. The criteria used to determine appropriate bargaining units typically include community of interest, history of bargaining, the interaction and degree of interdependence among departments, and the arrangement of labor-relations functions within the firm. Second, the NLRB conducts secret-ballot elections to determine whether or not a union will be certified to bargain with management. Albeit rare, the NLRB can certify a union without an election. In the *Gissel doctrine,* for example, the U.S. Supreme Court gave a stamp of approval for using authorization cards (i.e., cards signed by workers expressing their interest in having a union represent them) as a substitute for an election when an employer's actions amount to unfair labor practices. Third, the NLRB rules on unfair labor practices, which can be filed by either management or the union, claiming that the other party has violated the law or the terms of an agreement.

The laws governing labor-management relations in Canada are similar to those in the United States, yet the scope of federal regulations is much narrower, granting the provinces more power to regulate union-management relations. The Canada Labour code, administered by the Canada Labour Relations Board (CLRB) and the Federal Mediation and Conciliation Service, governs labor relations in the federal jurisdiction, which covers approximately 10 percent of the nation's workforce. The acts and authorities, in parentheses, for the provinces are as follows:

- Alberta Labour Relations Code (Alberta Labour Relations Board)
- British Columbia Labour Relations Code (British Columbia Labour Relations Board)
- Manitoba Labour Relations Act (Manitoba Labour Board)
- New Brunswick Industrial Relations Act (New Brunswick Labour and Employment Board)
- Newfoundland Labour Relations Act (Newfoundland Labour Relations Board)
- Nova Scotia Trade Union Act (Nova Scotia Labour Relations Board)
- Ontario Labour Relations Act, 1995 (Ontario Labour Relations Board)
- Prince Edward Island Labour Act (Prince Edward Island Labour Relations Board)
- Saskatchewan Trade Union Act (Saskatchewan Labour Relations Board)
- Quebec Labour Code (Office of the General Commissioner of Labour)

These laws generally allow their administrative agencies to certify unions as representatives of bargaining units; they also hear cases of unfair labor practices. Even though Ontario rejected the concept of automatic certification in 1998, many of the provinces in Canada still endorse it. However, the criteria for automatic certification vary among these provinces, although evidence of union support, which ranges from 51 to 55 percent, is typically required.

Membership in U.S. unions has been on the decline in the past 40 years, with a high of 35 percent in the early 1950s to a low of about 13.9 percent in 1998 (see Table 7.1). Two explanations for this decline are the economic shift from large manufacturing plants to small ones and a general view that unions have been a hindrance in determining appropriate terms and conditions of employment rather than a help. In recent times strikes have been a threat to rank-and-file workers, by allowing management to replace them permanently in the case of an economic strike or temporarily under an unfair-labor practice strike. By comparison, union membership in Canada is more than twice that of the United States. Major factors that account for this difference are the high levels of unionization of public sector and part-time employees in Canada, constituencies that the U.S. labor movement is now working hard to organize. Another explanation is that it is easier for a union to be certified in Canada than it is in the United States.

TABLE 7.1

1998 Union Membership in the United States and Canada (Percentages)

Selected Characteristics	United States		Canada	
	Union Member[1]	Union Coverage[2]	Union Member[1]	Union Coverage[2]
Total	13.9	15.4	30.7	33.3
Men	16.2	17.4	31.6	34.4
Women	11.4	13.1	29.8	32.0
Work Status				
Full-time	15.5	17.1	32.7	33.5
Part-time	6.5	7.5	21.9	23.6
Sector				
Private	9.5	10.3	21.6	23.9
Public	37.5	42.5	72.3	76.3

Sources: Bureau of Labor Statistics, Current Population Survey, January 25, 1999.
Statistics Canada, Selected Union Statistics, Special 1998 Labour Day Release.
[1] Data refers to members of a labor organization or employee organization similar to a union.
[2] Data refers to members of a labor organization or employee organization similar to a union as well as workers who report no union affiliation but whose jobs are covered by a union or an employee association contract.

Collective Bargaining Issues

Collective bargaining in the United States and Canada is much more de-centralized than it is in other regions of the world. Literally thousands of agreements are in place. Although some contracts involve multiemployer bargaining, where employers combine to negotiate a common agreement with a union, most of the contracts are between individual employers and unions. When many different employers and unions are involved across these two countries, contractual provisions are understandably highly varied. There are, however, limits on the scope of bargaining. The NLRA, for example, identifies three types of bargaining items. First, both parties are obligated to negotiate *mandatory items*, which consist of "wages, hours, and other terms and conditions of employment." Second, *permissive items* are subjects over which the parties can negotiate if both agree to do so. This type of item might include the product or service price. Third, the parties cannot negotiate *illegal items*, including featherbedding, discrimination in hiring practices, or a provision that would require individuals to join a union before they are hired.

Impasses can occur only with respect to mandatory issues. Several different impasse scenarios are possible. The parties can obviously agree to continue negotiations. Alternatively, either party can engage in economic sanctions in hopes of forcing an agreement. Unions can decide to go on *strike*. A major objective of all strikes is to achieve the total suspension of work within the employer's establishment. The most widely used secondary or subsidiary means of achieving this aim, invoked after the workers have quit work and left the business establishment, is the practice of picketing. Many labor unions maintain strike funds, which are used for the financial support of the strikers pending the settlement of the dispute. In some cases, striking unions appeal to other unions and to the public for financial support. In 1999 there were 17 strikes in the United States, a 53-year low. Of the 17 strikes, 12 were in the private sector; the remainder occurred in state and local governments, all in educational services. In the private sector, seven stoppages occurred in goods-producing industries and five occurred in service-producing industries. Canada has recently experienced approximately ten times the number of strikes as the United States, which is not too surprising given the significant higher union-membership rate in Canada. During 1999 notable strikes included: Calgary Herald employees in Alberta, grain handlers in Alberta and Manitoba, Cape Breton municipal employees in Nova Scotia, rotating strikes by doctors in British Columbia, strikes at nearly all B.C. ports that effectively closed seaports for 10 days, nurses in Quebec in July, and subway and bus workers in Toronto, Ontario in April.

When an impasse is reached over mandatory issues, an employer can impose a *lockout*. The right of employers to lock out employees is the analogue of the union's right to strike. But the power of employers to lock out their employees is qualified, especially inasmuch as employers have the power to counterbalance an economic strike by permanently replacing the strikers, stockpiling, subcontracting, and continuing operations with nonunion workers. A lockout is commonly used to prevent whipsawing, a union tactic of striking individual employers in a multiemployer bargaining unit to force a more favorable agreement.

During the life of a bargaining agreement, the parties are likely to have conflicts over the interpretation and application of certain provisions. For this reason, virtually all bargaining agreements in the United States and Canada have a grievance procedure, consisting of roughly four steps. The procedure typically begins when bargaining unit members believe that their contractual rights have been violated. Most grievances are resolved in the early stages. Those grievances that are not resolved by the union and employers themselves are in most cases submitted to binding arbitration, where a third party decides the issues. It is common to limit the authority of an arbitrator to interpreting the existing contract. The arbitrator is not allowed to change the content of the contract but merely to clarify and apply its provisions. Within this context, the arbitrator will hold a hearing, where both sides present their cases. In the end, the arbitrator issues a written decision and imposes a solution that both sides must honor.

Labor-management cooperation in the form of quality circles, work councils, or teams, although widely accepted in Europe, is controversial in the United States and Canada. The U.S. and Canadian labor movements have resisted such efforts precisely because they undermined the union's traditional role in the workplace. As a result, organized labor has challenged their legality on the basis that they are sham company unions that interfere with rights of workers to form legitimate unions. Indeed the NLRB ruled that teams at Elkhart Corporation, in Indiana, and safety committees at DuPont were in violation of the law. Recent developments, however, offer some support for labor-management cooperation activities. In 1994, for example, the Commission on the Future of Worker-Management Relations, chaired by John Dunlop, recommended that the U.S. Congress clarify labor laws so that a distinction is made between company unions, which should continue to be illegal, and employee involvement programs:

> On the basis of the evidence, the Commission believes that it is in the national interest to promote expansion of employee participation in a variety of forms provided it does not impede employee choice of whether or not to be represented by an independent labor organization. At its best, employee involvement makes industry more productive and improves the working lives of employees.

Congress responded by passing the Teamwork for Employees and Managers Act in 1996. Although President Clinton vetoed the bill, it showed that there is considerable support for overturning the NLRB decisions.

WESTERN EUROPE

Although there are many similarities between the labor movements in the United States and those in Western Europe, there are a couple of notable differences. First, they differ in terms of their fundamental philosophies of the role the labor movement should play in society. The labor movement in the United States is committed to working within a capitalistic system and to improving the economic conditions of union members through collective bargaining. West European labor movements, however, historically have been dedicated to reforming the social framework. It is not surprising, therefore, that in Western Europe, unions are more closely linked to political parties than they are in the United States. Accordingly, as Sauer and Voelker (1993) note, in most West European countries, "unions are a major controlling bloc within a socialist or labor party so that in the latter's policy-formulation process union interests must be given prime consideration" (p. 509).

Another difference is the administrative structure of the collective bargaining process. In general, collective bargaining occurs at the organizational level in the United States, thereby promoting a decentralized bargaining relationship between the parties. Collective bargaining in Western Europe, however, is more likely to take place at the industry or regional level, promoting a more centralized bargaining structure. Thus, in Western Europe, local unions have less autonomy and fewer functions than they do in the United States.

Although collective bargaining in Western Europe has long been centralized, recent developments suggest an erosion of this structure. In the United Kingdom, for example, pay for manufacturing workers covered by a collective bargaining agreement is now largely determined at the local level. Moreover, as Sparrow and Hiltrop (1994) note, "the incidence and impact of national and industry-level bargaining between the central labor and employer organizations has been significantly undermined in other countries where this type of bargaining was quite widespread and important in the past, such as Germany, Belgium, the Netherlands, and even Sweden" (p. 597). Indeed the impetus for this phenomenon has been as much a managerial desire to shift the control over the employment relationship from employees and unions to managers, as it has been a response to local economic conditions. In concurring with this observation, Baglioni and Crouch (1991) note that West European unions have been forced to retreat from certain decisions regarding terms and conditions of employment where they have traditionally played a central role.

As the data in Table 7.2 suggest, the percentage of workers that are unionized (union density) in Western Europe is quite impressive. To put this in perspective, as noted earlier, union density in the United States is roughly 14 percent. Indeed when the data were collected, only France had a lower rate than the United States. Low density is to some degree accounted for by adversarial relationships within or between the parties. For example, in France, where density is low, five major union confederations developed out of conflicting ideologies. Brunstein (1995) notes that "within companies, multi-unionism or multi-confederationism may be found, with union representatives who oppose and try to outdo each other over specific demands (higher salaries, reduced working hours, etc.) in order to attract as many members as possible" (p. 64). Yet such efforts have offended many employees, who eventually decided not to join a union. Sweden, with the highest density, provides an excellent example of a country where the spirit of cooperation between unions and management was famous from the 1930s through the 1970s. The recent movement toward decentralized bargaining, however, has soured union-management relations somewhat.

TABLE 7.2

Union Density in West European Countries, 1998

Country	Density (%)
Sweden	85.3
Denmark	73.2
Finland	71.0
Norway	55.1
Belgium	53.0
Ireland	52.4
Luxembourg	49.7
Austria	45.7
United Kingdom	41.5
Italy	39.6
Germany	33.8
Portugal	30.0
Switzerland	26.0
Netherlands	25.0
Greece	25.0
Spain	16.0
France	12.0

Source: Organization for Economic Cooperation and Development, 1991.

Even more important than using union density in assessing a labor movement's strength is union recognition by employers. Although union density is much higher in Western Europe than it is in the United States, union recognition for bargaining in the former is less formal than it is in the latter. Indeed with the exception of Sweden and France, employers are not required to bargain collectively with unions. And even in France, where the Auroux Law of 1982 obligates employers to bargain annually with certified unions, there is no requirement to come to an agreement. Moreover, the U.S. concept of exclusive representation does not generally exist in West European countries at all. Sauer and Voelker (1993) comment that these countries "provide for pluralistic representation through which a union legally represents only its members. If a union claims to represent 75 percent of an employer's workers, another union can attempt to get bargaining rights to the other 25 percent, and the employer can bargain with as many unions as represent its workers" (p. 514). Union security, in the form of union or closed shops, is also very rare in Western Europe.

Collective Bargaining Issues

Because most West European countries do not have legislation requiring employers to bargain collectively with a certified union, the issues over which the parties may negotiate are generally unspecified. In other words, there is no distinction made among mandatory, permissive, or prohibited issues, as is made in the

United States, albeit such provisions as union shops are commonly illegal. Ironically, therefore, bargaining issues and methods are both broader and narrower than those found in the typical U.S. bargaining agreement. This is nowhere more evident than in the status of bargaining agreements themselves. In the United States, bargaining agreements are legal contracts, enforced by the NLRB and the courts. And although most collective bargaining contracts in Western Europe are legally binding, there are notable exceptions. For example, in the United Kingdom, such contracts are not "legally enforceable; they are backed only by the relative power of the bargaining parties" (Bamber & Snape, 1987, p. 41). Moreover, an interesting aspect of European collective agreements is found in the practice of "extensions," whereby an agreement can be applied to parties that had no role in its negotiations. In France, for instance, an agreement between a group of employees and one of the most representative unions can be extended to the whole industry by the Ministry of Labor. In Germany, when employers employing a majority of the workers in an industry have signed the agreement, its terms are automatically applied to all employers in the industry.

Another difference between U.S. and West European bargaining issues involves contract length. A standard practice in the United States is to clearly define the duration of the contract, with *reopeners* specified in precise details. By comparison, although some contracts in the United Kingdom adopt this practice, it is common for them to be open ended. In addition, most French bargaining agreements include a length-of-contract provision, usually one year. But unless the duration is specified, the contract remains in effect until the parties agree to new terms. Sauer and Voelker (1993) also note that "French unions believe they can reopen negotiations at any time the balance of power shifts their way. For all practical purposes, then, French labor agreements are open-ended" (p. 515).

Social legislation in Western Europe has made it almost unnecessary to negotiate some of the basic terms regarding health care, work rules, and seniority clauses that are common in U.S. bargaining agreements. Specifically, as noted earlier, many countries offer comprehensive health care plans and statutes that require a specified number of days for vacation, holidays, and sick leave. To be sure, these accomplishments can be in part credited to labor movement efforts. Still, within recent times, unions have not had to address, through collective bargaining, what has already been gained by the legislative process. Growing antiunion sentiment may eventually require unions to become more active in protecting and advancing basic labor issues (Sauer & Voelker, 1993).

With the exception of France, Ireland, and Italy, wildcat strikes or unofficial-intracontract work stoppages are not permitted in West European countries (see Table 7.3). In most of these countries, unions are granted the right to strike as a means of pressuring management during negotiations over a new bargaining agreement. The incidence and duration of strikes, however, vary substantially. As Table 7.4 indicates, the southern countries and France tend to be the most militant in the use of strikes, in terms of the number of strikes, the number of workers involved in them, and production days lost from strike activity. In 1991, for example,

TABLE 7.3

Impasses Resolution Framework in Western Europe

Country	Official industrial strikes	Wildcat Strikes	Disruptive working action	Required strike notice	Employee lockouts	Third-party intervention	Penalties
Belgium	Recognized in law	Illegal	Legal	7 days	Not legally recognized	No compulsory council., med., arb.	Fees and dismissals for employees; civil suits against unions
Denmark	Not recognized in law	Illegal	Illegal	No notice required	Not legally recognized	Compulsory binding arb.	Fines may be imposed against employees or unions
France	Recognized in law	Legal	Illegal	No notice required	Legal under limited conditions	No compulsory council., med., arb.	Fines of 3-yrs. sentences and $3,000 can be imposed on employees or unions
Germany	Recognized in law	Illegal	Legal	No notice required	Legal	No compulsory council., med., arb.	No legally enforceable penalties
Greece	Recognized in law	Illegal	Illegal	1 day	Illegal	Compulsory binding arb.	Union organizers can be jailed; unions fined if court orders are not obeyed
Ireland	Not recognized in law	Legal	Legal	No notice required	Illegal	No compulsory council., med., arb.	No legally enforceable penalties

TABLE 7.3 (Continued)

Impasses Resolution Framework in Western Europe

Country	Official industrial Strikes	Wildcat strikes	Disruptive working action	Required strike notice	Employee lockouts	Third-party intervention	Penalties
Italy	Recognized in law	Legal	Not recognized in law	No notice required	Legal	No compulsory council, med., arb.	Fines/jail terms for illegal strikes
Luxembourg	Recognized in law	Illegal	Legal	Written notice required	Legal	Compulsory binding arb.	Token fines for union officials refusing to obey with court orders
Netherlands	Recognized in law	Illegal	Illegal	Reasonable notice	Legal	Compulsory binding arb.	No legally enforceable penalties
Portugal	Recognized in law	Illegal	Legal	5 days	Illegal	Compulsory binding arb.	Employers may be fined/jailed for lockouts or coercive methods to resolve disputes
Spain	Recognized in law	Legal	Illegal	5 days/10 days in public sector	Illegal	No compulsory council., med., arb.	Lockout fines up to $120,000
UK	Not recognized in law	Illegal	Illegal	No notice required	Legal	No compulsory council., med., arb.	Employers may fire employees who strike

Source: Wassell, T. (1993).

Spain lost 463 days per 1000 employees due to strikes, although Greece lost 452 such days (Sparrow & Hiltrop, 1994).

Table 7.4

Strike Activity in West European Countries

Rankings	Number of strikes	Number of workers in strikes	Number of work days lost in strikes
1	Spain	Italy	Spain
2	France	Spain	Greece
3	Italy	Greece	Italy
4	Greece	France	Ireland
5	United Kingdom	Germany	France
6	Germany	United Kingdom	Portugal
7	Portugal	Portugal	United Kingdom
8	Denmark	Netherlands	Denmark
9	Ireland	Denmark	Belgium
10	Belgium	Ireland	Netherlands
11	Netherlands	Belgium	Luxembourg
12	Luxembourg	Luxembourg	Germany

Source: Wassell, T. (1993).

When labor-management cooperation is mentioned in connection with West European countries, the first term that comes to mind is *codetermination.* Indeed Germany's experience with labor-management cooperation in the past provided a framework for codetermination legislation in such countries as Denmark, the Netherlands, Luxembourg, France, Austria, Norway, and Sweden. More recently, it has been the stimulus behind a proposed EU directive that would provide "information, consultation, and participation for employees." There are two key components to German codetermination: employee representation on company boards and on works councils.

German law requires employers to establish supervisory boards, with employee and management representatives as well as representation from appropriate unions; indeed among all of the EU countries, only Germany allows union representation on its board of directors (Fossum, 1995). The number of employee representatives is determined not only by the size of the organization, but by the industry; for example, the coal and steel industries are required to provide full parity on supervisory boards. When the company is unionized, the law stipulates that at least two or three representatives be union delegates. Oftentimes, these boards are divided into two types. The higher supervisory board (*Aufsichtsrat*) is responsible for developing managerial control measures and for selecting top-level managers. The lower supervisory board (*Vorstund*) analyzes the day-to-day operations of the firm and implements many decisions made by line managers (Katz & Kochan, 1992).

The success of worker participation on the board of directors in organizations outside of Germany is open to interpretation. Yet at least in Germany, it has not resulted in the adverse effects that were feared. Specifically, Fuerstenberg

(1977) observes that codetermination "had not led to revolutionary changes in company policy. Moreover, the boards function smoothly, and unanimity in decision making was the rule" (p. 51). Some even attribute the peaceful industrial relations during the 1950s and the 1960s to the implementation of codetermination policies.

The other channel of German codetermination is *works councils*. Although the intent of employee participation on supervisory boards is to provide employee input into the strategic and overall operations of the firm, works councils focus on the shop floor. Typically, therefore, management, union, and rank-and-file employees are represented on them. Precursors to works councils were joint management-labor committees, which first appeared in Germany during the late 1840s. The Works Council Act of 1972 draws a distinction among the four types of powers a works council can wield:

1. *The right to be informed.* Management has a duty to provide information about certain matters to works councils.
2. *The right to be consulted.* Works councils have a right to offer advice to management concerning selected issues.
3. *The right to investigate.* Management must allow and assist works councils in their investigation of certain matters.
4. *The right of codetermination.* Management cannot act on these matters without the agreement of works councils.

In general, issues that are subject to these powers are divided into economic and social matters. Economic matters include direction of firm operations, such as mergers, plant closings, expansions, or contractions of production; structure of organizations; and other business and financial decisions. Social matters involve such personnel issues as layoffs, wage payment systems, training options, pensions, holidays, and safety (Mills, 1989).

It is immediately obvious that many of these matters are dealt with through contract negotiations in the United States. In Germany, there is a dual labor-relations structure, one that incorporates union-management interactions and the other that includes the relationship of works councils with management. What even further complicates this arrangement is that although unions have the right to strike, works councils do not. In the past, separation of duties and responsibilities between these two labor-management institutions was fairly clear: Unions would negotiate industry and regional issues and works councils would deal with local issues. As the decentralization of bargaining continues in Western Europe generally and in Germany specifically, the division of responsibilities becomes less clear.

Besides codetermination, many countries in Western Europe have experimented with work cooperatives, teams, and quality circles. In the case of worker cooperatives, employees own the firms and hire managers who direct the company's strategies. Research in northern Italy found that cooperatives have higher productivity, lower pay differentials between rank-and-file and managers, more labor-intensive production facilities, and more peaceful labor-management relations than other private-sector firms (Bartlett, Cable, Estrin, Jones, & Smith, 1992).

EASTERN EUROPE AND THE NEW INDEPENDENT STATES

During the communist era, unions did exist in this region. Their role, however, was much different from that of unions in the United States or Western Europe. After all, the fact that East European and Soviet official unions were subservient to the Communist Party had two major implications for their structure and functioning. First, unions were organized along industry lines and were strongly centralized. And because official unions had ties to the Communist Party, top union leaders were likely to be members of the party and to be paid as well as top managers. Second, although the intent of unions was to represent the interests of individual members, they did so in only a limited way (e.g., handling social security claims and distributing holiday vouchers). Thus, official unions did not engage in the activities normally associated with Western-type collective bargaining. At this point, strikes, slowdowns, and other union-related protests were illegal (Jones, 1995).

Although there had been some efforts to reform unions under the old system, such as promoting improved member involvement in setting production targets and processing employee grievances, little success was achieved until the late 1980s and early 1990s. In fact, successor unions that began to appear during this period were not only interested in changing the structure of the labor movement, but in playing significant roles in ousting the Communist regimes in Eastern Europe and the Soviet Union. Perhaps the most notable instance occurred in 1989, when Solidarity gained political power in Poland. In Czechoslovakia, a brief general strike accompanied the 1989 *velvet* revolution. Finally, strikes by miners and others in Russia and the Ukraine during 1991 contributed to the demise of the Gorbachev administration. Today the successor unions have gained previously denied rights, including the right to organize and operate independently of their governments. They are also allowed to engage in collective bargaining and, in some industries, to strike (Cook, 1995).

The new unions have been somewhat effective in representing the rights of their members. For example, trilateral bargaining (i.e., negotiations involving unions, employer associations, and governmental representatives) has produced agreements in Russia that establish minimum-wage rates, take into account the effects of inflation on wages and pensions, and address dismissal issues. In addition, unions have been mildly successful in pushing for unemployment compensation, training and educational programs, and guaranteed subsidies for organizations threatened with bankruptcies. Furthermore, in 1986, a new Labor Code established in Bulgaria allowed limited worker participation in and collective bargaining at the local level through the worker brigades within organizations (Zic, 1998). Strikes have even helped to increase wages and benefits as well as to force new elections. To illustrate, the period from 1994 to 1996 saw an incessant series of major strikes by Romanian miners, oil refinery workers, railroad workers, public-sector employees, and metallurgy and utility workers, among others. These strikes were, in part, responsible for a change in government and a pledge by the new government to increase wages and to support tripartism (Zic, 1998).

Although unions in this region have experienced some momentary success in the transition of the economies of Eastern Europe and Russia, evidence indicates that their influence may be waning. There are several explanations for this. First, ideological differences and competition over resources, especially with regard to acquiring new members when overall membership is declining, have become sources of intense conflict within the labor movements. Second, some of the economic reforms of postcommunist governments, particularly price liberalizations and wage controls, run counter to union interests. Moreover, reformist policies designed to improve efficacy of production have produced a decline in the demand for labor. Finally, growth in nonunionzied industries and ongoing privatization of the state sector threaten to make existing union structures irrelevant in large sectors of these transitional economies. Further insight is provided over these problems by Cook (1995), who examined the labor movements in Poland, Russia, Ukraine, and the Czech Republic.

Cook accurately observes that Poland entered the postcommunist period with perhaps the strongest labor movement—epitomized by Solidarity. Solidarity came to power in 1989 as a political movement, but its political strength has been substantially weakened. One reason is that Polish workers generally and Solidarity members in particular felt the impact of economic transition, including an increase in unemployment, declining wages, and threats to the survival of organizations. Consequently, contradictions between the role of Solidarity as a trade union and its support of reforms generated internal clashes along with external challenges. In an effort to recapture its prominence, Solidarity adopted a more militant stance, and in the summer of 1993 engineered a major strike of public-sector workers, citing the government's violation of wage-indexing agreements. When the government stood firm, Solidarity called for a vote of confidence in the government, which led to new elections. Unfortunately for Solidarity, its platform of antireform intervention failed to achieve the 5 percent of the national vote required for parliamentary representation. As a result, the Polish labor unions, even the once strong Solidarity, have been dramatically weakened. To illustrate, Solidarity's membership dropped from a reported 2.5 million members in 1991 to 1.6 members in 1993. The OPZZ, Solidarity's major revival, also experienced a membership loss over this period.

In the past, practically all union members in the former Soviet Union belonged to the state dominated Russian Federation, which consisted only of industrial (branch) unions (Jones, 1995). After 1989, however, several unions began to emerge that were independent of the FNPR (the successor of the Russian Federation), including the inter-branch SOTSPROF (Association of Trade Unions), and the NPG (Independent Miners' Union) as well as such professional unions as the Russian Academy of Scientists Trade Union and Air Traffic Controllers Union. Efforts to establish federations in order to strengthen their positions relative to the FNPR, which remains the dominant union with two-thirds of Russia's labor force in its membership, have failed. Yet challenges still occur between the FNPR and the independent unions over seats on President Putin's Trilateral Commission and rights to control union property, collective-bargaining rights, and the authority to distribute social security funds.

The FNPR has adopted a combative approach to the government's policies on economic reform, especially in the areas of price liberalization and wage and income maintenance. The independent unions are somewhat militant and strike prone, but they generally support the government's policies, leading some workers to believe that independent unions are not responsive to the interest of their members. But neither approach has been truly effective in gaining political strength for their respective union organizations. In the 1993 election, for example, although the independent unions experienced meager success in their endorsed positions, the FNPR exercised little influence over their membership's voting behavior, with many workers refusing to support antireform issues.

Despite the threat of strikes by the FNPR, for example, the declaration in late 1996 to lead 66.5 million workers out in the country's first nationwide strike to protest unpaid wages, strikes generally have been waged by independent unions. According to Cook (1995), the government has resolved most of these strikes "with concessions, resulting in wage and other gains that have shielded militant workers from some of the harsher effects of reform" (p. 17). She also notes that these gains have been short-lived, with the real value of wages dissipating due to high inflation or the government's refusal to pay. Accordingly, even the most militant union members have become resigned to the fact that collective action is futile. This attitude is reflected in the decline in the number and length of strikes.

In the Ukraine, although the reformed official FPU (Federation of Ukrainian Unions) is the largest workers organization, with an estimated membership of 80 percent of the labor force, it is a weak workers' representative. VOST (the All-Union Association of Workers' Solidarity), the second largest labor organization in the Ukraine, is pro-reform, but so far has been ineffective in mobilizing its members. As in other East European countries, the postcommunist era generated several independent unions, some of which have been mildly effective in representing their memberships. The NPGU (Independent Miners' Union of Ukraine), concentrated in Donbass, with regional branches in other parts of the Ukraine, has been the most successful labor organization. Indeed the NPGU took a leading role in bringing about independence for the country.

The FPU and VOST generally have sided with the government on economic reform, which has developed more slowly in the Ukraine than in Poland, Hungary, Russia, and the Czech Republic. They also have been critical of the use of such economic tactics as strikes. By comparison, the NPGU has been highly critical of governmental policies, particularly those aimed at price liberalization and wages. Although the government has attempted to reduce tensions through negotiations over some of these issues, the NPGU, and a few other independent unions, remain skeptical about the government's intentions and, thus, have resorted to strikes. For instance, the NPGU engaged in a strike over unpaid wages of between $50 and $75 (per month) beginning in October of 1995. Ignoring government guarantees to pay at least some of the cash, the miners voted in February of 1996 to stay on strike. At one point, government officials claimed that the strike was crumbling, noting that only 70 of 251 mines were down, compared to the miners' assertion of 91. In a speech before 5,000 miners standing in temperatures of five below zero in the city of Donetak, Leonid Kolesnik, senior mining engineer, declared that the government "is trying to conceal the scale of the strike. . . . The government has promised us some money. Our aim is to maintain our strike and not to take these scraps" (Kulikov, 1996).

By and large, the Ukrainian labor movement has made some headway in representing the interests of its members. The gains have been restricted to specific regions, illustrating the distinctive feature of Ukrainian labor politics. In the east, the NPGU has been reasonably successful at pressing for its political agenda and at negotiating benefits for its membership. Unions in the less industrial, western region of the Ukraine do not support such an aggressive agenda, which may account for their ineffectiveness as worker representatives.

Most members of the labor movement in the Czech Republic belong to the CSKOS (Czech and Slovak Confederation of Trade Unions). The CSKOS was established in 1990 and split in December of 1992, when the Czech Republic and Slovakia emerged as separate countries, leaving the Bohemian and Moravian Chamber of Trade Unions in the Czech Republic. Although a few independent unions have surfaced, only the Moravian coal miners' union (OSCMS) has aggressively challenged the virtual monopoly of the CSKOS. Labor relations in the Czech Republic have been relatively conflict free, at least when compared with the experiences of the previous three postcommunist countries. Strikes have been few, brief, and industrially isolated, involving only mining and railway workers. As Cook (1995) points out, labor relations in the Czech Republic have been somewhat peaceful, partly because the cost of economic transition has been comparatively low, "with real wages remaining only about 13 percent below their 1990 level, unemployment at 2 to 5 percent despite significant production declines and layoffs in the state sector, and inflation low" (p. 18). Another key factor is the Czech Republic's separation from Slovakia, where a good deal of the antiquated heavy industry is located and consequently where reform costs have been high.

In sum, Cook's (1995) excellent analysis of the labor movements in four postcommunist countries reveals several important developments. First, unions in Poland and the Ukraine mounted strikes that significantly contributed to the downfalls of their governments, whereas the Czech Republic's unions have been rather sympathetic to the reform initiatives. Second, reformed unions throughout the region generally have been ineffective as collective-bargaining agents. Although some independent unions have led successful strikes against their respective governments, gains have been short lived at best, with inflation and other economic conditions cutting into them. Third, the common theme across the four countries is that unlike Western unions, East European unions have been unable to develop a unified political agenda, which has limited their effectiveness in representing the interests of their memberships. Cook (1995) explains that one reason for this is that "viable democratic parties have not developed in any of the countries reviewed here; so far unions have made electoral alliances either in a fragmented pattern (as in Russia) or with reformed communist parties (for instance, the OPZZ in Poland)" (p. 18).

Collective Bargaining Issues

Labor and management are adapting their relationship to the demands of a market economy, but experience in modern labor relations is still in its early stages. In Poland, organizational-level collective bargaining over wages and working conditions increasingly characterized the traditional labor-relations system. Although the Russian law provides for the right of collective bargaining, this right is not always protected. The law requires employers to respond to a trade union's initiative and negotiate with the union; however, the law does not require management to sign the agreement, even after both sides have signed protocols approving a draft text. As a result, the right to conclude a collective agreement is often not protected. In addition, employers often ignore the requirement to negotiate and refuse to come to the bargaining table at all. Even when agreements over bargaining issues have been achieved, a gap in the law, which fails to establish the employer's legal identity, often makes these agreements ineffective.

In terms of future bargaining issues in this region, the ILO has identified Hungary as a model of societal transition in several areas, including labor relations, dispute resolution, and the development of independent labor movements. The model was initiated when the Strike Act was passed in 1989. During a bargaining impasse, the act permits a two-hour warning strike. This tool is viewed as a means of prompting conciliation rather than as a weapon to force employers to comply with the demands of employees. Further strike activity cannot occur without first submitting the issue(s) to conciliation. That is, the parties must engage in mediation for at least seven days, after which the union can resume strike action. In light of the considerable and damaging impact of the diminishing real wage and the soaring unemployment rate, the two-hour strike and fewer long-term strikes yielded insignificant results. Accordingly, the 1992 Labor Code was amended to require alternative dispute resolution (ADR). Under this system, interest disputes must be mediated for at least seven days, during which time strikes or lockouts are illegal. If a resolution is not achieved, the parties may agree to an additional five-day mediation phase. Should mediation fail, the parties may resort to arbitration, where the arbitrator's decision is binding only if both parties agreed in writing before the arbitration. According to Fine (1999), although the 1992 Labor Code requires the establishment of an ADR service, it still only exits on paper. He concludes that even though there has been considerable advancement in Hungary's labor system, much of it has been in policy only, not necessarily in practice.

As in Western Europe, many countries in this region experience a conflict between labor-management cooperative efforts and the collective-bargaining process. To illustrate, the Ukrainian Law on Enterprises states that joint worker-management commissions should resolve issues concerning wages, working conditions, and the rights and duties of management at the enterprise level. Overlapping spheres of responsibility frequently interfere with the collective bargaining process (U.S. State Department, 2000).

THE MIDDLE EAST

As Table 7.5 illustrates, some countries in the Middle East are not supportive of organized labor. In Saudi Arabia and Libya, for example, labor organizations and collective bargaining are illegal and are viewed as "intermediaries between the revolution and the working forces" (U.S. State Department, 2000). Meanwhile, the data indicate that a majority of the Middle East countries recognize the right of workers to belong to unions or associations, but fewer than half of them recognize the right of labor organizations to negotiate bargaining agreements. Furthermore, only eight countries permit some form of strike activity. Thus, collective bargaining as it practiced in the United States, Canada, and in most countries in Europe, does not exist in this region of the world, perhaps with the exception of Israel. Accordingly, only a general discussion of labor relations is in order.

The most vibrant system of labor relations in this region is in Israel, which is one of the few countries in the region to feature multiparty parliamentary democracy. For many years, the labor movement has been led by the Histadrut (General Confederation of Labor in Israel), which covered trade unions and women's organizations, among other groups. It was also a major employer through an industrial conglomerate, which it controlled. Thus, at one time, virtually every employee in Israel was a member of the Histadrut. In recent years, the Histadrut has focused more on its trade union activities, a shift accompanying a loss of some 60 percent of its membership.

The structure of the labor movement in Israel is very similar to that of the United States. Indeed workers may join and establish labor organizations freely. Again, most unions belong to the Histadrut or to a much smaller rival federation, the Histadrut Haovdim Haleumit (National Federation of Labor). Both federations are independent of the government. As in the United States, unions regularly exercise their right to strike. Although unions are generally required to provide 15 days' notice before a strike, unauthorized strikes occur. Labor law protects union leaders from employment discrimination, even those organizing illegal strikes. In the case of essential public employees, the government may appeal to labor courts to enjoin the strike while the parties continue negotiations. During 1998, several strikes occurred in both public and private sectors. The primary strike issues were worker dismissals and the terms of severance arrangements.

Though other countries in the Middle East permit the existence of unions and the right for them to engage in collective bargaining and to strike, these activities are much more limited than they are in Israel. In Jordan, for example, labor laws mandate that workers must get permission from the government to strike. Unions are prohibited to call a strike if a labor dispute is under mediation or arbitration. If a settlement is not reached through mediation, the Ministry of Labor may, if both parties agree, refer the dispute to an industrial tribunal, an independent arbitration panel of judges, whose decisions are legally binding. If only one party agrees, the Ministry of Labor refers the dispute to the Council of Ministers and then to Parliament. Jordan experienced no strikes during 1998. Although employers are prohibited from discharging workers for their participation in labor disputes, the International Confederation of Free Trade Unions (ICFTU) does not adequately protect employees from antiunion discrimination.

TABLE 7.5

Management-Labor Legislation

Country	Right to Organize	Right to Bargain	Right to Strike
Algeria	X	X	X
Bahrain	X		
Egypt	X		
Iran	X		
Iraq	X		
Israel	X	X	X
Jordan	X	X	X
Kuwait	X	X	X
Lebanon	X	X	
Libya			X
Morocco	X	X	
Oman	X		
Qatar			
Saudi Arabia			
Syria	X		
Tunisia	X	X	
Turkey	X	X	X
United Arab Emirates			X
Yemen	X	X	X

Source: Constructed out of information presented in Ziskind, D. (1990), and by information presented in U.S. State Department (2000).

As Table 7.5 indicates, other countries that grant workers the rights to join unions, collectively bargain, and strike include Algeria, Jordan, Kuwait, and Yemen. Yet according to the U.S. State Department (2000), these rights are limited when compared to those in the United States and Western Europe. For example, in Algeria workers have the right to establish the trade unions of their choice. Indeed roughly two-thirds of the workers belong to unions. The General Union of Algerian Workers (UGTA), which dates from the era of a single political party, is the major labor federation. The UGTA encompasses national syndicates that are specialized by sector. There are also some independent unions, such as the (SPLA), covering airline pilots, the (SNTMA) representing airport technicians; and the (CNEX), which organizes teachers. Workers are required to obtain government approval to establish a union. The procedure mandates that the Labor Ministry must approve a union application within 30 days. The Autonomous Syndicates Confederation (ASC) has attempted since early 1996 to organize the autonomous syndicates, but without success. The application the ASC filed with the Labor Ministry still was pending at the end of 2000, although the ASC continues to function without official status. The law prohibits unions from associating with political parties and bars unions from receiving funds from foreign sources. The courts are empowered to dissolve unions that engage in illegal activities. Under the state of emergency, the government is empowered to require workers in both the public and private sectors to stay at their jobs in the event of an unauthorized or illegal strike. According to the 1990 Law on Industrial Relations, workers may strike only after 14 days of mandatory conciliation, mediation, or arbitration. The law states that arbitration decisions are binding on both parties. If no agreement is reached in arbitration, the workers may strike legally after they vote by secret ballot to do so.

Jordanian labor law permits workers in the private sector and in some state-owned companies the right to form and join unions. Unions, however, must be registered to be considered legal and only citizens of Jordan can belong to them. As of 1999, over 30 percent of the workforce was organized into 17 unions. Although union membership in the General Federation of Jordanian Trade Unions (GFJTU), the sole trade federation, is not mandatory, all unions belong to it. Substantial limits are placed on a union's right to strike. Indeed unions must obtain government permission to strike. While a labor dispute is under mediation or arbitration, strikes are illegal. If a settlement is not reached through mediation, the Ministry of Labor may refer the dispute to an industrial tribunal by agreement of both parties. Both parties are bound by a tribunal's decisions. If only one party agrees, the Ministry of Labor refers the dispute to the Council of Ministers and then to Parliament. In short, the government strongly encourages the parties to resolve their disputes without the use of such economic sanctions as strikes. As a result, most strikes tend to be illegal. During 1999, major illegal strikes occurred at Pepsi Cola Company and Jordan Cable and Wire Company:

> In July in protest over a recent contract between the Pepsi-Cola Company and The Food Workers Union, 255 of Pepsi's approximately 1,200 employees staged an illegal strike. The company issued two warnings to the workers and then dismissed them. After the Minister of Labor intervened, the company reinstated all but 115 of the employees and offered a severance package to the rest. After this agreement, the Ministry of Labor continued to urge the company to reinstate the remaining fired employees.
> In August the Jordan Cable and Wire Company laid off 20 of its 220 workers. In protest 100 other employees staged an illegal strike. A week later the company fired an additional 72 employees from among the strikers. Also in August, following an intervention from the Ministry of Labor, the company reinstated the 72 strikers. In November the Labor Court ruled that the initial 20 layoffs were illegal and ordered the company to reinstate those employees. The company had not done so at year's end. (U.S. State Department, 2000)

In Kuwait, workers have the right to join unions, but they can never be required to do so. Only one union is permitted in an industry, however, and only one federation of unions is allowed. In 1999, 12 of the 14 Kuwaiti unions belonged to the Kuwait Trade Union Federation (KTUF). Only about 5 percent of the total workforce, estimated at 1,100,000, belonged to a union. Although unions may strike, they are first required to refer labor disputes to compulsory arbitration. The law does not have any provision ensuring strikers freedom from legal or administrative action taken against them by the state. But sit-ins or other forms of moderate strikes are supported by the Ministry of Labor and Social Affairs for workers who face obvious wrongdoing by their employers.

Finally, the Yemen government passed a law in 1995 that provides workers with the right to organize and bargain collectively. Still the government seeks to influence unions by placing its own personnel inside them. All collective bargaining agreements must be registered with the Ministry of Labor, which reviews the agreements. Unions may negotiate wage settlements for their members and can resort to strikes or other actions to achieve their demands. Employers cannot dismiss an employee for union activities. When such dismissals occur, employees can appeal to the Ministry of Labor, which tends to be reasonably responsive. Employees also may take a case to the labor courts, which often are disposed favorably toward workers, especially if the employer is a foreign company.

U.S. State Department Reports (2000) also indicate that some countries in this region are anything but supportive of the rights of employees to join unions, bargain collectively, or strike. To illustrate, in 1995 Qatar and Saudi Arabia were suspended from the U.S. Overseas Private Investment Corporation (OPIC) insurance programs because of their lack of compliance with internationally recognized worker-rights standards, including the ability to form unions and bargain collectively. Moreover, in Syria, the right to organize and bargain collectively does not exist in any meaningful sense. In state-owned companies, union representatives negotiate hours, wages, and conditions of employment with representatives of the employers and the supervising ministry. Collective bargaining does exist in name only in the private sector, because any such agreement between labor and management must be ratified by the Minister of Labor and Social Affairs, who has effective veto power. The Committee of Experts of the International Labor Organization has long noted the government's refusal to abolish the minister's power over collective contracts.

Although the Egyptian government grants workers the right to join unions, such unions or workers' committees must belong to the Egyptian Trade Union Federation (ETUF), the only legally recognized labor federation. To the dismay of labor leaders, ETUF officials have close relations with members of the ruling government. Although the International Labor Organization has long objected to the requirement that labor organizations belong to a single federation, the Egyptian government has refused to change this policy. To be recognized as a legitimate labor organization by the government, a union must have at least 50 members. Today, most union members, about 27 percent of the labor force, are employed by state-owned organizations. Still the law prohibits "high administrative" officials in government and the public sector from joining unions.

Although the Iranian government grants the right to workers to belong to unions, there are no independent unions. Indeed a pseudo-labor organization known as the Worker's House, established in 1982, is the only authorized national labor organization. Its primary responsibility, however, is to exert government-imposed control over workers (U.S. State Department, 2000).

CHAPTER SUMMARY

To sum up this chapter is not easy, but some general conclusions can be advanced. In many parts of the world, the state and/or the employers (the latter sometimes dominated by the state as employer) dominate the industrial relations system, either directly by fixing the substantive rules or indirectly by so circumscribing the power of workers and their organizations that they have a negligible influence on outcomes. Throughout much of the Middle East, the weakness of the labor side is perhaps inevitable, given the overwhelming looseness of labor markets. Only in the United States and Canada do we find effective laws and regulations that require the parties to bargain collectively with each other. At the same time, in Western Europe, and some parts of Eastern Europe, there are meaningful long-term balances among the collective-bargaining players. But even in these regions, the basic "rules of engagement" are almost always fixed by the state. In the past, the British model of "voluntarism," where the two parties can do pretty much what they want, was adopted in few other places, but has long been abandoned everywhere, including its birthplace. To be sure, the balance and the basic rules have been tilting away from unions and workers for several decades. In Europe, where the balance had tended to be more tripartite, some of the same trends have taken place, although labor has on occasion been able to gain some strength through mergers or cooperative collaboration of formerly feuding ideological or confessional unions.

It is important to bear in mind that the labor movement is not just a cogged wheel in a machine that produces rules. It is and has been a social movement whose principal task has been to bring political and economic democracy to the lower strata of society. Some of their apparent lack of function (in Europe especially) is a partial index of how successful they have been over the past century-plus. Moreover, the core labor rights standards embedded in the key International Labor Conventions are there as a model of the rights of workers qua workers in a modern, democratic society—they were not handed down from Mount Sinai but emerged only after long struggles.

To have stressed that the labor movement is a social movement is not to assert that there are no movements, or trends, on the management side, but they seem of a different type. Expressed rather crudely, although labor's movements have been broadly class-oriented, management's seem to be more technique or principle oriented. In the United States, scientific management, introduced by Frederick Taylor via the Personnel Movement of the early 20th century, the acceptance of mature industrial relations in the 1950s and 1960s, and management's aggressive antiunion ideology and campaign over the recent decade provide adequate examples. No one could deny that all of these had major effects on managing labor relations.

CHAPTER 8

Conclusions

This book began by challenging the conventional practice of staffing certain positions in multinationals with expatriates, including parent-country and third-country nationals. In short, the argument is that expatriate assignments have proven to be too expensive, impractical, and obsolete. The question remains: Do multinationals have the ability and commitment to effectively identify and develop host-country workers in their foreign operations? The book at least partially answers this question by addressing the Human Resource Management (HRM) policies and practices of several regions of the world, where the need to develop global competitiveness necessitates an understanding of different perspectives, competences, and conventions. This is not to say that scholars and managers interested in expatriate-assignment issues will not benefit from the material presented here, but that the focus is on HRM in a variety of host countries. In what follows, a summary of the findings is presented regarding each of the HRM functions. Finally, limitations of the book are discussed.

ACQUIRING HUMAN RESOURCES

Countries vary widely in their technical sophistication regarding the acquisition of human resources. In part, as a legally preemptive strategy, organizations in the United States and Canada use comparatively advanced methods that emphasize empirical validation. By comparison, many countries located throughout Eastern Europe and the Middle East forego such sophistication in exchange for methods that rely heavily on the family or a religious group to provide the basis for transmission of job and employment information as well as for evaluating a prospective employee's qualifications, notably trustworthiness. In Western Europe, many organizations tend to recruit and select employees using traditional staffing methods. Yet even in this region striking exceptions occur. Consider, for example, the high proportion of French organizations that include graphology among their selection devises.

It was noted earlier that some groups have called for international standards of selection. For example, it has been proposed that International Labor Conventions might be viewed as international standards of best practice, and might present challenges to some U.S. ways of conducting business. So far, however, these standards do not seem to have fared very well. To illustrate, although some countries strongly endorse International Labor Convention No. 96, the *Fee Charging Employment Agencies Convention (Revised)* of 1949, providing for the progressive abolition of fee-charging agencies, other countries—including the United States—have outright rejected it.

DEVELOPING HUMAN RESOURCES

At the heart of a successful society in general and globally competitive organizations in particular is a well-educated or developed workforce. This has long been understood in the United States and Canada, where the conception of compulsory and free primary education was developed. It also has been acknowledge in Western Europe, where the human capital of German people accounted for the country's rebound from the devastation of World War II, and in Eastern Europe and the former Soviet states, where education is appreciated but is undergoing substantive change in light of the Soviet demise. In the Middle East, however, the educational starvation of some populations is all too commonplace.

According to many standards, the United States has the best-educated population in the world. Yet concerns remain regarding the overall development of its human resources, specifically in the area of certain basic skills and knowledge. This is because the U.S. government has yet to develop a comprehensive basic-skills policy. The prospective importance of human resource development policies is perhaps nowhere seen more clearly than in the case of the European Union. The announced intention of the EU is to build a European society based on three pillars: high wages, high solidarity, and high human resource development. High wages are essential so that Europeans may continue to enjoy the standard of living they have attained even if, as we saw in Chapter 2, those high wages may come at a cost in unemployment levels. High solidarity means a relatively even distribution of incomes in European society to generate the political support needed for a three-pillar policy. Finally, in recognition of the need to earn one's way in the world of trade, the feasibility of the whole policy will be based on high levels of effective and cutting-edge human resources development programs.

REWARDING HUMAN RESOURCES

In terms of performance appraisal, which is an integral process in rewarding workers, organizations in the United States and Canada tend to place the greatest emphasis on formal performance appraisal practices, often due to the legal ramifications associated with such decisions as dismissals or reprimands. There is a growing recognition in Western Europe regarding the importance of performance appraisals, though one is hard fought to find them used extensively in many southern countries in this region and in most East European countries.   What evidence exists for organizations in the Middle East suggests there is little use of performance appraisal systems in this region.

As was noted, most countries have legislation that addresses minimum-wage and, to a lesser extent, equal-pay issues.   In terms of minimum-wage laws, there are substantial differences in terms of their adequacy and in how they are administered.   Countries like the United States, Canada, France, Israel, and the Netherlands have comparatively high minimum wages, and although they provide the basics, they fall short of providing workers and their families with a solid standard of living.   Although most countries in Eastern Europe and the Middle East mandate minimum wages, they tend to be so low that they do not provide an adequate standard of living for workers.   Equal pay legislation is strongest in the United States and Canada.   Current trends indicate that many West European countries are beginning to adopted and enforce equal-pay laws. At the same time, women continue to be far less protected in Eastern Europe and the Middle East.

Comparisons of wages and salaries across countries are difficult for a variety of reasons.   Accordingly, a summary of such information is not straight-forward.   Yet what can be concluded is that overall wages in Eastern Europe and the former Soviet Union as well as most countries in the Middle East are comparatively low.   Moreover, although wages for production workers in the United States are somewhat higher than those of Canadian workers, they are substantially lower than for workers in Germany, Switzerland, Belgium, and Norway.

In terms of benefits, health care is perhaps the most controversial.   Although many countries offer national health care programs (e.g., the United Kingdom), others have opted for private insurance programs (e.g., the United States).   In both cases, however, the problem is how to manage the cost of health.   Retirement benefits also differ among the various countries.   In many countries, pensions are commonplace—even mandated; yet in others, retired workers must fend for themselves.   Regarding holidays and paid leaves, Western Europe tends to be the most generous, with countries like Austria and Denmark mandating six weeks of vacation for all employees.

PROTECTING HUMAN RESOURCES

The practice of protecting human resources involves preventing discrimination against *protected classes*, which typically include such characteristics as race, gender, national origin, age, and religion.   It also includes provisions to prevent the exploitation of children in the workplace as well as measures to ensure safe and healthy working conditions.   With regard to the discrimination against women, the United States and Canada are the world leaders in both effective laws and organizational policies, with many countries in Western Europe close behind.   The East European countries do not fare as well in terms of protecting women's rights in the workplace, but they are better than those countries in the Middle East.

The United States and Canada governments are also in the forefront in their commitments to provide protection in the workplace for the disabled as well as for individuals with other protected class attributes. To be sure, many countries have laws protecting people against discrimination in the workplace; other than in the United States and Canada, however, enforcement has generally been a problem. Almost every country in the world has laws that prevent the exploitation of children. Again outside of the United States and Canada, and to some degree Western Europe, problems in this area persist.

It is recognized that policies aimed at protecting human resources are and always have been controversial. The growth of industrialism in Britain was accompanied by extremely long hours of work—often governed more by the length of available daylight than anything else. Twelve-hour days were very common and even longer hours on occasion. Today the laws in many countries are much more rigid. For example, the Fair Labor Standards Act requires U.S. organizations to limit the workweek to 40 hours, beyond which overtime must be paid. Moreover, in 1998, the French president signed legislation, effective January 2000, lowering the legal workweek to 35 hours for firms with more than 20 employees. Yet little change has occurred in some East European and the Middle East countries. To be sure, countries in these regions generally have laws limiting required workweek hours, but they are poorly administered. To illustrate, although Russian law prohibits required work beyond 40 hours per week, it is essentially ignored by employers.

Most countries also have made progress at ensuring worker protection against unsafe or unhealthy working conditions. Indeed many EU directives have been passed that deal with safety in the workplace. As noted earlier, however, much work in this area of protecting human resources remains in some East European and Middle East countries.

MANAGING LABOR RELATIONS

The practice of collective bargaining in its purest form occurs in very few countries of the world. Regarding the countries examined in this book, only the United States and Canada support a labor-relations environment that permits decentralized contract negotiations. Evidence was presented, however, that certain countries in Western Europe are moving in this direction. For example, in the United Kingdom, pay for manufacturing workers covered by a collective bargaining agreement is now largely determined at the local level. Certainly, with the exception of Israel, traditional labor relations do not exist in the Middle East. Indeed in Saudi Arabia and Libya labor organizations and collective bargaining are illegal.

In terms of labor-management cooperation efforts, Western Europe provides the most successful model. For example, the concept of codetermination, consisting of employee representation on company boards and on works councils, was developed in Germany. The legality of such ventures has been challenged by the labor movements in the United States and Canada. And it is this resistance that has stifled their advancement.

A FINAL NOTE

A limitation of this book is that it examines HRM practices and policies in only four regions of the world. Obviously, a book covering the world would have been more informative. Indeed the HRM polices and practices in Australia, Japan, and New Zealand, would have offered some interesting comparisons with those in the countries included in this analysis. Moreover, the HRM developments in Sub-Saharan Africa and in South America are worthy of investigation. It is submitted, however, that the regions studied provide a broad perspective on the different HRM environments, policies, and practices.

Another limitation of the book concerns its timeliness regarding certain data. It is unfortunate that a book that attempts to provide current information on such a dynamic topic as global HRM is practically out of date by the time it is published. For this reason, an appendix is included that provides many Web sites where updated information and data can be obtained.

Resources for Global Human Resource Management Policies and Practices

What is evident from the material presented in this book is that the field of international human resource management is very dynamic. The intent of this appendix, therefore, is to provide the reader with a variety of sources where updates in this field commonly appear. The specific sources will be grouped into three categories: Web pages, journals, and other resources.

WEB SITES

The following are the best sites in terms of dealing with global human resource management issues, but they are by no means the only ones. Sites will be categorized according to the regions for which they have the greatest application. A final category will include sites that have cross-regional applications.

United States and Canada

http://www.bls.gov/
The Bureau of Labor Statistics provides an impressive amount of information about the U.S. labor context. Moreover, it provides comparative labor information for several countries. Specifically statistics are presented on productivity and unit labor costs; compensation; labor force, employment, and unemployment; and consumer prices. From this web site, you also have access to the *Monthly Labor Review*, a journal that periodically publishes articles on labor issues in various countries.

http://strategis.ic.gc.ca/
This Web page is run by Industry Canada. The information includes
economic indicators, monthly and quarterly economic data, economic
newsletters, and publications, some of which deal with comparative labor economic issues.

Europe and the New Independent States

http://www.oecd.org/
At this Organization for Economic Cooperation and Development Web
site, you have free access to some documents and statistics on education, economics, and labor for OECD member countries. However, full
access will require you to register with them or to purchase documents
from them.

http://europa.eu.int
The European Commission Web site provides information on European
Union countries regarding social, economic, and education policies.
Moreover, economic data are presented for each of these countries.

http://www.eubusiness.com/
This Web page provides information on EU laws and business developments. It also offers up-to-date information on EU programs as well
as documents regarding doing business in Europe. Finally, statistics on
economic and financial conditions are available. Free registration is
required in order to have access to most of its features.

http://www.ucis.pitt.edu/reesweb/
REESWEB is a site supported by the University of Pittsburgh. This
site is a comprehensive index of electronic resources on the Balkans,
the Baltic states, Central Europe, Eastern Europe, the Russian Federation, and the former Soviet Union. You will find almost every web
site that deals with economic and social issues in this region listed in
this resource.

Middle East

http://www.trade.gov/SmapFrameset.html
The International Trade Association, a program within the U.S. Department of Commerce, supports this Web site. It provides up-to-date
statistics and documents dealing with economic conditions of the countries located in the Middle East and North Africa.

<u>Arab.net</u>
While it is not clear how often it is updated, Arab.net provides information regarding the governments, economies, cultures, and businesses in 20 countries in the Middle East.

<u>http://www.cbs.gov.il/</u>
The Central Bureau of Statistics is an Israeli government agency. Its Web page offers a wealth of statistics on education, economic, and social factors.

Cross-Regional Web Sites

<u>http://www.ihrim.org/</u>
The International Association for Human Resource Information Management (IHRIM) provides the knowledge and solutions to help you manage information and technology to accomplish the strategic goals of your company. To access most of their features, however, you must become a member of the IHRIM.

<u>http://www.state.gov/www/global/human rights/</u>
In this Web page, the U.S. State Department provides annual reports on human rights practices throughout the world. In particular, it updates changes in laws affecting employment discrimination based on gender, national origin, age, and religion. Moreover, there is information regarding child-labor laws, the rights of employees to unionize, and acceptable working conditions.

<u>http://www.ilo.org/</u>
The International Labor Organization provides a wealth of information on standards, principles, and rights in the workplace. It also supports a number of databases, including LABORSTA, a database on labor statistics covering economically active population (data since 1945) employment, unemployment, hours of work, wages, labor costs, consumer prices, occupational injuries, occupational accidents, and strikes and lockouts (data since 1969).

<u>http://www.auckland.ac.nz/lbr/stats/offstats/OFFSTATSmain.htm</u>
OFFSTATS is a resource offered by the University of Auckland. It lists web sites offering free and easily accessible social, economic, and general data from official or similar "quotable" sources, especially those that provide both current data and time series. The country lists are mainly Web pages provided by statistical offices, central banks, and governmental departments and agencies, whereas the topics list is comprised of links to the statistics pages of international organizations and associations and a few commercial sites.

http://unescostat.unesco.org/
The UNESCO Institute for Statistics is the statistical branch of the
United Nations Organization for Education, Science and Culture. It was
established in July 1999 in order to reform UNESCO's statistical ca-
pacities. The Web site provides statistics for countries throughout the
world concerning national education systems, institutions, teaching
staff, and enrollment by level of education. It also presents data on literacy rates and access to schooling.

http://ciber.bus.msu.edu/busres.htm
Michigan State University supports this Web page. It lists a substantial
number of web pages dealing with a variety of topics, including human
resource management for countries throughout the world. The Web
page is nicely designed and user friendly.

On-line or Hard-Copy Publications

http://www.aom.pace.edu/
As a member of the Academy of Management, you will receive or have
access to three major journals: *Academy of Management Journal,
Academy of Management Review*, and *Academy of Management Executive*. While the Journal and Review contain scholarly articles, the Executive is aimed at the practitioner. Membership also allows you to receive information from Divisions or Groups, one of which is International Management.

http://www.mcb.co.uk/hrmid.htm
The *Human Resource Management International Digest* can be purchased either on-line from the above address or in hard copy. This service gathers informative articles from hundreds of publications
throughout the year and will keep you up to date with the very latest in
HR concepts, applications, comment, and research. It will provide you
with a unique opportunity to understand and monitor developing HR
trends and ideas around the world and to apply them to your own practice with confidence.

http://www.jibs.com
Currently, the *Journal of International Business Studies* (JIBS) is available only in hard copy. In the near future, however, subscribers will be
able to access this publication from the above address. JIBS is a refe-
reed journal that publishes the results of social science research and
other types of articles that advance the understanding of business, including human resource management.

http://www:routlege.com

The International Journal of Human Resource Management is the forum for HRM scholars and professionals. Concerned with the expanding role of strategic human resource management in a dynamic global environment, this resource focuses on future trends in HRM, drawing on empirical research in the areas of strategic management, international business, organizational behavior, personnel management and industrial relations. Articles include a wide range of issues: employee participation, human resource flow, reward systems and high commitment work systems. Published in London by Routledge.

References

A&G Information Services (1996). July level of unemployment in Russia reached 9.2% of the country active population of the country, August 27.

Abdalla, I., & Al-Homound, M. (1995). A survey of management training and development practices in the state of Kuwait. *Journal of Management Development* 14: 14-26.

Abdel-Halim, A., & Ashour, A. (1995). Early employment and mobility behaviors of business graduates in the Arab Gulf region. *International Studies of Management & Organization* 25: 67-87.

Addison, J., & Siebert, W. (1994). Vocational training and the European community, *Oxford Economic Papers* 46: 696-723.

Adkins, D. (1995). All work and no play. *World & I* 10: 376.

Adler, N. (1991). *International Dimensions of Organizational Behavior*. Boston: PWS-Kent.

Ahlen, K. (1989). Swedish collective bargaining under pressure: Inter-union rivalry and incomes policies. *British Journal of Industrial Relations* 27: 330-346.

Amerah, M. 1990. Major employment issues in Arab countries. Mimeo. *The Royal Scientific Society Seminar on Employment Policy in Arab Countries*. Amman, Jordan: June.

Applebaum, E., & Batt, R. (1994). *The New American Workplace*. Ithaca, NY: LR Press.

Assennara (1998), Arab Employees in Israel. Retrieved January 20, 1998 from the World Wide Web: http://www.assennara.com.

Bachler, C. (1996). Global inpats—don't let them surprise you. *Personnel Journal* 75 June: 54-56

Baglioni, G., & Crouch, C. (1991). *European industrial relations: The Challenge Flexibility*. London: Sage.

Baldi, S., Khalaf, G., Perie, M., & Sherman, J. (2000). International education indicators: A time series perspective, 1985-1995. *National Center for Education Statistics*. Washington D.C.: U.S. Department of Education.

Bamber, G., & Snape, E. (1987). British industrial relations. In G. Bamber and R. Lansbury (Eds.), *International and Comparative Industrial Relations*. London: Allen and Unwin.

Bartlett, C., & Ghoshal, S. (1987). Managing across borders: New organizational responses. *Sloan Management Review* 29: 43-53

Bartlett, W., Cable, S., Estin, D. Jones, C., & Smith, S. (1992). Firms in northern central Italy: An empirical comparison. *Industrial and Labor Relations Review* 46: 103-118.

Belobaba, E. (1994). Economic recovery takes hold in Eastern Europe. *Canadian Business Review* 21: 32-35.

Black, J., Mendenhall, M., & Oddou, G. (1991). Toward a comprehensive model of international adjustment: An integration of multiple theoretical perspectives. *Academy of Management Review* 16: 291-317.

Blanchard, O., & Jimeno, J. (1995). Structural unemployment: Spain versus Portugal. *American Economics Review* 85: 212-218.

Blondal, S., & Scarpetta, S. (1998). Retire early, stay at work? *OECD Observer* June-July: 15-20.

Bournois, F. (1993). France. In C. Brewster, A. Hegewisch, J. Lockhart, and G. Holden (Eds.), *The European Human Resource Management Guide*. London: Academic Press.

Bournois, F., Chauchat, J., & Roussillon, S. (1994). Training and management development in Europe. In C. Brewster and A. Hegewisch (Eds.), *Policy and Practice in European Human Resource Management*. London: Routledge.

Boyacigiller, N. (1990). The role of expatriates in the management of interdependence, complexity, and risk in multinational corporations. *Journal of International Business Studies* 21: 357-381.

Brewster, C. (1995). Towards a European model resource management. *Journal of International Business Studies* 26: 1-22.

Brewster, C., & Hegweisch, A. (Eds.). (1994). *Policy and Practice in European Human Resource Management*. London: Routledge.

Brewster, C., Hegewisch, A., & Mayne, L. (1994). Trends in European HRM. In P. Kirkbride (Ed.), *Human Resource Management in Europe*. London: Routledge.

Brunstein, I. (1995). *Human Resource Management in Western Europe*. Berlin: de Gruyter.

Bureau Development (1991), Support for the disabled in Sweden. *Countries of the World* 23: 123-126

Bureau of Labor Statistics (1997). At http://www.stats.bls.gov/news.release.

Bureau of Labor Statistics (1999). National compensation survey: Occupational wages in the United States, 1998. Washington, D.C.: U.S. Department of Labor.

Bureau of Labor Statistics (2000). International Comparison Statistics. Washington, D.C.: U.S. Department of Labor.

CanadaOnline (2000). Retrieved on July 8, 2000 from the WWW. http://canadaonline. about.com/ newsissues/canadaonline/library/bl/blminwage.htm

Carnevale, A., Gainer, L., & Meltzer, A. (1990). *Workplace Basics: The Essential Skills Employers Want*. San Francisco: Jossey-Bass.

Casio, W. (Ed.). (1989). Human Resource Planning Employment and Placement, ASPA/ BNA Series No. 3, Washington, DC: The Bureau of National Affairs, Inc.

Civil Rights Act of 1964, Title VII, Section 103a.

Cohen, B., & House, W. (1996). Labor market choices, earnings, and informal networks. *Economic Development & Cultural Change* 44: 589-619.

Colton, T. (2000). Union of Soviet Socialist Republics, *Microsoft Encarta Encyclopedia* Microsoft Corporation. All rights reserved.

Commission of the European Community, Maastricht Treaty, 1991.

Commission on the Future of Worker-Management Relations, U.S. Department of Labor.

Cook, L. (1995). Labor unions in post-communist countries. *Problems of Post Communism* 42: 13-19.

Courpasson, D., & Livian, Y. (1991). Training for strategic change: Some conditions of effectiveness. A case in the banking sector in France. Paper presented at the 6th Workshop of strategic human resource management, EIASM, St. Gallen, Switzerland, March.

Cowen, R. (1996a). Fund of disappointment. *Economist* 338 (January 27): 46-47.

Cowen, R. (1996b). A gradual goodbye. *Economist* 338 (January 27): 5-8.

Cradden, T. (1993). Trade unionism, social justice, and religious discrimination in Northern Ireland. *Industrial and Labor Relations Review* 46: 480-501.

Cremer, J. (1989). Common Knowledge and the Coordination of Economic Activities. In M. Aoki, B. Gustafsson, and O. Williamson (Eds.), *The Firm as a Nexus of Treaties*. London: Sage Publications.

Cui, G. (1998). The evolutionary process of global market expansion: Experiences of MNCs in China. *Journal of World Business* 33: 35-79.

Czinkota, M., Rivoli, P., & Ronkainen, I. (1990). *International Business* (2nd ed.). Fort Worth, TX: Dryden Press.

Dany, F., & Torchy, V. (1994) Recruitment and selection in Europe: Policies, practices, and methods. In C. Brewster and A. Hegewisch (Eds.), *Policy and Practice in European Human Resource Management*. London: Routledge.

DED. (1986). Equality of opportunity in employment in Northern Ireland: Future strategy options–a consultative paper. Belfast: Department of Economic Development.

Department of Labor (1996). Employment and Training Survey. Washington, DC: U.S. Department of Labor

Derr, C. (1988). Managing high potentials in Europe: Some cross cultural findings. European Management Journal 22: 72-80.

Digh, P. (1997). Shades of gray in the global marketplace. *HRMagazine* 42: 90-94.

Diwan, I., & Squire , L. (1992). Economic and social development in the Middle East and North Africa. *Middle East and North Africa Discussion Paper Series,* No. 3. Washington, DC, World Bank.

Duane, M. (1996). *Customized Human Resource Planning: Different Practices for Different Organizations*. Westport, CT: Quorum Books.

Dunlop, J. (1958). *Industrial Relations Systems*. New York: Holt.

Earley, P., & Singh, H. (1995). International and intercultural management research: What's next? *Academy of Management* 38: 327-340.

Edstrom, A., & Galbraith, J. (1977). Transfer of managers as a coordination and control strategy in multinational organizations. *Administrative Science Quarterly* 22: 248-63

Education at a Glance: OECD indicators (2000) Organization for Economic Cooperation and Development Education Database.

Fairclough, G. (1996). It isn't black and white. *Far Eastern Economic Review* 159: 54-59.

Feher, J. (1991). Kritikus pontok a teljesitmenyertekelesi rendszerek hatekony alkalmazasaban. *Humanpolitikai Szemle* 78: 13-22.

Fetherston, D. (1995). CITY & CO: Consultant reads between the lines. *Newsday* January 23: C03.

Fey, C., Engstrom, P., & Bjorkman, I. (1999). Doing business in Russia: Effective human resource management practices for foreign firms in Russia. *Organizational Dynamics* Autumn: 69-75.

Filella, J. (1993). Is the there a Latin model in the management of human resources? In A. Hegewisch and C. Brewster (Eds.), *European Developments in Human Resource Management*. London: Kogan Page.

Filella, J., & Hegewisch, A. (1994). European Experiments with Pay and Benefits Policies. In C. Brwester and A. Hegewisch (Eds.), *Policy and Parctice in European Human Resource Management*. London: Routledge.

Fine, C. (1999). Strike law and ADR in Hungary: A model for labor movements in Central and Eastern Europe. *Labor Studies Journal* 24: 29-42.

Fisher, C., Schoenfeldt, L., & Shaw, J. (1993). *Human Resource Management* (2nd ed.). Boston: Houghton Mifflin Company.

Flolrz-Saborido, I., Gonzallez-Rendoln, M., & Alcaide-Castro, M. (1995). Spain. In I. Brunstein (Ed.), *Human Resource Management in Western Europe*. New York: de Gruyter.

Folletti, S., Giacomello, G., & Cooper, J. (1993). Recruitment, reform and the Italian labour market. In A. Hegewisch and C. Brewster (Eds.), *European Developments in Human Resource Management*. London: Kogan Page.

Forster, N. (2000). The myth of the international manager. *International Journal of Human Resource Management* 11: 126.

Fossum, J. (1995). *Labor Relations* (6th ed). Chicago: Irwin.

Fox, L. (1995). Can Eastern Europe's old-age crisis be fixed? *Finance & Development* 31: 34-38.

Fuerstenberg, F. (1977). West German experience with industrial democracy. *The Annals* 431: 51.

Gause, F. (1997). The political economy of national security in the GCC States. In Gary Sick and Lawrence Potter (Eds.), *The Persian Gulf at the Millennium: Essays in Politics, Economy, Security, and Religion*. New York: St. Martin's Press.

George, L. (1995). Russia: Neither jobs nor justice–state discrimination. *Women's International Network News* 21: 29-34.

Golbar, D., & Deshpande, S. (1997). HRM practices of large and small Canadian manufacturing firms. *Journal of Small Business Management* 35: 30-38.

Gordon, E., Ponticell, J., & Morgan, R. (1989). Back to the basics. *Training and Development Journal August*: 73-76.

Groh, K., & Allen, M. (1998). Global staffing: are expatriates the only answer? (Special Report on Expatriate Management). *HR Focus* 75: S1(2).

Guzda, H. (1993). Getting richer, getting poorer. *Economist* 326: 52-53.

Hedlund, Gunnar. 1986. The hypermodern MNC—A heterarchy? *Human Resource Management* 25: 9-25.

Hay Group (1987). Performance Appraisal in French Firms. Retrieved on March 8, 1999 from the WWW on March http://www.haypaynet.com/

Hegewisch, A. (1993). The decentralization of pay bargaining: European countries. In A. Hegewisch and C. Brewster (Eds.), *European Developments in Human Resource Management*. London: Kogan Page.

Hegewisch, A., Brewster, C., & Koubek, J. (1996). Different roads: Changes in industrial and employee relations in the Czech Republic and East Germany since 1989. *Industrial Relations Journal* 27: 50-64.

Hegewisch, A., & Mayne, L. (1994). Equal opportunities policies in Europe. In C. Brewster and A. Hegewisch (Eds.), *Policy and Practice in European Human Resource Management: The Price Waterhouse Cranfield Survey*. London: Routledge.

Henderson, P. (1996). In the new Russia, racism is rising to the surface. *San Francisco Chronicle* January 13: A10.

Heneman, H., Schwab, D., Fossum, J., & Dyer, L. (1989). *Personnel/Human Resource Management*. Homewood, IL: Irwin.

Hiatt, F. (1994). Russia's new rich turn to private schools. *Washington Post* September 30: A31.

Hill, C. (1997). *International Business* (2nd ed.). Chicago: Irwin.

Hinterhuber, H., & Stumpf, M. (1990). Human resource management in Italy. In R. Pieper (Ed.), *Human Resource Management: An International Comparison.* Berlin: de Gruyter.

Hofstede, G. (1980). *Cultural Consequences: International Differences in World-related Values.* London: Sage.

Hofstede, G. (1984). *Culture's Consequences.* London: Sage.

Holden, L., & Livian, Y. (1993). Does strategic training policy exist? Some Evidence from ten European countries. In A. Hegewisch and C. Brewster (Eds.), *European Developments in Human Resource Management.* London: Kogan Page.

Hoskins, D. (1996). Social security in the 90s: the imperatives of change, *Social Security Bulletin* 59: 72-78.

Housemann, S. (1995). Part-time employment in Europe and Japan. *Journal of Labor Research* 16: 249-251.

Human Resources Development Canada (2000). Overview of the Old Age Security Program. Retrieved on July 12, 2000 from the WWW. http://www.hrdc-drhc.gc.ca/Isp/oasind_html.

IBM/Towers Perrin (1992). *Priorities for Gaining Competitive Advantage: A Worldwide Human Resource Study.* London: Towers Perrin.

ILO Report III (1998). *Vocational Rehabilitation and Employment of Disabled Persons.* Geneva: International Labour Organizations.

ILO Report (1999). *World Report of Employment.* Geneva: International Labour Organizations.

InterPress Service English News Wire. (1996). Finance: Transition to market brings poverty, inequality June 27.

IPR Strategic Business Information Database (2000). Lebanon: Old age Pension bill. Info-Prod (Middle East) Ltd.

Israel Business Today (2000). Average Gross Monthly Wage in Israel $1,716. Vol. 14, p. 6.

ITAR-TASS. (1996). Russia Raises Minimum Wage April 25.

Ivancevich, J. (1995). *Human Resource Management.* Chicago: Irwin.

Jones, D. (1995). Successor unions in traditional economies: Evidence from St. Petersburg. *Industrial and Labor Relations Review* 49: 39-45.

JSOURCE (2000). Health Services. Retrieved on August 16, 2000 from the WWW. http://www.us-Israel.org/jsource/Health/health_services.html.

Katz, H., & Kochan, T. (1992). *An Introduction to Collective Bargaining and Industrial Relations.* New York: McGraw-Hill.

Kiriazov, D., Sullivan, S., & Tu, H. (2000). Business success in Eastern Europe: Understanding and customizing HRM. *Business Horizons* 43: 39.

Kishlansky, M, & Weisser, H. (2000). The United Kingdom. *Microsoft Encarta Encyclopedia.* Microsoft Corporation.

Kmitch, J., Laboy, P., & Van Damme, S. (1995). International comparisons of manufacturing compensation costs. *Monthly Labor Review* 118: 3-9.

Kobrin, S. 1988. Expatriate reduction and strategic control in American multinational corporations. *Human Resource Management Journal* 27: 63-75.

Koubek, J. (1993). Vyvoj systému personàlni pràce v podnikovà afé (Development of personnel management systems in companies), a research study Praha. *Vysokà skolà ekomomichkà,* 56.

Koubek, J., & Brewster, C. (1995). Human resource management in turbulent times: HRM in the Czech Republic. *The International Journal of Human Resource Management* 6: 223-247.

Kovach, R. (1995). Matching assumptions to environment in the transfer of management practices. *International Studies of Management and Organization* 24: 83-95.

Kubeš, M., & Benkovic, P. (1994). Realities, paradoxes and perspectives of HRM in Eastern Europe. In P. Kirkbride (Ed.), *Human Resource Management in Europe: Perspectives for the 1990s*. London: Routledege.

Kulikov, Y. (1996). Ukraine miners stay on strike despite cash offer. *Reuters* February 2.

Lancet, The (1999). Health care in Iraq (Letter to the Editor) June 5: 976.

Landau, D. (1992). More new OLIM are working according to recent survey. *Jewish Telegraphic Agency* October 23: PG.

Lavy, V., & Spratt, J. (1997). Patterns of incidence and change in Moroccan literacy. *Comparative Education Review* 41: 120-22.

Leupold, J. (1987). *Management Development*. Landsberg am Lech: Verlag Moderne Industrie.

Levy, F. (1990). Employee compensation and benefits: Canada vs. U.S. *Business Quarterly* 54: 20-26.

Levy-Leboyer, C. (1994). Selection and assessment in Europe. In H. C. Triandis, M. D. Dunnette, & L. M. Hough (Eds.), *Handbook of Industrial and Organizational Psychology* (2nd ed.). Palo Alto, CA: Consulting Psychologists Press.

Logger, E., Vinke, R., & Kluytmas, D. (1995). Compensation and appraisal in an international perspective. In A. Harzing and J. Ruysseveldt (Eds.), *International Human Resource Management*. London: Sage.

Lynch, L., & Black, S. (1998). Beyond the incidence of employer-provided training. *Industrial and Labor Relations Review* 52: 64-80.

Maclean's (2000). *Financial Outlook* May 8: 35.

Mathis, R., & Jackson, J. (1997). *Human Resource Management* (8th ed.). Minneapolis/St. Paul: West Publishing.

McIvor, G. (1994). Norway acts positive after the no vote. *Guardian* December 3: 7.

Milkovich, G., & Boudreau, J. (1994). *Human Resource Management* (7th ed.). Burr Ridge, IL: Irwin.

Mills, D. (1989). *Labor-Management Relations* (4th ed.). New York: McGraw-Hill.

Minehan, M. (1996). Skills shortage in Asia. *HRMagazine* 41: 152

Mitchell, A. (1998). *Strategic Training Partnerships Between the State and Enterprises*. Geneva, Switzerland: ILO report.

Morrison, A., & Roth, K. (1992). A taxonomy of business-level strategies in global industries. *Strategic Management Journal* 13: 399-418.

Moskovskie Novosti (1996). Russia: Absence of trained personnel limits further growth of computer markets. January 21: V29.

Muco, M. (1996). Income policy and labor market development in Albania: Some distribution and living standard implications. Colloquium sponsored by the Estonian Ministry of Foreign Affairs.

Nakhoul, S. (1996). Bahrain tries to find more jobs for its nationals. Reuters (on-line), July 26.

Nelson, D. (2000). Romania. *Microsoft Encarta Encyclopedia*. Microsoft Corporation.

Noe, R., Hollenbeck, J., Gerhart, B., & Wright, P. (2000). *Human Resource Management: Gaining a Competitive Advantage* (3rd ed.). Burr Ridge, IL: Irwin.

Organization for Economic Cooperation and Development (OECD) (1991). *Employment Outlook*. Paris: Organization for Economic Cooperation and Development.

Organization for Economic Cooperation and Development (OECD) (1994). *Finland*. Paris: Organization for Economic Cooperation and Development.

Organization for Economic Cooperation and Development (OECD) (2000). *Education at a Glance*. Organization for Economic Cooperation and Development Education Database.

Organización Internacional del Trabajo (OIT) (1998). New institutional picture of training in the region. Retrieved on February 8, 1999 from the WWW: http://web-dev.260cintespa.cinterfor.org.uy/rct/eng/doc1/capii.htm

Osborn, A. (2000) No-Frills approach keeps costs in check. *Europe* February: 42-44.

Palestinian National Authority (1998). Palestinian labor and employment. Retrieved on February 20, 1998 from the WWW: http://www.pna.net/facts/pal_labor_employ.htm.

Papalexandris, N. (1993). Human management in Greece. In A. Hegewisch and C. Brewster (Eds.), *European Developments in Human Resource Management*. London: Kogan Page.

Peak, M. (1995). I think I'll go work in France. *Management Review* 84: 7-8.

Pearce, J. (1991). From socialism to capitalism: The effect of Hungarian human resource practices. *Academy of Management Executive* 5: 76-82.

Porter, M. (1998). *The Competitive Advantage of Nations*. New York: Free Press.

Possehl, S. (1995). Russian brain drain flows directly into U.S. science talent reservoir. *Los Angeles Times* February 26: A51-52.

Price Waterhouse/Cranfield. (1990). *The Price Waterhouse Cranfield Project on International Strategic Human Resource Management: Report 1990*. London: Price Waterhouse.

Price Waterhouse/Cranfield Project (1991). Report on international strategic human resource management.

Price Waterhouse/Cranfield Survey (1994). In C. Brewster and A. Hegewisch (Eds.), *Policy and Practice in European Human Resource Management*. London: Routledge.

Prieto J., Blasco R., & Quintanilla, I. (1991). Recrutement et selection du personnel en Espagne. *Review of European Psychological Applications* 41: 47-62

Prokopenko, J. (1994). The transition to a market economy and its implications for HRM in Eastern Europe. In P. Kirkbride (Ed.), *Human Resource Management in Europe: Perspectives for the 1990s*. London: Routledge.

Puffer, S. (1994). Compensating local employees in post-communist Russia. *Compensation and Benefits Review* 26: 35-43.

Purcell, J. (1991). The rediscovery of the management prerogative: The management of labour relations in the 1980s. *Oxford Review of Economic Policy* 7: 33-43.

Quinn, S. (1996). Jobs sex bias hits men. *Guardian* May 6: S1(6).

Rafaeli, A. (1999). Pre-employment screening and applicants' attitudes toward an employment opportunity. *Journal of Social Psychology* 139: 700-713.

Reynolds, C. (1986). Compensation of overseas personnel. In J. J. Famulato (Ed.), *Handbook of Human Resource Administration*. New York: McGraw-Hill.

Roberts, K. (1998). Managing the global workforce: Challenges and strategies. *The Academy of Management Executive* 12: 93-10

Rojot, J. (1990). Human resource management in France. In P. Herriot (Ed.), *Assessment and Selection in Organizations: An International Comparison*. Berlin: de Gruyter.

Russell, S., & Al-Ramadhan, A. (1994). Emigration & immigration: IRAQ-Kuwait crisis, 1990-1991. *International Journal of Middle East Studies* 26: 569-581.

Russia: New educational system in the works (2000). IPR Strategic Business Information Database Feb 6: NA

Sachs, J. D., & Stone, G. L. (1999). Ten trends in global competitiveness in 1998. (Geneva, Switzerland: World Economic Forum).

Saporta, M. (1990). Coca-Cola gives $150,000 to help train Polish workers. *Atlanta Constitution*: B(10).

Saudhouse (2000). Lack of Women's Rights in Saudi Arabia. Retrieved on May 8, 2000 from the WWW: http://www.saudhouse.com/ hrights/women/women.htm.

Sauer, R., & Voelker, K. (1993). *Labor Relations: Structure and Process* (2nd ed.). New York: Macmillan.

Shaban, R., Assaad, R., & Al-Qudsi, S. (1995). The challenge of unemployment in the Arab region. *International Labour Review* 134: 65-91.

Shackleton, V., & Newell, S. (1991). Management selection: A comparative survey of methods used in top British and French companies. *Journal of Occupational Psychology* 64: 23-36.

Shimmin, S. (1989). Selection in a European context. In P.Herriot (Ed.), *Assessment and selection in organizations: Methods and practice for recruitment and appraisal*. Chicester: John Wiley.

Simon, S. (1996a). Job Hunt's wild side in Russia. *Los Angeles Times* January 2: A(1).

Simon, S. (1996b). Willing and Able in Russia. *Los Angeles Times* January 13: A(1-2).

Sloane, P., & Mackay, D. (1997). Employment equity and minority legislation in the UK after two decades: a review. *International Journal of Manpower* 18: 597-621

Smith, J., & Robertson, I. (Eds.). *Advances in Selection and Assessment*. Chichester: Wiley.

Soderstrom, M. (1992). Sweden. In G. Brewster, A. Hegewisch, J. Lockhart, and P. Holden (Eds.), *The European Human Resource Management Guide*. London: Academic Press.

Sparks, C., & Greiner, M. (1997). U.S. and foreign productivity and labor costs, *Monthly Labor Review* February: 26-35.

Sparrow, P., & Hiltrop, J. (1994). *European human resource management in transition*. Englewood Cliffs, NJ: Prentice Hall.

Stanley, A. (1994). In Russian education: Growing class distinction. *New York Times* May 22: 1(3).

Statistics Canada (1997). Employee training: An international perspective.

Steiner, D., & Gilliland, S. (1996). Fairness reactions to personnel selection techniques in France and the United States. *Journal of Applied Psychology* 81: 134-141.

Swaak, R. (1995). Expatriate failures: Too many, too much costs, too little planning. *Compensation and Benefits Review* 27: 47-55.

Thach, L. (1996). Training in Russia. *Training & Development*, 50: 34-40.

Thompson, J. (1993). Promotion of employee ownership through public policy: The British example. *Journal of Economic Issues* 27: 825-840.

Travis, A. (1993). Sex bias claims increase by 47 percent. *Guardian* June: 1(4).

Treu, T. (1992). Labour flexibility in Europe. *International Labour Review* 131: 497-512.

Tully, D. (1990). *Labour, Employment and Agricultural Development in West Asia and North Africa*. Dordrecht, Kluwer Academic Publishers.

Tung, R. (1987). Expatriate assignments: Enhancing success and minimizing failure. *Academy of Management Executive* 1: 117-126.

Tyson, S. (1989). 1992: An investigation of strategies for management development. Paper presented at the seminar: Europe without frontiers. Amsterdam, November.

UN/ECE. (1996). Economic survey of Europe in 1994-1995. United Nations Economic Committee for Europe.

United Nations (1995). *The World's Women 1995: Trends and Statistics*. New York: Statistics Division of the United Nations.

U.S. State Department (2000). Annual Country Reports on Human Rights Practices.

Venkat, A. (1995). One step backwards? *Harvard International Review* 17: 66-74.

Vicente, C. (1993). Human resource management in Spain: Strategic issues, the economic and social framework. In S. Tyson, P. Lawrence, P. Poirson, L. Manzolini, and C. Vincente (Eds.), *Human Resource Management in Europe*. London: Kogan Page.

Wassell, T. (1993). Job-cutter's axe chips away at power of Labour. *The European* October 21: pp. 40-41.

Wieviorka, M. (1996). The seeds of hate. *UNESCO Courier* 49: 10-12.

Wilkinson, F. (1994), Equality, efficiency and economic progress: the case for universally applied equitable standards for wages and conditions of work. In *Creating Economic Opportunities: The Role of Labour Standards in Industrial Restructuring*. Geneva, Switzerland: International Institute for Labour Studies

Wolfson, M., & Murphy, B. (1998). New views of inequality trends in Canada and the United States, *Monthly Labor Review* 121: 3

Woodward, S. (1995). *Socialist Unemployment: The Political Economy of Yugoslavia*. Princeton: Princeton University Press.

World Bank, Retrieved on August 8, 2000 from the WWW: http:// www.worldbank.org/ data/databytopic/databytopic.html.

Yip, G. (1989). Global strategy ... in a world of nations? *Sloan Management Review* Fall: 29-41.

Zic, Z. (1998). From lambs to lions: The changing role of Bulgarian and Romanian labor unions in the course of democratic transition. *Perspectives on Political Science* 27: 155-161.

Ziskind, D. (1990). *Labor Laws in the Middle East: Tradition in Transition*. Los Angeles, Calif.: Litlaw Foundation.

Zitaner, E. (1992). Variable pay programs: tracking their direction, *Compensation and Benefits Review* 24: 8-16

Name and Source Index

A&G Information Services, 21
Abdalla, I., 73
Abdel-Halim, A., 50
Addison, J., 40, 59
Adkins, D., 40
Adler, N., 2
Ahlen, K., 89
Alcaide-Castro, M., 39, 97
Al-Homound, M., 73
Allen, M., 5
Al-Qudsi, S., 23
Al-Ramadhan, A., 28
Amerah, M., 26
Applebaum, E., 75
Ashour, A., 50
Assaad, R., 23
Assennara, 127

Bachler, C., 4
Baglioni, G., 136
Baldi, S., 54
Bamber, G., 138
Bartlett, C., 2
Bartlett, W., 143
Batt, R., 75
Belobaba, E., 22
Benkovic, P., 19, 102
Bjorkman, I., 48
Black, J., 2
Black, S., 56
Blanchard, O., 13
Blasco R., 43
Blondal, S., 97

Bournois, F., 45, 65
Boyacigiller, N., 2
Brewster, C., 13, 19, 21, 39, 40, 46, 48,
    59, 70, 79, 93, 94, 100, 115-117
Brunstein, I., 136
Bureau Development, 118
Bureau of Labor Statistics, 10-11, 15,
    58, 83, 87, 90-91, 133, 161

Cable, S., 143
CanadaOnline, 81
Carnevale, A., 53
Casio, W., 34
Chauchat, J., 65
Colton, T., 69
Commission of the European
    Community, 60
Commission on the Future of Worker-
    Management Relations, 135
Cook, L., 143-146
Courpasson, D., 60
Cowen, R., 60, 118
Cradden, T., 117
Cremer, J., 49
Crouch, C., 136
Cui, G., 4
Czinkota, M., 12

Dany, F., 38, 41-42, 44, 49
DED, 117
Department of Labor, U.S., 4, 56, 91
Derr, C., 65
Deshpande, S., 32

Digh, P., 4
Diwan, I., 23
Duane, M., 31, 79
Dunlop, J., 7, 131, 135

Edstrom, A., 2
Engstrom, P., 48
Estin, D. 143

Feher, J., 80
Fetherston, 43
Fey, C., 48
Filella, J., 45, 94
Fine, C., 147
Fisher, C., 32
Flolrz-Saborido, I., 39, 97
Forster, N., 5
Fossum, J., 141
Fox, L., 102
Fuerstenberg, F., 142

Gainer, L., 53
Galbraith, J., 2
Gause, F., 27
George, L., 120-121
Gerhart, B., 2
Ghoshal, S., 2
Gilliland, S., 43, 45
Golbar, D., 32
Gonzallez-Rendoln, M., 39, 79
Gordon, E., 53
Greiner, M., 91
Groh, K., 5
Guzda, H., 21, 99

Hay Group, 79, 83
Hegewisch, A., 13, 21, 39, 40, 89, 94-
    95, 116-117
Henderson, P., 121
Hiatt, F., 69
Hill, C., 2, 5
Hiltrop, J., 45, 79, 81, 92-94, 119, 136,
    141
Hinterhuber, H., 79
Hofstede, G., 43, 50
Holden, L., 60, 62-64, 66-67
Hollenbeck, J., 2
Housemann, S., 94
Human Resources Development
    Canada, 84

IBM/Towers Perrin, 79
International Labor Organizations, 14,
    26, 28, 129
InterPress Service English News Wire,
    121
IPR Strategic Business Information
    Database, 108
Israel Business Today, 106
ITAR-TASS, 21
Ivancevich, J., 83

Jimeno, J., 13
Jones, C., 143
Jones, D., 143-144
JSOURCE, 107

Katz, H., 141
Kiriazov, D., 69, 71
Kishlansky, M, 95
Kmitch, J., 15-17
Kobrin, S., 2
Kochan, T., 141
Koubek, J., 19, 21, 46, 48, 70, 79, 100
Kovach, R., 48, 80
Kubeš, M., 19, 102
Kulikov, Y., 146

Laboy, P., 15,
Landau, D., 48
Lavy, V., 73
Leupold, J., 61
Levy, F., 85
Levy-Leboyer, C., 40, 43, 45
Livian, Y., 60, 62-64, 66-67
Logger, E., 16, 92
Lynch, L., 56

Mackay, D., 90
Maclean's, 83
Mayne, L., 13, 94, 117
McIvor, G., 12
Meltzer, A., 53
Mendenhall, M., 2
Mills, D., 8, 131, 142
Minehan, M., 4
Mitchell, A., 55
Morgan, R., 53
Morrison, A., 2
Moskovskie Novosti, 70
Muco, M., 100
Murphy, B., 11

Nakhoul, S., 27
Newell, S., 43, 45
Noe, R., 2, 32, 36, 45, 56, 65, 78, 80, 85, 112

Oddou, G., 2
Organization for Economic Cooperation and Development (OECD), 37, 59, 68, 137
Osborn, A., 95-96

Palestinian National Authority, 127
Papalexandris, N., 43, 79
Peak, M., 97
Pearce, J., 80, 100, 104
Ponticell, J., 53
Porter, M., 1
Possehl, S., 48
Price Waterhouse/Cranfield (PWC), 37, 46, 49, 61
Prieto J., 43
Prokopenko, J., 48
Puffer, S., 101, 103-104
Purcell, J., 89

Quinn, S., 115
Quintanilla, I., 43

Rafaeli, A., 50
Rivoli, P., 12
Roberts, K., 5
Robertson, I., 43
Rojot, J., 79
Ronkainen, I., 12
Roth, K., 2
Roussillon, S., 65
Russell, S., 28

Sachs, J. D., 54
Saporta, M., 71
Saudhouse, 74
Sauer, R., 136-138
Scarpetta, S., 97
Schoenfeldt, L., 32
Shaban, R., 23, 25-27
Shackleton, V., 43, 45
Shaw, J., 32
Shimmin, S., 45
Siebert, W., 40, 59
Simon, S., 47, 123

Sloane, P., 90
Smith, J., 43
Smith, S., 143
Snape, E., 138
Soderstrom, M., 89
Sparks, C., 91
Sparrow, P., 45, 79, 81, 92-94, 119, 136, 141
Spratt, J., 73
Squire, L., 23
Stanley, A., 69
Statistics Canada, 53, 83
Steiner, D., 43, 45
Stone, G. L., 54
Stumpf, M., 79
Sullivan, S., 69
Swaak, R., 4

Thach, L., 69
Thompson, J., 94
Torchy, V., 38, 41-42, 44, 49
Travis, A., 115
Tu, H., 69
Tully, D., 26
Tung, R., 5
Tyson, S., 65

United Nations Economic Committee for Europe (UN/ECE), 18, 20-21
United Nations, 26, 70, 72-73, 108, 119, 121
U.S. State Department, 88, 90, 99, 103, 105-106, 114-115, 119-121, 123-124, 126, 129, 130, 148-149, 151-152

Van Damme, S., 15,
Venkat, A., 48
Vicente, C., 43
Voelker, K., 136-138

Wassell, T., 140-141
Weisser, H., 95
Wieviorka, M., 117
Wolfson, M. 11
Woodward, S., 21
World Bank, 55, 70, 102, 106, 121
Wright, P., 2

Yip, G., 2

Zic, Z., 143-144
Ziskind, D., 104, 109, 149
Zitaner, E., 84

Subject Index

Age Discrimination in Employment
Act, United States, 111-112
Air Traffic Controllers Union, 144
All-Union Association of Workers'
Solidarity, 145
Americans with Disability Act, United
States, 111-112
Anderson Consulting, 56
Autonomous Syndicates Confederation,
150

Bohemian and Moravian Chamber of
Trade Unions, 146

Canada Labour Relations Board, 132
Canadian Charter of Rights and
Freedoms, 113
Child labor laws: in Eastern Europe and
the New Independent States, 123-
124; in the Middle East, 128-129; in
the United States and Canada, 113;
in Western Europe, 119
Civil Rights Act, United States, 111-
112
Collective bargaining issues: in Eastern
Europe and the New Independent
States, 147; in the United States and
Canada, 134-135; in Western
Europe, 137-142
Commission on the Future of Worker-
Management Relations, 135
Compensation: in Eastern Europe and
the New Independent States, 98-

Compensation—Cont.
100; in the Middle East, 104-106; in
the United States and Canada, 81-
84; in Western Europe, 88-95
Confederation of Greek Workers, 89
Czech and Slovak Confederation of
Trade Unions, 146

Discrimination laws: in Eastern Europe
and the New Independent States,
120-123; in the Middle East, 125-
128; in the United States and
Canada, 111-113; in Western
Europe, 114-119

Economic and Monetary Union, 12
Elkhart Corporation, 135
Employee benefits: in Eastern Europe
and the New Independent States,
100-104; in the Middle East,106-
110; in the United States and
Canada,84-88; in Western Europe,
95-97
Employee Share Ownership Plans, 92-
94
Equal Employment Opportunity
Commission, United States, 111-
112
Equal Opportunities Commission,
United Kingdom, 90, 115
Equal Pay Act: in the United Kingdom,
89-90; in the United States, 111

European Coal and Steel Community,
     12
European Court of Justice, 89-90, 114
Expatriate failure, 2-5
Exxon, 1

Fair Employment (Northern Ireland)
     Act, 117
Fair Labor Standards Act, the United
     States, 82, 113
Federal Express, 56
Federation of Ukrainian Unions, 145

General Electric, 1-2, 56
General Federation of Jordanian Trade
     Unions, 150
General Motors, 1
General Union of Algerian Workers,
     149
Gross Domestic Product, 9, 23, 28, 96,
     102
Gulf War, 26-27

Hewlett-Packard, 70
Histadrut, 148
Human resource planning: in Eastern
     Europe and the New Independent
     States, 46; in the United States and
     Canada, 31; in Western Europe, 37

Independent Miners' Union of Ukraine,
     145

Job Training Partnership Act, 54

Kuwait Trade Union Federation, 151

Lunar European Demonstration
     Approach, 15

Maastricht Treaty, 12-13, 15, 60
Management by objective, 78-79
Matsushita, 2
Minimum wages: in Eastern Europe
     and the New Independent States,
     98-99; in the Middle East, 105;
     in the United States and Canada,
     81-82; in Western Europe, 88-89

National Labor Relations Act, United
     States, 131-132, 134

National Labor Relations Board,
     United States, 132, 135, 138

Occupational Safety and Health Act,
     United States, 114
Old Age Security Act, Canada, 84-85
Ontario Employment Standards Act,
     87, 113
Overseas Private Investment
     Corporation, United States, 151

People with Disabilities Discrimination
     Act, United Kingdom, 118
Performance appraisal, 77-81
Philips NV, 2
Procter & Gamble, 2
Protection of Young Persons Act,
     Ireland, 119

Railway Labor Act, United States, 131
Recruitment: in Eastern Europe and the
     New Independent States, 46-48; in
     the Middle East, 49-50; in the
     United States and Canada, 32; in
     Western Europe, 37
Russian Academy of Scientists Trade
     Union, 144

Selection: in Eastern Europe and the
     New Independent States, 48; in the
     Middle East, 49-50; in the United
Social Charter, 12, 60, 118
Social Security Act, United States, 84
Solidarity, 143-145

Texas Instruments, 56
Treaty of Rome, 12, 89, 114

Ukrainian Law on Enterprises, 147
Unemployment: in Eastern Europe and
     the New Independent States, 19-21;
     in the Middle East, 23-28, 49, 144,
     146-147; in the United States and
     Canada, 10-11; in Western Europe,
     13-15, 17, 38, 89
U.S. Robotics, 56

Variable pay, 83-84, 92, 95, 100

Wildcat strikes, 138-140

Workplace regulations--Cont.:
    in Eastern Europe and the New
    Independent States, 124; in the
    Middle East, 129-130; in the United
    States and Canada, 113-114; in
    Western Europe, 119-120
Works Councils, 141-142

About the Author

MICHAEL J. DUANE is Associate Professor of Management at North Central College, Naperville, Illinois. Recipient of various awards for his scholarship, he has taught courses in industrial relations and has served as an associate professor of management and director of the MBA program at Mercy College, Detroit. Dr. Duane is author of several articles and two previous books published by Quorum: *The Grievance Procedure in Labor-Management Cooperation* (1997) and *Customized Human Resource Planning* (1996).